The Quality of Society

Adolfo Figueroa

The Quality of Society

Essays on the Unified Theory of Capitalism

palgrave
macmillan

Adolfo Figueroa
Economics Department
Pontifical Catholic University of Peru
Lima, Lima, Peru

ISBN 978-3-030-11655-2   ISBN 978-3-030-11656-9 (eBook)
https://doi.org/10.1007/978-3-030-11656-9

Library of Congress Control Number: 2018967282

© The Editor(s) (if applicable) and The Author(s), under exclusive license to Springer Nature Switzerland AG 2019
This work is subject to copyright. All rights are solely and exclusively licensed by the Publisher, whether the whole or part of the material is concerned, specifically the rights of translation, reprinting, reuse of illustrations, recitation, broadcasting, reproduction on microfilms or in any other physical way, and transmission or information storage and retrieval, electronic adaptation, computer software, or by similar or dissimilar methodology now known or hereafter developed.
The use of general descriptive names, registered names, trademarks, service marks, etc. in this publication does not imply, even in the absence of a specific statement, that such names are exempt from the relevant protective laws and regulations and therefore free for general use.
The publisher, the authors and the editors are safe to assume that the advice and information in this book are believed to be true and accurate at the date of publication. Neither the publisher nor the authors or the editors give a warranty, express or implied, with respect to the material contained herein or for any errors or omissions that may have been made. The publisher remains neutral with regard to jurisdictional claims in published maps and institutional affiliations.

This Palgrave Macmillan imprint is published by the registered company Springer Nature Switzerland AG
The registered company address is: Gewerbestrasse 11, 6330 Cham, Switzerland

Acknowledgements

A reviewer appointed by Palgrave contributed through critical comments and suggestions to the shaping of the book in its final form. The economics department, Catholic University of Peru, contributed with research assistants to the completion of the research work. Javier Vásquez contributed with technical assistance in the final stages of the book production, including the preparation of the final submission of the book. The author wishes to express his deep gratitude to all of them.

Contents

1	**Introduction**	1
	Book Content	7
2	**The Unified Theory of Capitalism: An Overview**	11
	The Facts to Be Explained	12
	Seeking Scientific Explanations	15
	Unified Theory of Capitalism: Foundations	17
	The Evolutionary Model	21
	Quality of Society	30
	Science-Based Public Policies	34
	Comparisons with Standard Economics	38
	References	39
3	**Science Is Epistemology**	43
	The Alpha–Beta Method	44
	Causality in Mechanical Processes	48
	Causality in the Evolutionary Process	58
	On Alternatives to the Alpha–Beta Method	67

	Against Deductivism and Inductivism	71
	The Complexity of Accepting/Rejecting Economic Theories	74
	Conclusions	79
	References	81
4	**Path Dependence and the Economic Process**	83
	Some Analytical Distinctions	84
	Economic Theory of Colonialism: An Outline	86
	Colonial Legacy in the Unified Theory of Capitalism	90
	Endurance of Colonial Institutions Under Capitalism	94
	Explaining the Origin of Western Economic Supremacy	100
	Path Dependence and Institutions	104
	Conclusions	109
	References	112
5	**Population and the Quality of Society**	115
	A Dynamic Model with Exogenous Population	115
	Dynamic Model with Endogenous Population	122
	Economic Growth as Entropic Process	128
	Population Density Effect	130
	Conclusions	134
	References	136
6	**Unified Theory of Capitalism and Bio-Economics**	139
	Foundations of Bio-Economics	141
	Capitalist Model of Bio-Economics	145
	The Workings of the Model	151
	Beta Propositions	157

Comparing the Unified Theory of Capitalism and Bio-Economics	165
Conclusions	168
References	171

7 Individualism in the Anthropocene Age — 173
The Nature of Economic Growth Under Capitalism — 174
Human Behavior Evolution — 176
The Myth of Competition — 179
The Freedom Discourse — 185
Individual Freedom and Social Responsibility — 188
   Corporate Social Responsibility (CSR) — 190
   Crime Responsibility — 191
Individualism Question in the Anthropocene Age — 194
Individualism and Quality of Society — 202
Conclusions — 204
References — 205

8 Science-Based Public Policies — 207
Positive and Normative Propositions — 207
The Case of Neoclassical Economics — 213
The Case of Unified Theory of Capitalism — 217
Poverty vs Inequality — 223
Income Redistribution Effect vs Economic Growth Effect — 230
Conclusions — 235
References — 236

9 Redistribution Through Labor Markets — 237
A Short Run Sigma Model of the Labor Market — 238
   Introducing Legal Minimum Wage — 240
   Empirical Consistency — 245
The Legal Minimum Wage Effect — 246

    Endogenous Three-Tier Labor Incomes   247
    Unemployment Insurance Policy   251
    Introducing a Guaranteed Minimum Income
    (gmi)   252
    Conclusions   258
    References   259

10 Epilogue: New and Old Economics   261
    What Is the Nature of the Unified Theory of
    Capitalism?   261
    What Is the Major Novelty of the Unified Theory
    of Capitalism?   263
    How Does the Capitalist System Operate?   264
    What Are the Policy Implications of the Unified
    Theory?   269
    What Is the Value of Epistemology?   274

Author Index   279

Countries Index   281

Subject Index   283

List of Figures

Fig. 3.1 Diagrammatic representation of an abstract process — 45
Fig. 9.1 The low-skilled labor market in the sigma society — 239

List of Tables

Table 4.1 Formation of capitalist institutions   107
Table 6.1 Bio-economic process: growth and the
           environment   148

CHAPTER 1

Introduction

What is the unified theory of capitalism about? It is a positive economic theory that seeks to explain the functioning of the capitalist system. It is unified in the sense that it seeks unity of knowledge, rather than fragmentary and inconsistent knowledge. It assumes that the capitalist system is constituted by two qualitatively different types of societies, the *First World* and the *Third World* countries. Thus, the unified theory of capitalism pursues to explain each group of countries taken separately—through partial theories—and then the system taken as a whole through a unified theory.

It is unified theory in another important sense. It seeks to integrate the ecological system and the capitalist system into a single economic process. It assumes that the production of goods is constraint by the laws of nature. The production of goods is not an isolated system. Hence, the unified theory seeks to explain the economic growth process, which is seen as evolutionary, with quantitative and qualitative outcomes—not as a mechanical process, with quantitative outcomes only.

The unified theory intends to be a scientific economic theory. Therefore, it seeks to give epistemological justification to its findings. Science is epistemology. The *composite epistemology*—which combines two epistemologies, the *abstract process* and *falsificationism*—is utilized for that purpose. The composite epistemology deals with the logic of scientific knowledge in hyper-complex realities, such as the social world. According to this logic, scientific knowledge requires a scientific theory as abstract representation of the real social world, which, by construction, is falsifiable or testable.

The economic process is therefore the abstract representation of the social economic activity, which refers to the production of goods and its distribution among social groups in human societies. What are the ultimate factors that explain the observed production and distribution outcomes in human societies? This is the scope of economics.

The principles of the composite epistemology are too general to be operated; hence, practical and operational rules for scientific research need to be derived from the composite epistemology. This is given by the *alpha–beta method*, which constitutes the practical rules to construct testable scientific theories so that they can be either accepted or rejected in economics and the social sciences. One of these rules says that economic theories are falsifiable through the use of models, which, by assuming a particular social context under which people interact, constitute a more operational representation of the economic process and are then falsifiable.

The unified theory assumes that the economic process under capitalism is separable into three models: static (for the short run), dynamic (for the long run), and evolutionary (for the very long run). The unified theory ensures that the findings in each model are consistent with each other.

Hence, the theory is unified, leading to unity of knowledge, in this analytical sense as well—one world, one explanation.

Therefore, theoretical models of the unified theory have been constructed to represent the capitalist system and then submitted to empirical refutation, following the rules of the alpha–beta method. The results have shown that the empirical predictions of the models are consistent with the available data. Therefore, on epistemological grounds, the unified theory has been accepted as a valid theory of the capitalist system; that is, the abstract world that the unified theory has constructed is a good approximation of the real world capitalism.

In particular, the evolutionary model of the unified theory is able to explain the fundamental fact of capitalism: the outcome of the economic growth process includes a continuous rise in the income levels of capitalist countries, but accompanied by qualitative changes—higher degrees of income inequality and continuous degradation of the bio-physical environment—, the consequences of which are social maladies.

Considering social order as a public good, increasing income inequality is a social malady for it is conductive to stronger social conflicts and thus to significant social disorder conditions. Environment degradation also constitutes a social malady. Depletion, pollution, and climate change leads to a more hazardous human life and to more intense social conflicts and social disorder within the current generation; moreover, the wellbeing of future generations and the very survival of the human species are also put at high risk.

The income effect of economic growth on the quality of society is positive, but the social maladies effect is negative. What is then the net effect of economic growth upon social wellbeing?

According to the evolutionary model, in the first stages of economic growth the positive effect dominates, but in later stages the negative effect will. As the economic growth process is repeated, the environment problems of pollution and depletion become more acute, and one of them—whichever comes first—will set the limits to growth. At some period, the economic growth process will collapse and switch to another type of process. Economic growth is thus *unsustainable*. Moreover, economic growth ultimately puts the very survival of human species not only at risk, but the higher the growth rate, the sooner the collapse period will occur.

What are the ultimate factors explaining the fact that the economic growth under capitalism is accompanied by social maladies? Democracy is one of the fundamental institutions of capitalism. Why do social maladies persist under democracy? This is certainly a paradox.

According to the evolutionary model, the power structure is the ultimate factor explaining this outcome. The power structure includes two components: the initial inequality in the individual endowments of economics and social assets and the fundamental institutions of capitalism, markets and electoral democracy. Markets imply the rule of voluntary exchange of goods. Electoral democracy in turn imply the rule that governments must be elected by voting. The implication is that electoral democracy is a mechanism by which the political power of the people (the workers) granted by democracy is transferred to the political elite who is able to capture the state by buying votes and for its own benefit.

Given these institutions, the initial inequality in asset distribution leads to the existence of economic and political elites, and then to a concentrated power structure, for these elites exercise their power through the institutions of market and electoral democracy. Thus, the power elites have incentive to promote economic growth, for they are the main beneficiaries, not only in their income shares but in maintaining their privileged position in society. Furthermore, economic growth with social maladies will be reproduced period after period as long as the power structure remains unchanged. Democratic capitalism is not a self-regulating system regarding social maladies. The paradox is thus solved.

Finally, the evolutionary model takes as criterion of social wellbeing the category of *quality of society*, which combines income levels and social maladies. Along the economic growth process, the quality of society will depict a particular trajectory, which has an inverse-U shape: At the initial stages of economic growth, the positive effect of rising income levels upon quality of society dominates, but ultimately the negative effect of social maladies will become dominant, which ultimately leads to the collapse of the economic growth process.

This empirical prediction is consistent with the available facts of the world society since the 1950s. Given that the capitalist system is predominant in the world society, the predictions of the model can be extended to the latter. Indeed, quality of society measured by the variable *healthy life expectancy* (life expectancy corrected by disease days lost) have started to decline around 2010. Pollution is already among the top ten killers in the world.

Earth scientists have shown that the planet has already entered into a new age, replacing the Holocene age, which is called the *Anthropocene age*, for it originates on human activities. "Human activities" can be defined more precisely as the economic growth process. Therefore, this scientific finding is also consistent with the predictions of the evolutionary model of the unified theory.

What are the choices that human society has in the Anthropocene age? Science-based policies have been derived from the unified theory. Given the side effects of economic growth, the current pro-growth policies must be dethroned; hence, the only choice left is to enthrone public policies that seek the improvement of the quality of society instead. However, these new public policies are against the interests of the current power elites. Therefore, the new public policies require the dethroning of the current power structure—the ultimate factor in the economic growth process—with which capitalism operates.

Taking into account that the capitalist system is becoming the dominant form of social organization in the world society, these conclusions of the unified theory can be extended to the world society as well. The world society should follow public policies that promote the improvement in the quality of society instead of the current pro-growth policies, which have become universal.

In sum, the empirical predictions of evolutionary model of the unified theory have been proven to be consistent with available facts. Then, on epistemological grounds, the unified theory has been accepted as a valid theory that explains the real capitalist system. However, in accord with the composite epistemology, this acceptance can only be provisional, until new data are produced, superior economic theory is invented, or superior epistemology is created. On epistemological grounds, it can also be said that the unified theory is superior to standard economic theories, in the sense that the unified theory is able to explain the facts that the other economic theories can, but it explains facts that the others cannot. Economic growth with social maladies is one of these facts.

Book Content

The unified theory of capitalism has recently been presented as a new scientific endeavor in economics in several books. The present book is a kind of new volume of the series. It presents a set of essays. The essays seek to further the implications of the unified theory. For a new scientific endeavor, this objective seems justified.

The book-review articles on the previous books have praised their achievements but have also raised some specific questions, but none of epistemological significance as to merit some major revisions. Therefore, the theoretical and empirical findings of the unified theory presented earlier have been left untouched in this set of essays.

What do these essays intend to add? The essays mostly seek to further the implications—about explanatory and policy issues—of the evolutionary model of the unified theory, which deals with the fundamental economic problem of our time: *the fall in the quality of human society and the risk of collapse of the human species, as we know it.* The essays intend to remain in the realm of science.

The book as a whole is intended to be self-contained. The first essay presents an overview of the unified theory; thus, the reader should be able to understand the issues under discussion, even if she or he is not familiar with the unified theory. Each essay is also intended to be self-contained by indicating the basic findings of the unified theory or giving a cross reference with the previous books. Some repetitions across the essays were then inevitable.

The essays and the questions they intend to answer are as follows:

Chapter 2: An overview of the unified theory of capitalism is presented. This is just to provide the reader with a handy reference to follow the rest of the essays, and thus make the book self-contained. However, the reader will be referred to the specific places of the previous volumes for further reading and formal proofs whenever the arguments presented are more involved.

Chapter 3: The unified theory has been accepted under the epistemological rules of the alpha–beta method. In addition, the relative superiority of the unified theory to alternative economic theories have also been established applying this method to all. Has this method left unanswered some epistemological problems that affect those results?

Chapter 4: According to the evolutionary model, the most relevant exogenous variable to explain economic growth with social maladies is the initial inequality in the individual endowments of economic and social assets. Historically, where would this initial inequality come from? What is the role of the European colonial legacy in the functioning of today's capitalism? Does this history matter?

Chapter 5: Is population growth cause or consequence of the outcome of economic growth with social maladies? What is the role of population in the Anthropocene age?

Chapter 6: The evolutionary model analyses the interactions between human activities and the bio-physical environment in the economic process. This is also the scope of the new bio-economics school. Are these two theories consistent with each other?

Chapter 7: The relation between individual freedom and the common goods is one of the fundamental questions about capitalism. This relation has been studied for centuries. What is the nature of this relationship now under the Anthropocene age?

Chapter 8: Science-based public policies have been derived from the unified theory. This derivation has an epistemology justification. However, what is its ethical justification? What was the implicit normative theory?

Chapter 9: Public policies of no-growth have been derived from the unified theory. How could real wage rates increase in a no-growth capitalist society?

Chapter 10: The main findings and further implications that can be derived from the essays are summarized here.

By giving answers to these questions, the set of essays presented in this book should make the implications of the unified theory and its derived public policies much more understandable, not only for students and researchers of economics, but for other scientists, and the general reader as well. The book does not require previous knowledge of the unified theory of capitalism. It does require, however, scientific thirst for understanding the fundamental social problems of our time in the new Anthropocene age.

CHAPTER 2

The Unified Theory of Capitalism: An Overview

The unified theory of capitalism has recently been presented as a new scientific endeavor in economics in several books. The first version (Figueroa 2009) was followed by a book containing the central theoretical and empirical findings (Figueroa 2015, Vols. I and II), which then was followed by a third book dealing with the public policy implications of the unified theory (Figueroa 2017). This is a fourth book in the series, dealing with further questions and implications of the unified theory.

The book-review articles on the previous books have in general praised their achievements; in addition, they have also raised some specific questions, but none of epistemological significance as to merit some major revisions (Bulmer-Thomas 2010; Goodwin 2016; Barrón et al. 2016; Charles 2018). Some authors have criticized the assumption of the unified theory. On epistemological grounds, the assumptions of a theory cannot be judged a priori, but only a posteriori, by testing the consistency between the empirical predictions of the theory with facts. Others have pointed out that more statistical testing is needed before accepting the theory.

Certainly, more testing of a theory is always welcome. The unified theory presents another view of society, with new relevant variables, datasets of which are scarce. Given the available datasets and empirical studies, the most salient facts of capitalism are consistent with the predictions of the unified theory, as will be summarized in this chapter.

On epistemological grounds, any scientific theory is accepted only provisionally, until new datasets, new statistical theories, new epistemologies, or new and superior scientific theories become available. This is also the case of the unified theory.

This chapter presents the unified theory of capitalism in its most elementary form. The idea is to make the book self-contained and thus help the reader to follow the essays of the book by understanding the foundations of unified theory; therefore, this chapter includes the primary assumptions of the unified theory and its relevant models. The predictions of these models are then shown to be consistent with the basic facts of capitalism.

The emphasis is on the evolutionary model, as the essays of the book deal mostly with the economic growth process under social and environmental stress, which constitutes the fundamental problem of our time—including the fate of the human species. The public policy implications of the model are also presented in its most elementary form. Because the unified theory departs from standard economics, basic comparisons between the two are also presented. This should also help the reader to understand better the content of the book.

The Facts to Be Explained

Economics is the social science that deals with the production of goods and its distribution in human societies. Capitalism is one of these societies. Economics could explain the functioning of capitalism if the empirical regularities of production and distribution under capitalism were known. Fortunately, there exists a set of facts that is undisputable as a set of empirical regularities, which can be utilized for that purpose (Figueroa 2015, Vol. I, Chapter 2). They are:

Fact 1: Income gaps between First World and Third World countries are persistent and tend to increase over time.
Fact 2: Income inequality degree is persistently higher in the Third World than in the First World.
Fact 3: Existence and persistence of unemployment in the First World.
Fact 4: Existence and persistence of underemployment and unemployment in the Third World.
Fact 5: Existence and persistence of income gaps by ethnic groups in the Third World. Those ethnic groups who are the descendants of the populations under domination in the European colonial period tend to be the poorest.
Fact 6: In the short run, real and nominal variables are not independent neither in the First World nor in the Third World.
Fact 7: In the long run, real wage rates rise together with per capita income in both First World and Third World countries.
Fact 8: In the long run, rising income levels are accompanied by degradation of the biophysical environment in both First World and Third World countries.

Economic growth—the rise of per capita income or income levels over time—has characterized the two centuries of capitalist development. However, the growth rates of total output since the end of the World War II have been significant, reaching values never seen before. These rates have also been higher than the population growth rates, leading to significant growth rates in output per capita. This performance has been observed in both the First World and the Third World, the two major components of the capitalist system. In historical perspective, the last seven decades of capitalism may be called the economic growth age. The social consequences of the continuous rising in income levels have led to improvements in the social wellbeing, such as increase in life expectancy and decrease in poverty everywhere in the capitalist system. Empirical data show these features (World Bank 2017).

However, the economic growth age has also been accompanied by qualitative changes in society, such as the persistence or aggravation of unemployment, underemployment, income inequality, and the degradation of the biophysical environment (World Bank 2017; IPCC 2018). These side effects of output growth have led to social maladies, such as increasing social conflicts, social disorder, and rising risks in human health, more hazardous human life.

Social disorder refers to behavior of people not in agreement with the institutions of capitalism (property rights, market [voluntary] exchange, and democracy), such as illegal behavior with violence (trading, robbery, migration, and terrorism). Data on social disorder is very scarce. The United Nations world crime trends show that the number of prisoners per 10,000 population has been rising in the period 2003–2015 in Latin America, less markedly in Asia, and stable in Europe (no data on Africa); that is, this ratio and its increase is higher in more unequal societies.

Social disorder makes human life more hazardous. Environment degradation does too. Overall economic losses caused by natural disasters, associated to climate change—earthquake, flooding, drought, storm, wildfire—are increasing worldwide (Munich RE reports). Pollution is among the top factors of morbidity and among top killers in the world (World Bank and IHME 2016).

If the social wellbeing is measured in terms of life expectancy, the social progress seems indeed spectacular, as said above. If life expectancy is corrected by the health conditions of the people, the new indicator of healthy life expectancy shows little or no social progress in the last decades (IHME 2016). People indeed live longer but a sicker life. In sum, empirical data also show economic growth with social maladies.

Therefore, two sets of facts have been observed in the economic growth age. Set one: output growth and per capita output growth, declining poverty, and rising life expectancy. Set two: the same as set one, plus persistent unemployment, underemployment, rising income inequality, together with the continuous degradation of the biophysical environment (depletion and pollution together with climate change) and a more hazardous human life. The first set alone indicates economic growth with social progress, the second, economic growth with social maladies.

Two economic theories seek to explain the process of economic growth under capitalism: Neoclassical theory and the unified theory, the first explains the first set of facts and the latter the second set. The unified theory would seem to be superior to neoclassical theory, but this comparison requires epistemology, and a common epistemology.

Seeking Scientific Explanations

Science is epistemology. Scientific knowledge requires epistemological justification. This requirement is stronger in economics and the other social sciences than in natural sciences.

The reason is that the social world is much more complex than the physical world. In addition, when dealing with capitalist societies, scientific knowledge in economics can hardly be class-neutral, as class interests also play a role in research and publications. This makes the need of epistemological justification even stronger in economics.

The unified theory of capitalism has been presented as a new scientific endeavor in economics. Therefore, it had to meet the requirement that science is epistemology. Which epistemology? It has been shown (Figueroa 2016) that the best methodology, with the lowest degree of error among known methodologies, to be utilized in economics is the composite epistemology, a combination of two epistemologies: the abstract process, proposed by Nicholas Georgescu-Roegen (1971) and falsificationism, by Karl Popper (1968).

According to composite epistemology, scientific knowledge of hyper complex realities can be attained by transforming the real social world into an abstract social world, which takes the form of an abstract process. In economics, this transformation is made by using a set of assumptions (a scientific theory) about the components of the abstract economic process, which includes endogenous and exogenous variables, and the structure-mechanisms by which exogenous variables affect the endogenous variables, such that this relationship is falsifiable or testable by construction.

However, the composite epistemology—as any epistemology—only provides general principles of knowledge, such as, no scientific theory, then no explanation of reality; the use of abstraction makes a scientific theory in principle false. Then to make the composite epistemology operational a research method, logically derived from it, is needed. This is the alpha–beta method. The alpha-propositions constitute the assumptions of the scientific theory, whereas the beta-propositions are the derived empirical predictions of the alpha-propositions, which are falsifiable by construction. Hence, this method gives us rules for scientific research in economics, namely, rules to accept or reject scientific theories in economics (Figueroa 2016).

The unified theory and the neoclassical theory were thus submitted to the same rules, the alpha–beta method. Indeed, both economic theories are in accord with the requirements of the alpha–beta method, as they both assume that the economic process is composed of exogenous and endogenous variables and a given structure-mechanisms by which the exogenous variables affect the endogenous. In addition, both theories assume the same elements in the structure: institutions (private property rights, market systems, and electoral democracy), people's technological knowledge, and people's preferences. Finally, the economic process is analyzed through models of each theory. The difference between neoclassical theory and unified theory comes from assuming different processes, not only different endogenous and exogenous variables.

Unified Theory of Capitalism: Foundations

The set of primary assumptions (alpha propositions) of the unified theory of capitalism can be summarized as follows:

> *Institutional context.* The institutions of capitalist society include private property rights, markets, and electoral democracy. Because market exchange requires private property rights, the fundamental institutions of capitalism are markets and electoral democracy. Walrasian and non-Walrasian markets constitute the market system, where labor markets are of the second type.

Initial conditions. Individuals participating in the economic process are unequally endowed with economic and social assets. This is called the *initial inequality*. Individuals are separated by class and citizenship. The concentration of capital ownership implies the existence of class society (capitalists and workers), whereas the inequality in social assets implies the existence of first and second class citizens. The existence of initial inequality in conjunction with the institutions lead to a concentrated power structure, to a power elites, who run the society.

The unified theory also assumes that the capitalist system is not homogeneous, as different types of capitalism exist. Ontological universalism does not exist even within capitalism. Two types of capitalism are assumed: sigma society and epsilon society, such that in the latter case social assets are equally distributed and citizenship is not a social marker. Whereas sigma is a society of classes and citizenships, epsilon is a society of classes only.

In order to explain capitalism, sigma and epsilon constitute partial scientific theories, which will explain each type of capitalism, taken separately. Epsilon theory is intended to explain the First World and sigma theory the Third World. Then a unified theory will be needed to explain the capitalist system, taken as a whole, which is a sigma society.

Economic rationality. Workers act guided by the motivation of self-interest. In addition, they tolerate inequality but up to some limits only. When the degree of income inequality goes beyond their thresholds of tolerance, individuals will react and seek to restore it to a tolerable y situation, the actions of which will lead to social disorder, that is, to illegal behavior.

Capitalists operate through firms and seek to maximize profits. Politicians operate through political parties and seek to capture the state for their own benefits. To be sure, electoral democracy is a mechanism by which the political power of the people that is granted by the principle of democracy is transferred to the political elites, who then seek to buy votes to capture the state. Electoral democracy is business too. Economic and political elites constitute the power elite and they seek to exercise their power through the institutions of capitalism, markets and electoral democracy, for their own benefits.

Economic process is entropic. Finally, the unified theory assumes that the economic process is not an isolated system, independent of the ecological system. Humans as biological species are part of the ecological system. The economic process of production and distribution is subject to the laws of nature, such as photosynthesis and thermodynamics. This assumption implies that the outcome of the economic process includes not only goods but depletion and pollution of the environment, for waste is also an irrevocable outcome. In addition, pollution leads to climate change. Human health tolerance to pollution is limited; that is, if pollution concentration in the atmosphere reach a value that is beyond the threshold of human health tolerance, the fate of the human species is put to the risk of collapse.

The abstract capitalist societies so constructed are, of course, not equal to the real world society, as only some factors, those considered essential to its functioning, have been taken into account. Hence, the unified theory, as any scientific theory, is in principle false. The scientific question is of a different nature: does the abstract capitalist world, as constructed by the unified theory, *resemble well* the real capitalist world? This calls for empirical testing.

The direct testing of the unified theory is, however, unviable, for it is too abstract to be operational. According to alpha–beta method, the testing of a scientific theory in economics is attained through the construction of models of the theory: the very high abstract world is placed into a particular context to make it testable by the introduction of auxiliary assumptions. Unity of knowledge requires that the auxiliary assumptions should be logically consistent with the primary assumptions of the theory. The theoretical models so constructed allow us to derive empirical predictions about the relations between endogenous and exogenous variables. These predictions are the beta propositions of the model. They are falsifiable by construction and can then be used to test the model and either accept or reject it.

Three models are the most relevant: static for the short run, dynamic for the long run, and evolutionary for the very long run. The concept of "run" does not refer to chronological time, but to logical time, to what are assumed as givens. The longer the run, the fewer the factors that are considered as givens, and then the more adjustments that are allowed in the economic process; hence, the higher the number of the endogenous variables and the fewer the number of the exogenous variables that the economic process contains.

These three models of the unified theory have been constructed and submitted to the falsification task. The short run model seeks to explain production, employment, and distribution with capital and labor endowments as givens. The model is able to explain the Facts 3, 4, and 6 listed above. Capitalism operates with excess labor supply, which takes the form of unemployment in the First World and underemployment together with unemployment in the

Third World. Excess labor supply is a necessity for profit maximization, for it is the device to extract human effort.

The long run model or dynamic model is intended to explain the process of economic growth. Physical and human capital are now endogenously accumulated. The endogenous variable output per worker will increase over time. The dynamic model, as the static one, assume mechanical processes; hence, they can continue forever.

In the evolutionary model, the economic process is entropic. Depletion and pollution set limits to the reproduction of the growth process. In an evolutionary process, quantitative and qualitative changes take place in the economic process; in addition, the existence of qualitative changes and threshold values of the endogenous variables are assumed, such that when these threshold values are reached the process breaks down and a new process follows.

The Evolutionary Model

The evolutionary model of the unified theory will allow us to answer the qualitative changes that also take place in the economic growth process, in particular changes in the initial conditions, such as, does the initial inequality tend to decline?, does sigma society become epsilon society? The evolutionary model that was developed in a previous book (Figueroa 2017, Chapter 6) is now summarized.

According to unified theory, economic growth is not a mechanical process, but an evolutionary one. The economic process is entropic, subject to the laws of nature, including the laws of thermodynamics, which deals with the relations between matter and energy. Therefore, the economic process is evolutionary, for it will be accompanied by qualitative changes in the biophysical environment.

In the economic growth process, in the very long run, the interactions of man and nature are among the essential elements. Therefore, the evolutionary model can only refer to the capitalist system taken as a whole. Actually, it will refer to the world society, and to the world output, in which capitalism is the most significant system.

The evolutionary economic growth process is complex as it includes feedback effects. It also includes the existence of threshold values of tolerance, which set limits to the reproduction of the economic growth process. When the values of the endogenous variables go beyond the threshold values, the economic growth process comes to an end, to a collapse, and switches to a new process. Quantitative changes accompanied by qualitative changes take place in the economic growth process. Therefore, the economic growth process cannot go on forever. Economic growth is unsustainable.

The economic growth process seen as an evolutionary process is then represented by an evolutionary theoretical model, by including auxiliary assumptions to the alpha propositions of the unified theory. Hence, the evolutionary model assumes as exogenous variables the initial factor endowments, the initial stocks of renewable and non-renewable natural resources, and the initial inequality in asset endowments, whereas output per worker, degree of income inequality, and degree of degradation of the environment are the endogenous variables. The structure elements of the process include the institutions of capitalism (market and electoral democracy) in conjunction with the initial people's preferences and the initial level of people's technological knowledge—for these will be subject to endogenous change in the economic growth process.

Analytically, in the evolutionary model, the quantitative endogenous variables go through dynamic equilibrium situations over time, which imply particular trajectories. The use of dynamic equilibrium is only a logical artifice, for it is temporary only. The objective of the evolutionary model is to show the possible breakdown of the dynamic equilibrium due to the qualitative changes that accompany the quantitative changes. This will be kind of *supporting* dynamic model of the evolutionary model.

In the economic growth process, the relevant quantitative endogenous variable is output per worker—as it comprises changes in total output and in total population. The dynamic equilibrium or steady state trajectory of output per worker is called the growth frontier curve of society. As structural equations of the dynamic model, the level of the growth frontier curve depends upon the investment rate, the level of education of workers, the growth rate of population, and the initial technological level, whereas its slope depends upon the growth rate of technological change.

The model assumes that more equal societies constitute better environments for investment in both physical and human capital, for they are societies with higher social order, and thus less risky, and more prone to education as rights. Therefore, the investment rate and the education level are both higher in epsilon society than in sigma society. In addition, more equal societies care more for social protection policies, which lead to lower growth rates of population.

As to technology differences, the model assumes that the initial level of technology is higher in epsilon than in sigma. New technologies grow at a given rate over time (g), which is exogenously determined. The *adoption* of new technologies in each society grows at the same rate (g). Sigma society is overpopulated and thus operates with two sectors: capitalist and subsistence, where the residual workers generate their own incomes as self-employed. Technological adoption takes place in the capitalist sector only, for the subsistence sector is residual.

The technology adoption rate therefore corresponds to the behavior of the capitalist sector in each society. The assumption is that the adoption rates in both capitalist sectors proceed at equal rates, which is also equal to the rate of technological change; hence, this behavior maintains unchanged the initial gap in levels. Education equalization is the factor that can equalize technological levels.

Given the differences in their initial inequality, there will be a difference in the levels of the growth frontiers: that of the epsilon society lies at a higher level compared to that of the sigma society. The output per worker of each society moves along their particular growth frontier curves over time, growing at the same rate, but starting from different levels.

Assuming stability conditions in the dynamic equilibrium, it follows that from any initial situation of output per worker, a capitalist society's output per worker will move spontaneously towards its growth frontier curve. This is called the *transition dynamics*, which also constitutes a trajectory, for it takes time to reach the frontier. In epsilon society, once the growth frontier is reached, output per worker will travel along the frontier curve. In sigma society, the growth frontier curve will be reach if, and only if, the subsistence sector has been absorbed by the capitalist sector; otherwise, the frontier will only be approached.

The growth frontier curve is unobservable. It represents the dynamic equilibrium conditions. What is observable is the transition dynamics. It starts from the given value of output per workers and moves towards the growth frontier curve at a growth rate that is higher than that of the frontier (g), otherwise the catching up would be unviable.

The epsilon society and the sigma society will move towards their corresponding growth frontier curves from their particular initial situations: initial higher output per worker in epsilon.

The economic growth process does not imply the equalization in income levels between sigma and epsilon. The transition dynamics curves move towards different growth frontiers, different destinations, as they are placed at different levels. If there were a unique growth frontier curve for both societies, then they would move towards the same destination even departing from different starting points, and income levels would eventually be equalized. In this model, however, the economic growth process takes place under different frontiers; hence, the model predicts that income level differences will persist in the long run.

The relevant exogenous variable that keeps the growth frontier curves apart is the differences in the initial inequality in asset endowments of each society. Initial inequality is higher in sigma than in epsilon. Therefore, income level equalization between these societies would require equalization in the degree of initial inequality, which is exogenously determined. The initial inequality can change, but only exogenously.

Another prediction of the model is the persistence of the excess labor supply. Along the growth frontier curve of epsilon, excess labor supply in the form of unemployment rate remains positive. In sigma society, the rate of excess labor supply is also positive, and takes the form of unemployment and underemployment, which is equal to the self-employment in the subsistence sector. The economic growth process, no matter how high the growth rate is or for how long, will not eliminate the excess labor supply. The reason is that excess labor supply is required for the functioning of capitalism, for it is the device to extract effort from workers.

Regarding changes in income inequality in the economic growth process, the model predicts that it will remain unchanged in epsilon society. Profit maximizing capitalist firms will pay real wage rates that are equal to the marginal productivity of labor, which is a fraction of the average labor productivity, which is identical to output per worker. Therefore, real wage rates will grow at the same rate of that of output per worker. Wage share in total income will remain constant and so will profits share.

In sigma society, output per worker in the capitalist sector is higher than in the subsistence sector. Their growth rates will be different: higher in the capitalist sector than in the subsistence. Income distribution between capitalists and workers in the capitalist sector will not change (for the same reasons given for the case of epsilon). However, the income gap between the real wage rate and the average income in the subsistence sector will increase. Therefore, income inequality will tend to increase.

The subsistence sector is not homogeneous. It includes the group of workers who is not only endowed with low physical and human capital, but is also second class citizens. This group is called *z-workers*. This group is the poorest in society and its output per worker in the z-subsistence sector grows at the lowest rate compared to the other sectors. In sigma society, the economic growth process is accompanied by higher income inequality, which includes higher income inequality among workers as well (Figueroa 2015, Vol. II and Chapter 5).

It follows that the economic growth process will not transform the sigma society. The subsistence sector will remain. The differences in social entitlements—first class and second class citizens—will also persist. The sigma society will not endogenously become epsilon society.

Taking into account the capitalist system as a whole, output per worker is the highest in the epsilon society, followed by that in the capitalist sector of sigma, and the lowest in the subsistence sector of sigma. The model has no prediction over the growth rates of the two capitalist sector, as they refer to the transition dynamics. However, the model predicts that the subsistence sector will grow at the lowest rate. Therefore, income inequality will tend to increase over time. The capitalist system, takes as a whole, tends to behave like a sigma society.

The final prediction of the model is that, in the long run, income inequality degree depends upon the initial inequality in assets endowments. This is the exogenous variable of the model. Exogenous increases in the initial inequality in epsilon will cause a higher income inequality. The power elites will concentrate higher degree of power and will be able to exercise their power with greater force through markets and electoral democracy. In sigma society, an increase in the initial inequality will shift upward the curve showing income inequality rising over time. The same conclusion applies to the capitalists system as a whole.

Since epsilon and sigma theories intend to represent in abstract form the First World and the Third World, the evolutionary model is able to explain Facts 1–2 listed above. Moreover, and predicted by the model, income inequality in the capitalist system as a whole tends to increase over time endogenously and also due to the effect of increases in the exogenous variable *initial inequality* (higher concentration of capital), as shown for the case of rich countries by Piketty (2014, Chapter 5).

The model also explains Facts 3–4, for economic growth proceeds with excess labor supply. Fact 5 is also explained because in the Third World the z-workers are the populations that are descendants of the dominated people in colonial times who are mostly in the subsistence sector and thus constitute the poorest groups among workers. Finally, the model is able to explain also Fact 7, for growth generates rising real wage rates (Fact 6 was explained by the short run model, as shown earlier).

The evolutionary model has thus explained the basic long run facts of capitalism listed above, except Fact 8. To this we now turn.

In order to study the connection of the economic process with the ecosystem, the model will assume a capitalist system that is dominant in the world economy. Then the model assumes that mineral resources is the main source of matter and energy inputs required in the economic process. (The other source is sun energy.) The model also assumes a fixed coefficient, technologically determined, in the relation between mineral resource inputs and total output.

What does happen to the biophysical environment in the production process? The relations between mineral resource inputs and total output (material output) are subject to the physical laws of thermodynamics, dealing with relations between matter and energy. According to the first law, the conservation law, material inputs (copper) utilized in production enter part into the material output and part must become waste; similarly, energy inputs (oil) utilized in production enter part to produce work and part must become dissipated energy. Therefore, production of goods must be accompanied by waste.

According to the second law, the entropy law, this waste leads to pollution of the atmosphere, which implies a qualitative change in the biophysical environment. There are natural sinkers—oceans and forests—that can absorb part of the pollution emissions, but the production process generates pollution above that. The model assumes a fixed coefficient, technologically determined, in the relation between the mineral resource inputs and the flow of pollution, net of the removal by natural sinkers. The flow of pollutants are then concentrated in the atmosphere. In addition, the stock of mineral resources are continuously depleted. Therefore, entropic economic process means production of goods with depletion and pollution of the biophysical environment.

Pollution leads to climate change. Pollutants include greenhouse gases (CO_2), the increase of which raises the temperature in the Earth's surface. The natural climate—and the natural niche of human species—is maintained by the greenhouse effect, without which the surface temperature would be much cooler on average. Although the physics of climate is a hyper complex system, with many feedback effects, pollution through the greenhouse effect leads ultimately to rising temperatures. Climate change then implies not only extreme temperatures, but changes in the patterns of rainfalls, flooding, drought, and so on, and thus human life becomes more hazardous.

The two fixed coefficients that have been assumed above imply an aggregate fixed coefficient in the relation between mineral resource inputs and total output and the accompanying waste. Therefore, the model predicts that as output per worker increases over time, which implies increases in total output, then the pollution flow will also increase proportionally to total output, and the concentration of pollution in the atmosphere will increase over time as well. The higher the growth rate of total output, the higher the growth rate of the pollution flow, and the higher the pollution concentrations in the atmosphere. Thus the evolutionary model is able to explain Fact 8.

Quality of Society

According to the evolutionary model of the unified theory of capitalism, the economic growth process generates increasing output per worker, a quantitative outcome, accompanied by qualitative changes: rising income inequality and rising pollution and climate change. Increasing income levels lead to higher consumption levels of the population and thus to higher wellbeing of society. But the qualitative changes imply degradation in both social and biophysical environments, which in turn implies a higher degree of social disorder and a more risky and hazardous human life, and thus lower degree of wellbeing of society. Social maladies are thus increasing at each period along the growth frontier curve of society.

What is then the net effect of economic growth upon the quality of society? The model predicts that at the first stages of economic growth the positive effect dominates, but ultimately the negative effect will. Hence, the quality of society will depict an inverse-U shape curve over time for a given power structure.

The evolutionary model predicts the breakdown of the current economic growth process. The limits to the economic growth process could come from the threshold values of human tolerance for income inequality, depletion or pollution, whichever comes first. Income inequality cannot increase forever, for there are limits to the social disorder and the social conflicts that higher degrees of inequality generate. Degradation of the environment refers to pollution of the atmosphere and climate change, which cannot go on forever either: the human health tolerance for the concentration of pollution is limited. Finally, depletion of non-renewable natural resources (minerals) cannot go on forever either, because it constitutes a given stock on the crust of the earth.

Pollution and depletion limits would imply the risk of collapse of human society, as we know it.

The evolutionary model predicts that the breakdown of the economic growth process will come from the limits given by pollution, for this is a *problem of the commons* and thus no social actor has incentives to control it. Pollution concentration in the atmosphere increases in the process of economic growth and there will exist a time $T = T^*$, at which the threshold limit of human tolerance for pollution will be reached. The breakdown of the process will occur at this period and a new process with de-growth will follow.

The facts that we know about the economic growth process tend to be consistent with the predictions of the evolutionary model of the unified theory: The outcome of the economic growth includes rising income levels but accompanied by social maladies, as said above. In particular, the summary indicator of healthy life expectancy suggest that the downward sloping part of the quality of society curve has already been reached.

In addition, Earth scientists have shown that indeed the planet has already entered into a new age—replacing the Holocene age—beginning around the 1950s, which is properly called the Anthropocene age, as the change originates mostly from human activities—namely, from rapid economic growth. These scientists have also shown that global warming is *likely* to reach 1.5 °C of increase—the threshold value to avoid big natural disasters—between 2030 and 2050 if it continues to increase at the current rate (IPCC 2018). This scientific finding is also consistent with the predictions of the evolutionary model of the unified theory: The negative net effect of the economic growth process upon the quality of society appears to be already dominant.

Is the end of the economic process irreversible? Yes, that is what an evolutionary model says. According to the laws of thermodynamics, degradation of the environment can go only in one direction, degradation is irreversible—a cup falling from a table will become a broken cup, but the broken cup could not possibly return to the initial cup. Therefore, the economic growth process is an entropic process, generating waste and degradation of the environment, which cannot continue forever. Economic growth is *ecologically unsustainable*. The economic growth process has an end period of collapse, at which it will be replaced by another. Then the fundamental problem or our time is not our social maladies only; the very survival of the human species is now at stake.

The only choice with which human society is now left is to retard the collapse period ($T = T^*$). Could the retardation of the economic growth collapse occur endogenously?

The evolutionary model assumes the existence of a power elite, who run the capitalist society, as they exercise their power through the institutions of capitalism, market and electoral democracy, but following their own interests. Then the elites have the power to change technology, an exogenous variable of the evolutionary model. Thus, technological innovations can be controlled and changed through investment in innovations. However, the incentive is greater for labor saving innovations, which will imply higher profits than capital saving. Therefore, along the growth frontier curve, technological change that is labor saving is taking place.

The incentives to invest in mineral saving technologies are less significant. The biophysical environment degradation is the problem of the commons. Unless profits are increased in doing something to reduce the degradation, such as higher relative price of minerals to induce the innovations, the power elite would let the current economic growth process to continue, even if that choice is suicidal. Furthermore, the mineral extraction industry will oppose any technological change that is mineral saving.

Would workers press for changing the current economic growth process? Workers also act guided by self-interest. Then they also see the environment degradation problem as the commons problem. Even if they had the incentives, they do not have the power.

From biology we know that human behavior is the result of both nature (genes) and nurture (social influence); moreover, we humans are endowed with two drives: egotism and altruism. Then on the evolution of human behavior, the relative strength of these two drives is not fixed by nature, but by the influence of society. The biological theory implies that Human behavior can be controlled and changed. We humans are vulnerable to manipulation.

How does the human behavior evolution operate under capitalism? Power elites are able to change workers' behavior in directions that benefit the elite's interests by applying behavioral engineering techniques. They have the incentives, the power, and the instruments to do so. The egotistical drive of human make-up is constantly exacerbated and the altruistic drive is weaken. Therefore, in each period along the growth frontier curve of society, workers' preference systems are continuously induced to change towards consumerism, modernization of life style, and become more egotistic, opportunistic, individualistic, and less altruistic in their behavior (Figueroa 2017, Chapters 3–5).

Workers are thus losing autonomy over time. Individuals are endowed with two human drives: egotism and altruism, and the combination is socially determined. Therefore, it is not that workers are naturally highly egotists, they have become so by the influence of capitalism. Therefore, workers have neither the power not the incentive to change the current economic growth process, as they have become part of it.

Science-Based Public Policies

According to the evolutionary model, the current economic growth process will continue as long as the power structure remains unchanged. The outcome of this process is higher income levels over time, but accompanied by social maladies. In a democratic society, such as capitalism, this outcome is certainly a paradox. The unified theory is able to explain this paradox. Firstly, democracy under capitalism takes a particular form, electoral democracy. Secondly, the initial inequality in assets distribution implies the existence of economic and political elites. Markets and electoral democracy constitute the mechanisms through which these elites can exercise power over society. Hence, the institutions of capitalism together with the initial inequality create a concentrated power structure, a power elite in society.

Thirdly, the power elite has the incentive to promote pro-growth public policies, for they are the major beneficiaries of economic growth, not only maintaining absolute and relative income but also maintaining their privileged social position. Moreover, the power elites have induced changes in human drives; workers have increasingly become more egotists. The environmental problem is the problem of the commons, for which the increasing egotism of the elites and workers will not be of help. Egotism leads to blind behavior regarding its social consequences. In sum, the capitalism is not a self-regulating system. This is why we have reached the current dramatic situation. Thus, the paradox is given an explanation.

New public policies are then needed. The economic growth process is entropic and thus evolutionary. It is not mechanical, that is, it cannot go on forever. It is ecologically unsustainable. It is subject to a breakdown. The collapse period (T^*) depends upon the rate of output growth—the higher this rate, the sooner the collapse. In order to delay the collapse period, therefore, the current pro-growth policies should be dethroned and public policies that seek to improve the quality of society—free of social maladies—should be enthroned instead. Higher quality of society would also be the legacy for the next generations as well.

In the evolutionary model, the criterion of social wellbeing is quality of society. This is the common good. This criterion is far from the individualistic wellbeing principle, such as Pareto optimality, utilized in standard economics. Under the situation of collective risk of survival, as the human species is facing now, the common good should prevail over the individual interest. This may be called the *common good principle*. Thus, on this normative principle, science-based public policies have been derived from the unified theory of capitalism.

The no-growth public policies would then reduce the pollution emissions and thus retard the collapse period. Technology innovations that are mineral saving would also be needed, so that the flow of pollution be reduced further. As a result, human life would be less hazardous due to climate change. However, the no-growth policy will maintain unchanged the current degree of income inequality. Congealing this high degree of inequality would also maintain social disorder. Therefore, reducing social maladies and having a higher quality of society would need policies to redistributive income, within and between the First and Third Worlds. More equal societies are high quality societies.

These new public policies are against the interests of the power elites. They would not be viable, unless the power structure with which capitalism operates is changed.

The current power structure is a combination of the initial inequality (exogenous variable) and the institutions of capitalism (structure elements). However, any policy seeking the redistribution of physical capital endowments would be socially unviable—it would go against the institution of private property rights, thus it would call for a revolution. Redistribution of human capital is obviously unviable. Eliminating the differences in social entitlements—the existence of first and second class citizens—would require breaking with history, for this is the European colonial legacy. This would be a socially complex operation.

On institutional changes, the market system is part of the core of capitalism and must remain. Actually, market is a mechanism to solve voluntary exchange of goods in society. The market theory assumes that it operates like a big computer, solving the system of equations that imply individual behavior, and coming up with a set of prices and quantities of equilibrium. This is how the market works now, even with a power elite. In more equal society (free from power elites), the equations of the market system would be different and the big computer will come up with a different solution of prices and quantities of equilibrium, which imply new income distribution.

What about electoral democracy, which is a particular form of democracy? Political power originates in the electoral democracy, for it is the mechanism by which the workers' political power—granted by the principle of democracy—is transferred to the political elites, who are then able to capture the state and use it for their own benefits. Economic elites exercise their power not only through markets but also through electoral democracy. Therefore, electoral democracy is a distortion of the way in which democracy is defined.

Replacing electoral democracy by a form of workers' democracy—in accord with the democracy principle of *the government of the people, for the people, and by the people*, for under capitalism the people are the workers—would then change the current power structure to a more balance one. Economic elites would maintain their economic power through markets, but now workers would have the political power and the control of the state.

A workers' democracy is an institutional change. It does not change the concentrated distribution of physical and social assets. In particular, inequality in social entitlements remains unchanged. First and second class citizens are still part of the system. Workers' democracy would not lead to a break with history. It would not transform a sigma society into an epsilon society. However, it would make capitalism operate under weaker power relations and under a new set of public policies. Thus, higher quality of society would be achievable.

The fact that economic growth with social maladies is an outcome of a democratic capitalism is certainly a paradox. Democracy should make the system self-regulating. The unified theory explains why this is not the case: Democratic capitalism operates with electoral democracy, which is also business, plutocracy; therefore, democratic capitalism operates with a power structure.

Replacing the institution of electoral democracy for another form of more direct democracy in which political power is given back to workers would then lead to a new power structure, which would make viable the new public policies needed for the new Anthropocene age. The solution to the fundamental problem of our time thus requires an institutional innovation of capitalism, a re-foundation of capitalism.

Comparisons with Standard Economics

The unified theory of capitalism is able to explain the functioning of this system. The empirical predictions of the models of the theory are consistent with the list of eight basic empirical regularities of capitalism, as shown above. In particular, the evolutionary model is able to explain the outcome of economic growth with social maladies. Science-based policies has been derived from this model to cope with the challenges of the Anthropocene age.

Comparisons with standard economics—neoclassical and Keynesian economics—are in order. The set of facts that standard economics can explain are also explained by the unified theory: existence and persistence of excess labor supply and economic growth with poverty reduction and rising life expectancy. However, standard economics cannot explain the fact that economic growth is accompanied by social maladies.

The difference, of course, lies in the set of primary assumptions (the alpha propositions). Standard economics ignores what the unified theory assumes as essential factors, namely, power relations in society, the social consequences of excessive income inequality, and the entropic nature of the economic process; that is, these factors may exist and have an effect upon the economic process, but the assumption of standard economics is that their effect is small and thus they can be ignored. Instead, standard economics assumes a society where competition is a significant force in the functioning of a free society, such as capitalism. Any economic or political power will in the long run be eliminated by the force of competition.

According to standard economics, economic growth is seen as a mechanical process and can thus go on forever. According to unified theory, economic growth is seen as an evolutionary process; then it cannot go on forever and is subject to a breakdown.

Differences in public policies also follow. Standard economics implies public policies that keep promoting economic growth—"business as usual." The discourse is that the existence of social problems just reflects the need of higher growth rates. Unified theory implies de-growth and income redistribution, which in turn implies a re-foundation of capitalism. Whereas standard economics assumes that we still live in the Holocene age, where natural resources were abundant, unified theory says that we already live in the new Anthropocene age. Standard economics is clearly the old economics, whereas unified theory is the new.

In sum, the basic facts about capitalism are consistent with the predictions of unified theory and refute those of standard economics. On epistemological grounds, therefore, standard economics would have to be rejected. This conclusion means that the assumptions of standard economics (alpha propositions) are proven to be inappropriate as abstract representation of the real world capitalism, as they lead to predictions (beta propositions) that are refuted by facts. Standard economics ignores some factors that are essential to understand capitalism.

References

Barrón, M., Silva Macher, J. C., Dancourt, O., & Jiménez, F. (2016). Book symposium on *Growth, employment, inequality, and the environment: Unity of knowledge in economics* by Adolfo Figueroa. *Economía, 78*, 151–186.

Bulmer-Thomas, V. (2010). *A unified theory of capitalist development* by Adolfo Figueroa. *Journal of Human Development and Capabilities, 11*(2), 359–361.

Charles, A. (2018). *Economics of the Anthropocene age* by Adolfo Figueroa. *Journal of Development Studies*, 54(8), 1472–1473.
Figueroa, A. (2009). *A unified theory of capitalist development*. Buenos Aires: Cengage Learning.
Figueroa, A. (2015). *Growth, employment, inequality, and the environment: Unity of knowledge in economics*, Vols. I and II. New York, NY: Palgrave Macmillan.
Figueroa, A. (2016). *Rules for scientific research in economics: The alpha-beta method*. New York, NY: Palgrave Macmillan Springer.
Figueroa, A. (2017). *Economics of the Anthropocene age*. Cham, Switzerland: Palgrave Macmillan Springer.
Georgescu-Roegen, N. (1971). *The entropy law and the economic process*. Cambridge, MA: Harvard University Press.
Goodwin, G. (2016). *Growth, employment, inequality, and the environment: Unity of knowledge in economics* by Adolfo Figueroa. *Journal of Human Development and Capabilities*, 17(4), 606–607.
Piketty, T. (2014). *Capital in the twenty first century*. Cambridge, MA: Harvard University Press.
Popper, K. (1968). *The logic of scientific discovery*. London, UK: Routledge.

Data Sources

Institute for Health Metrics and Evaluation (IHME). (2016). *Global burden of disease*. http://www.healthdata.org/gbd.
Intergovernmental Panel on Climate Change (IPCC). (2018). https://www.ipcc.ch/.
Munich RE. https://www.munichre.com/topics-online/en/climate-change-and-natural-disasters/natural-disasters/climate-facts-2015.html.
United Nations Economic and Social Council. (2017). *World crime trends and emerging issues and responses in the field of crime prevention and criminal justice*. https://www.unodc.org/.../reports-on-world-crime-trends.html.

World Bank. (2017). *World development indicators.* https://data.worldbank.org/indicator.

World Bank & IHME. (2016). *The cost of air pollution: Strengthening the economic case for action.* Washington, DC: The World Bank.

CHAPTER 3

Science Is Epistemology

Epistemology is the logic of scientific knowledge in factual sciences. Then it is seen as a formal science—or as part of logic—and giving rationality to the knowledge in factual sciences. Factual sciences could not establish their own rationality because the criterion to accept or reject the existence of relations between facts cannot be based on the facts themselves. Epistemology is thus the science of sciences.

Analytically, epistemology takes the form of a *theory of knowledge*: A set of assumptions about those requirements that give scientific knowledge in factual sciences a logic, a rationale to determine its validity and limits. As in any theory, the set of assumptions of an epistemology must constitute a logical system, free of internal contradictions. In addition, the set of assumptions should be able to generate a set of practical rules for doing scientific research. The knowledge so attained in factual sciences will be scientific in the sense that the risk of error is minimized.

Seeking to produce scientific knowledge without epistemology is just like searching for something in a dark room. Epistemology constitutes the required light.

Economics is a science that deals with the social world, which is a highly complex reality. Then, the more fundamental is the role of epistemology in the development of scientific knowledge in economics—and in the social sciences in general. The unified theory of capitalism has been developed following the rules of the alpha–beta research method, which has logically been derived from the composite epistemology, which in turn is a combination of the epistemologies of abstract process (Georgescu-Roegen 1971) and falsificationism (Popper 1968). Therefore, the accepted validity of the unified theory—including its relative superiority to standard economics—depends on the logical validity of the alpha–beta method. Some further elaborations and clarifications on the properties of the alpha–beta method are then presented in this essay.

The Alpha–Beta Method

The epistemology of the abstract process assumes that a hyper complex real world—as the social world—can be understood if it can be transformed into an abstract world, a much simpler world, such that the abstract world takes the form of an *abstract process*. The elements of the abstract process include endogenous variables (Y), exogenous variables (X), and the mechanisms (M) by which the exogenous variables affect the endogenous variables; moreover, in order to have this influence the exogenous variables act upon a given structure (S) of society. The role of the structure was only implicit in the previous presentations of the alpha–beta method (Figueroa 2016), and will now be made explicit.

What is this structure S? Consider anatomy and physiology, which are inseparable elements in the functioning of human body, although we may call them structure and mechanism respectively. As this example indicates, there is a correspondence between the two, the structure (anatomy) implies a mechanism (physiology) and vice-versa. In the abstract process, the structure-mechanism elements play similar roles. They refer to those traits that make society identifiable, as a well-defined type of society, and thus susceptible of scientific knowledge.

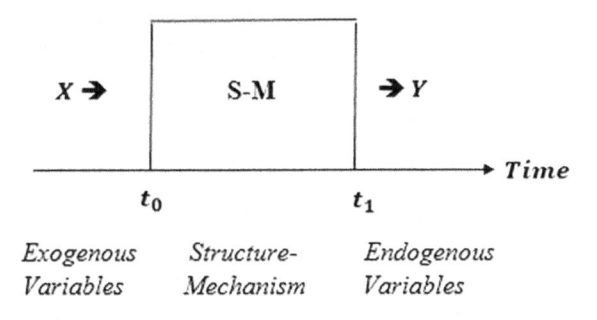

Figure 3.1 shows the diagrammatic representation of an abstract process. What an abstract process says is that changes in the exogenous variables (X), acting upon the structure (S), and through the mechanism (M), will modify the endogenous variables (Y) in particular directions. The process has a given duration ($t_0 - t_1$), which is repeated period after period.

How do we establish the elements of the abstract process? Not by empirical observations, for the objective of the abstract process is precisely to explain those observations—by determining the underlying factors. This is just to confirm that epistemology cannot be constructed from factual sciences themselves, as said above.

Exogenous and endogenous variables must satisfy the definition of a *variable: the changes of which are measurable,*

Fig. 3.1 Diagrammatic representation of an abstract process

countable, and can be assigned a meaningful "size." In contrast, the elements of the process that are not variables belong to the structure elements of *S–M*. They are qualitative, uncountable elements, which are supposed to be the underlying factors operating in the observed relations between endogenous and exogenous variables.

According to alpha–beta method, the elements of the abstract process—endogenous and exogenous variables and the structure elements—are established by a set of assumptions, called the *alpha propositions*, which constitutes the scientific theory. The transformation of a hyper complex real world into an abstract world thus requires a scientific theory.

The scientific theory transforms the real world into an abstract world by making assumptions about what is essential and what is not in the functioning of society; hence, the theory retains the first and ignores the second. It follows that the construction of the abstract world constitutes a distortion of the real world. Therefore, the scientific theory is in principle empirically false. Whether the abstract world is a *good approximation* of the real world requires confronting the theory against facts, which in turn requires that the scientific theory be falsifiable or refutable. This is the principle of falsificationism.

The theory to be scientific must then be able to generate a set of propositions that are observable and falsifiable, which are called the *beta propositions*. Therefore, beta propositions constitute the empirical predictions about the relations between the endogenous and exogenous variables that are derived logically from the alpha-propositions, from the set of assumptions of the theory. Hence, if beta propositions fail (are refuted by facts), then the set of alpha propositions fails and then the scientific theory fails as a good approximation of the real world, for its assumptions were proved to be inappropriate.

The objective of a scientific theory is to *explain* the real world. Scientific explanation can only mean that the scientific theory is able to establish *causality relations: what causes what.* The alpha–beta method allows us to answer this fundamental scientific question, for causality relations refer to the effect of exogenous variables upon endogenous variables.

The alpha–beta method is thus logically consistent with the composite epistemology. The alpha-propositions constitute the set of assumptions of the theory by which a complex reality is transformed into an abstract process, from which beta-propositions are logically derived, and constitute, by construction, the empirical predictions of the theory and are falsifiable. Furthermore, the alpha–beta method allow us to establish causality relations in hyper complex worlds.

A scientific theory will then fail to explain the real social world on two accounts: either because its set of assumptions is inappropriate or because the nature of the real world under study is not amenable to transformation into an abstract process, an orderly abstract world. This would be the case of social worlds that are chaotic in some periods, such as wars and hyperinflations.

Now consider economics. It is a social science that studies the activity of production and distribution of goods in human societies. This is done by constructing an abstract society that is intended to represent fairly well the real social world. The real social world is seen through an *abstract economic process*. The elements of the economic process are established by assumptions, by a scientific economic theory.

It follows that in order to derive beta propositions from alpha propositions, these must not be tautological propositions. For example, no empirical prediction can be obtained from a proposition that is unobservable but tautological, such as "capitalists seek what they desire" (for whatever capitalists do, it must always be what they desire to do!).

This is a useless assumption because it cannot generate falsifiable empirical predictions, unless it states what exactly is "what people desire." Consider instead the assumption "capitalists seek to maximize profits," which is unobservable and also non-tautological, for in principle it could be false; hence, beta propositions can be derived from it.

In economics, a scientific theory is too general to be submitted directly to falsification. The alpha-proposition about capitalists' motivation stated above can hardly be tested, unless the capitalists are placed in a particular social context in which they operate, such as monopoly, oligopoly or perfect competition markets, or in a context of given capital stocks (in the short run) or capital accumulation (in the long run). Hence, in dealing with the social world—a hyper complex reality—falsification requires the construction of *models* of the theory, which place the theory in a particular context, at a lower level of abstraction, to make them falsifiable, subject to the condition that the number of models be finite. An economic theory is then a family of models.

Consider the case of the unified theory. Its set of assumptions (alpha propositions) transforms the real world capitalism into an abstract capitalist society. In order to make the theory falsifiable, theoretical models were utilized. Three forms of economic processes leading to corresponding models were: static model, for the short run, and dynamic model, for the long run, are defined as mechanical processes; then there is the evolutionary model, for the very long run.

Causality in Mechanical Processes

Static and dynamic theoretical models assume the existence of structural relations, that is, relations between all variables of the process, which constitute the structural equations. From these, we obtain the reduced form equations, which show the endogenous variables as function of the exogenous variables alone, given the structure S. This is the general equilibrium solution of the model, showing the market prices and quantities of equilibrium, and the consequent solution of production and distribution in the capitalist society.

Consider firstly a static model, which represents a corresponding static process in the short run in the capitalism system. The static process refers to the case in which the relations between endogenous variables in the structural equations are contemporaneous; moreover, in the reduced form equations, the *values* of the endogenous variables remain unchanged as long as the *values* of the exogenous variables also remain unchanged.

In the static model of the unified theory, the endogenous variables (Y) include total output and income distribution and the exogenous variables (X) include factor endowments, initial inequality, and the international terms of trade. About the components of the structure elements of the abstract process, the static model assumes the following:

- Institutions: markets (S_1) and electoral democracy (S_2),
- People's technological knowledge (S_3), and
- People's preference systems (S_4).

Therefore, this set of assumptions implies $S = (S_1, S_2, S_3, S_4)$. Changes in structure implies a different set.

The passage from alpha to beta propositions is a logical one, namely, it requires a theorem. This theorem can be stated as follows:

Static Process Theorem
If

1. Given theory α, let $\alpha°$ be a static model of α, such that $\alpha° = \alpha + A$, where A is the set of auxiliary assumptions

that refer to the particular social context of the static process.
2. The structural equations of the model are given by the following implicit functions, for n endogenous variables

$$\Phi_j(X, Y_j; S) = 0, j = 1, 2, \ldots, n$$

3. Static equilibrium exists and is stable, such that Y_0 are the values of equilibrium.

Then

The reduced form equations are

[β] $\quad Y^0 = F(X; S),\ F_{ij}$ is either $> 0,\ < 0, = 0,$ or $= (?)$ (3.1)

Function F says that the equilibrium values of the endogenous variables (Y^0) depend upon the values of the exogenous variables (X), given the structure elements of the process (S). This set of relations between endogenous and exogenous variables is clearly defined and are thus testable. Therefore, the reduced form equations show the beta propositions of the model at the same time.

Causality relations in the static process (and in the short run) can be defined as the effect of changes in the exogenous variables (X) upon the equilibrium values of the endogenous variables (Y^0), given the structure elements of society (S). Causality relations are thus given by the beta propositions of the model.

To be sure, the causal effect of a particular exogenous variable (X_j) upon a particular endogenous variable (Y_r) means that the value of the other exogenous variables and the structure of society remain unchanged. In mathematical terms, the causality relation is given by the partial derivative of Υ_j with respect to X_j, represented by F_{ij}, the values of which could be positive, negative, nil (0), or undetermined (with the interrogative sign).

It follows that causality relations in static models can only be established under *givens*. Therefore, causality refers to the *marginal* effects—not to the *total* effects—of changes in each exogenous variable upon changes in the endogenous variables. The causality relations and the beta propositions can then be represented by a matrix (F_{ij}), with the signs of the partial derivatives in each cell.

Causality is thus an analytical concept, derived from a theoretical model. It refers to *what causes what*, and thus separates the cause from consequence. It is not a statistical concept, neither a philosophical one.

Consider now a dynamic model, which corresponds to a dynamics process, in the long run. It assumes that there exists inter-temporal relations between endogenous variables in the structural equations, which implies that in the reduced form equations each endogenous variable moves along a particular trajectory over time, given the *values* of the exogenous variables and given the structure S. Again, the passage from alpha to beta propositions is a logic one, and thus requires a theorem. This theorem can be stated as follows:

Dynamic Process Theorem
If

1. Given theory α, let α^* be a dynamic model of α, such that $\alpha^* = \alpha + A^*$, where A^* is the set of auxiliary assumptions that refer to the particular social context of the dynamic process.

2. The structural equations of the model are given by the following implicit functions, for n endogenous variables:

$$\Psi_j(X, Y_{jt}, Y_{jt-1}; S) = 0, \, j = 1, 2, \ldots, n$$

3. Dynamic equilibrium exists and is stable, such that Y_t^* are the values of equilibrium over time t.

Then
The reduced form equations are

$$Y^*(t) = G(t; X; S) \tag{3.2}$$

$$[\beta] \quad Y(t) = G'(t; X; S; Y_0) < Y^*(t) \tag{3.2'}$$

The dynamic equilibrium trajectory is represented by Eq. (3.2). Function G is the set of reduced form equations of the dynamic model and says that the equilibrium values of the set of endogenous variables (Y^*) follow a particular trajectory over time (t), for given values of the exogenous variables (X) and given the structure elements of the process (S). To be sure, dynamic equilibrium of an endogenous variable is not a particular value of the variable, but a succession of values over time, that is, a particular trajectory or path, a curve over time.

In Eq. (3.2'), function G' represents the *transition dynamics* toward the dynamic equilibrium trajectory, which refers to the spontaneous adjustment of the dynamic equilibrium, whenever it is out of equilibrium. The transition dynamics is assumed to be a trajectory as well, for the full adjustment takes time, that is, it takes time to reach the dynamic equilibrium curve from any situation out of equilibrium. Transition dynamics starts from the initial conditions of society (Y_0) and moves spontaneously to converge to its dynamic equilibrium curve. Therefore, function G' becomes function G when convergence is attained, as the endogenous variables now move along the dynamic equilibrium path.

In Eq. (3.2), changes in the exogenous variables and in the structure elements will modify the trajectory of the dynamic equilibrium in particular directions. Furthermore, the exogenous changes will also modify the trajectory of the corresponding transition dynamics, now moving to the new dynamic path or curve, as indicted in Eq. (3.2′).

Function G is unobservable, for it is still part of the assumptions of the model—the existence of dynamic equilibrium. Therefore, function G cannot be submitted to falsification; that is, in this case the set of reduced form equations is not the set of beta propositions of the model. The beta propositions are given by the transition dynamics (function G'), for it is observable. However, it should be clear from the Eqs. (3.2) and (3.2′) that the transition dynamics reflects fully the corresponding dynamic equilibrium conditions and that changes in exogenous variables or structure elements will change the dynamic equilibrium of the endogenous variables and thus the corresponding dynamic transition trajectories in the same directions. Therefore, the dynamic model can be tested by the transition dynamics; if the latter fails, the former does too.

Given that the causality relations derived from the dynamic equilibrium and from the transition dynamics are equivalent, as shown above, then the beta propositions of the dynamic model—which are observed through the transition dynamics—also provides the causality relations of the dynamic model. In sum, the transition dynamics is then observable and testable by construction. Therefore, transition dynamics shows the set of beta propositions and of causality relations of the dynamic model.

In order to illustrate this property, consider the dynamic model of the unified theory of capitalism. The dynamic model of the unified theory assumes as endogenous variables (Y) output per worker and income inequality and as exogenous variables (X) the initial factor endowments and the initial inequality. The structure elements of the process are just those of the static model. The dynamic equilibrium of output per worker (y^*) is a rising curve over time, which is called the *growth frontier curve*.

In the structural equations, the level of this curve (the intercept) is determined by the rate of investment in physical capital, the human capital per worker (measured as average years of schooling), and the population growth rates; then, the model assumes that these variables are determined by the initial inequality in society (δ). The slope of the curve is determined by the growth rate of technological change (g), which is unobservable, and thus has to be assumed to remain unchanged. In the reduced form, the determinants of the level of the frontier curve ultimately depend upon the initial inequality only.

The growth frontier curve is unobservable because it is still part of the assumptions of the model—the existence of dynamic equilibrium. The transition dynamics is the observable trajectory. The initial condition of society is given by the observed output per worker or output per capita (y_0), which depends upon the initial factor endowments, namely, the ratio capital per worker and technology level. The transition dynamics is determined by the initial output per worker and the exogenous variable of the growth frontier curve. Therefore, changes in the initial inequality (δ), the only exogenous variable, will change the growth frontier curve and so will the trajectory of the transition dynamics, for it will now be moving towards the new frontier.

Could the structure elements of the abstract process be logically allowed to change exogenously? Technology refers to people's knowledge about how to produce goods. Technological change means change in technological knowledge in society, which leads to increases in productivity in the economic process—more output will be produced with the same dose of machines and workers. It also implies a change in the structure S; therefore, the new technology will modify the structure of society, which in turn will modify the beta propositions and the causality relations.

Technological knowledge in society is not a variable. It is a qualitative concept. Technological knowledge to produce goods is incorporated in machines, the stocks of which are observable; it is also incorporated in workers' productive skills, which are also observable. Hence, the stock of machines and of human capital (years of schooling) are measurable and can play the role of endogenous or exogenous variables, but they do not constitute the technology of society.

Changes in technological knowledge are recognizable by the introduction of new types of machines, new types of skills, and new types of material inputs in the production process, all forms of technological modernization, but these changes are not measurable. Technological knowledge is not quantifiable; certainly, changes in the growth rate of technological knowledge is not either. The characteristics of changes in technology can only be established by assumptions of the model, the testing of which will be done only indirectly, through the beta propositions of the model.

As to people's rationality, the unified theory assumes that the observed human behavior is the result of people's rational behavior. Rational behavior is just the assumption that there exists a logical consistency between means and ends in human behavior. Individual economic behavior is thus the result of the combinations of two effects: constraints (observable) and the forces that motivate individuals to act and choose among alternatives, summarized in the term *preference system*. Preference systems—including here motivations, aversions, tolerance thresholds, beliefs, and human drives—constitute the mechanisms through which the exogenous variables act upon the endogenous variables.

Exogenous changes in preferences will change the structure S, which means that people will change their behavior even if their constraints remain unchanged, for they are now seeking different ends—and still behaving rationally. This change in behavior would give rise to new causality relations. However, people's preference systems are not variables. Changes in preference systems are recognizable by the introduction of new types of goods and consumption modernization, and new types of social practices, but these changes are not quantifiable. The characteristics of changes in preferences can only be established by assumptions of the model, the testing of which will be indirect, through the beta propositions of the model.

Institutions include rules and organizations. Rules, as prescribed guides for human conduct, can be formal and informal. However, the rules that people actually seek to take into account in their behavior can hardly be observable, for it is similar to knowing their preference system. What is observable is people's behavior, what they do, not what is underlying that behavior. The rule of law (formal) is observable, and the individual cost of obeying or disobeying the law are observable as well. Therefore, the assumptions about institutions refer to the institutional structure of society, from which only some are taken into account as essential factors in the economic process, ignoring the rest.

The unified theory assumes two basic institutions of capitalism: the market system—and the private property rights that it requires—and the electoral democracy. The unified theory assumes that in the exchange of goods people follow the market rules and that the behavior of governments and citizens follow the rules of electoral democracy. If these institutions change, the structure will too, and so will the structural equations, given the new incentive systems that the change brings about, which will generate new reduced form equations. Although institutions are not variables, the qualitative *changes* in the prescribed norms contained in the rule of law are observable.

Consequently, exogenous changes in the structure elements of the economic process can be analyzed only in the case of formal institutions. These institutional changes are qualitative but can be subject to analysis by the logical artifice of transforming them into *fictitious variables*, usually called "dummy variables".

Changes in technology or preferences are unobservable and thus cannot be subject to this type of analysis. What we can observe is what people do under a given situation, not about what people would do under different situations. The production function and the utility function in society are both unobservable. Therefore, the common method of calculating the changes in total consumption or total output, and explaining them by the changes in the explanatory variables, and then attributing *the residual* to the effect of changes either on preferences or technology has no epistemological justification. The residual method is not about falsifying the theory, for under this method the theory could never be rejected; it is rather about protecting the theory.

According to alpha–beta method, introducing exogenous changes in preferences or in technology—or in the rate of technological change—will make the model unfalsifiable (similar to the use of the category "expectations" in macro-models, which is very common). Any inconsistency between the predictions of the model and facts could then be attributed to those (unobservable) changes to save the model. The model would thus become immortal, as these changes would constitute a protection belt of the model against rejection.

Causality in the Evolutionary Process

An evolutionary economic process refers to the very long run. It assumes intertemporal relations among the endogenous variables in the structural relations; in addition, the evolutionary process assumes feedbacks (as in dynamic processes) and the existence of threshold values in the endogenous variables, which put limits to the reproduction of the process, such that the process cannot be repeated forever, eventually will come to a collapse, and then will be switched to another process. Then the evolutionary process contains a dynamic process, but only as a logical artifice, for the dynamic equilibrium will only be *temporary*.

In order to simplify the presentation, and without loss of generality, consider the unified theory as an example. The unified theory assumes that the economic growth process is not mechanical but evolutionary. The evolutionary model of the unified theory assumes as the set of endogenous variables (Y) output per worker, degree of income inequality, and degree of environment degradation. The set of exogenous variables (X) include factor endowments (labor and capital, including physical and human), natural resource endowments (dowry of nature), and the initial inequality. The initial structure elements (S) are similar to those of the dynamic model.

The evolutionary model assumes that the economic growth process is subject to the laws of nature, such as photosynthesis and thermodynamics, which operate as constraints. Production of goods requires matter and energy and thus waste is an irrevocable outcome. There is no way to produce goods without generating depletion and pollution; moreover, double of output implies roughly double of depletion rates and pollution emissions.

It also assumes that technological change is endogenous, as firms have incentives to invest part of their profits in technological innovations that are labor saving (for given relative factor prices), for their effect will be to increase further their profits. Some firms may also have incentives to invest in research to find new technologies that are mineral saving, which can reduce the flow of pollution emissions per *unit of output*; however, other firms, which make profits by exploiting mineral resources will have different incentives. The net effect may ultimately be positive but will be too small to reduce the total pollution flow, for *total output* will increase continuously in the growth process.

About changes in the people's preference systems, the evolutionary model assumes that the power elites have the incentive and the means—through the use of behavioral engineering techniques and the media that they also control—to manipulate human behavior, so as to induce changes in people's preferences in directions that are in the elites' own interests. These include (a) changes in the human drives that make people become more and more egotists and opportunists and (b) changes in their consumption behavior, making workers more addict to consumption, to modernization, especially to exosomatic gadgets that come with it—known as consumerism. Thus, the model predicts that consumption rates will tend to increase in the growth process—workers' saving rates will thus tend to decline. Therefore, changes in the people's preference systems are also endogenous.

Given that technology knowledge and preferences are unobservable, how can one justify that a theoretical model may assume their endogenous changes? Firstly, assuming that both elements of the structure change endogenously does not mean that they have become endogenous variables. They are changed endogenously, but remain part of the structure S of the process. Secondly, the evolutionary model assumes that these endogenous changes depend upon observable elements—the output per worker, which is an endogenous variable—and that these relations are part of the structural equations. These assumptions will then be reflected in the reduced form equations of the model. Thus the empirical refutation of the model will prove those assumptions wrong or its acceptance may prove them right.

As to institutional changes, private property rights and the market system could hardly be changed if capitalism is to be maintained. New institutions setting limits to capital concentration would be opposed by the power elite. Similarly, electoral democracy could hardly be changed, for it is in the interest of the power elite to maintain it, as this is the mechanism through which the political power granted to the people by the principle of democracy is transferred to the political class. Markets and electoral democracy constitute the mechanisms through which the power elites exercise their power. Hence, institutional changes would occur only exogenously.

On the structure elements, therefore, the evolutionary model assumes two groups. In the first group, technological knowledge (S_3) and preferences systems (S_4) are initially given, but they change endogenously with the economic growth process; in the second group, the institutions of market system (S_1) and electoral democracy (S_2) remain exogenously given.

In order to obtain the beta propositions and causality relations in the evolutionary model, consider the dynamic process theorem, shown above, as representing the *temporary dynamic equilibrium* of the economic growth process, now seeing as a component of the evolutionary process. Hence, we may write the set of reduced form equations of the model as follows:

$$Y^{**}(T) = H(T; \delta; S_1, S_2), Y < Y' \quad (3.3)$$

$$[\beta] \quad Y(T) = H'(T; Y_0; \delta; S_1, S_2), Y(T) < Y^{**}(T) \quad (3.3')$$

In Eq. (3.3), function H represents the reduced form of the evolutionary model. It shows that the endogenous variables (Y) change just with the passage of time along given trajectories, where Time (T) now refers to historical time (T), not to mechanical time (t). The dynamic trajectory is only temporary, for the process cannot go on forever; that is, the economic growth process collapses and switches to another process when the threshold value Y is reached. This trajectory is marked Y^{**} (T) to indicate that the underlying dynamic equilibrium is now temporary. The exogenous variable in function H is the initial inequality (δ) and the structure elements that are exogenously given include the two fundamental institutions of capitalism, markets (S_1) and electoral democracy (S_2).

Technological knowledge (S_3) and preference systems (S_4) are still elements of the structure, for the causality relations will operate through them, but they change endogenously in the economic growth process. They play a role as part of the structural equations of the model, as the effect of the exogenous variable will operate through them, which are already internalized in the reduced function H.

In Eq. (3.3′), function H' represents the transition dynamics. From the initial condition (Υ_0), the endogenous variables move spontaneously towards the dynamic equilibrium curve. For the particular case of the endogenous variables output per worker (y), the transition dynamics starts from the initial condition (y_0), which in turn depends upon the initial level of technology and factor endowments of society, and moves spontaneously to the growth frontier curve, function H.

Analytically, the evolutionary model works through a dynamic model. Therefore, the properties of the dynamic model presented earlier apply in the case of an evolutionary model, but subject to two conditions: (a) for the quantitative endogenous variables, dynamic equilibrium is temporary only; (b) along the temporary dynamic equilibrium curve, qualitative changes in the other endogenous variables take place along the temporary dynamic equilibrium. The transition dynamics—Eq. (3.3′)—is observable and testable and thus it provides the beta propositions and the causality relations of the evolutionary model.

In this particular case of the evolutionary model of the unified theory, the transition dynamics trajectory of output per worker describes a curve that is increasing over time, at a rate that is faster than the growth rate of the frontier curve (g), for this is a necessary condition for the catch up. The collapse of the process occurs at the period ($T = T^*$) in which $y = y'$, that is, when the threshold value of human health tolerance for pollution has been reached.

In sum, output per worker will travel along the transition dynamics, approaching toward the growth frontier curve, and along the frontier once it is reached, given the exogenous variables and the structure elements of the process that are exogenous. As long as these exogenous factors—called the *ultimate factors*—remain unchanged, the transition dynamics will continue over time until, eventually, the collapse period is reached.

In terms of the other components of the endogenous variables, their particular trajectories are as follows: the degree of income inequality and the degree of environment degradation also increase over time; that is, the quantitative increase of income level over time is accompanied by these qualitative changes, which constitute social maladies.

In order to visualize the evolutionary process, consider the transition dynamics trajectory of output per worker as a curve that is rising over time. Along this curve, in every point of it, the two qualitative endogenous variables (income inequality and environment degradation, measured by total pollution flow) can be marked as reaching ever increasing values, until the threshold values of human tolerance is reached, which will imply the breakdown of the evolutionary process. A given degree of concentration of the power structure remains fixed along the curve. This is a simple way to represent the idea of an evolutionary model, in which quantitative changes are accompanied by qualitative changes, which eventually put limits to the reproduction of the process.

In the evolutionary model, the combination of the initial inequality and the institutions of market and electoral democracy have led to a concentrated power structure in society (ρ), that is, $\rho = (\delta; S_1, S_2)$, which remains unchanged in the economic growth process. This power structure implies the existence of a power elite. The power elites exercise their power through the markets and electoral democracy, the basic institutions of capitalism; hence, the power elites have the incentives to defend and promote these institutions of capitalism.

The power elites promote economic growth policies because it is in their own interest to do so. They are the main beneficiaries of economic growth, as they are able to reproduce both their high income position and their privileged social position. Economic growth with social maladies under capitalism is thus explained by the concentrated power structure; it is the ultimate factor. Therefore, changes in the power structure will affect the endogenous variables of the evolutionary model, function H will change, which in turn will change function H'.

The outcome of the economic growth process is higher income levels together with social maladies. Let us define *quality of society* (QoS) as the combination of output per worker and the qualitative variables income inequality and environment degradation. The former component has a positive effect upon QoS whereas the second effect is negative. The model assumes that the first effect is dominant at the first stages of economic growth, but the second become dominant at later stages. Therefore, the evolutionary model predicts a trajectory of QoS that has the shape of a U-inverse curve (Figueroa 2017, Chapter 6, Fig. 6.1, p. 193).

The evolutionary process is then reduced to quality of society (QoS) as the only endogenous variable and to power structure (ρ) as the only ultimate factor. Then, function H'—Eq. (3.3′) above showing the transition dynamics–can be written as follows:

$$[\beta] \quad \text{QoS}(T) = J'(T; Y_0; \rho), \, T < T^*, \, T^* = f(\rho) \quad (3.4)$$

In Eq. (3.4), function J' says that, for a given power structure (ρ), there will be a particular trajectory of the QoS curve, which is U-inverse shaped, before the collapse period T^* is reached; hence, changes in the power structure will change both the trajectory of the QoS curve and the extent of T^*. Function J' is observable and testable. Therefore, Eq. (3.4) shows both the beta proposition and the causality relations of the evolutionary model.

What is changeable in the power structure? The initial inequality in the individual distribution of economic and social assets is exogenously determined. It can change, but only exogenously. What would it take to redistribute the economic and social assets? The redistribution of physical capital ownership from capitalists to workers would not be socially viable, for it would require a change in one of the fundamental institutions of capitalism: the private property rights. Human capital cannot be redistributed. Capitalism operates not only with class differences, but also citizenship differences. To eliminate first class and second class citizenship would require a break with history, as this difference comes from the way capitalism was originated, namely from colonialism.

What would it take to change institutions? The market system can hardly be changed, as it constitutes the core of capitalism. It is not needed either. The market theory assumes that markets operate like a big computer, solving the system of equations that imply the voluntary exchange of goods in society, and coming up with a set of prices and quantities of equilibrium. This is how it works now, even with a power elite. In more equal society (free from power elites), the equations of the market system would be different and the big computer will come up with a different solution, but the market system would be needed.

We are then left with electoral democracy. This institution is consistent with the core of capitalism. Electoral democracy is, however, just a particular form of democracy. Electoral democracy is the mechanism by which the political power of the workers (the people) granted by democracy is transferred to the political elites and allow them to capture the state for their own benefits. Electoral democracy is business too. It is a distortion in the principle of democracy.

Dethroning the electoral democracy and enthroning another form of democracy that gives workers back the political power would imply a reduction in the concentrated power structure. Economic elites would maintain economic power but workers would now have the political power, as they would control de state. Therefore, replacing electoral democracy by other more direct form of democracy would be socially viable, as it would retain the capitalist system, although it would imply a re-foundation of capitalism, a break with history.

The new power structure would have incentives to promote new public policies, directed to improve the quality of society rather than persisting on the perverse and suicidal economic growth. It then follows that, according to unified theory, public policies are endogenous, as they depend on the interests of those who run the society, of those who concentrate the power structure.

Generalizing, it follows that causality relations in the evolutionary process are more complex than in mechanical processes. In static and dynamic models, changes in the exogenous variables will cause changes in the endogenous variables, either in their values (static, in the short run) or in their trajectories (dynamic, in the long run), for a *given* structure. In the evolutionary model (in the very long run), some of the structure elements will change endogenously (and contribute to the qualitative changes in the process) and some will remain exogenously determined. Therefore, changes in the value of the exogenous variables will cause changes in the temporary trajectories of the endogenous variables, as well as in the collapse period, for *given* elements of the structure; furthermore, changes in structure elements will change the temporal trajectories of the endogenous variables, as well as in the collapse period, *given* the exogenous variables.

In static models, the reduced form equations show at the same time the beta propositions; however, in dynamic and evolutionary models, the beta propositions are indicated by the transition dynamics, not by the reduced form equations alone. In all cases, beta propositions are falsifiable and show causality relations as well.

On Alternatives to the Alpha–Beta Method

The alpha–beta method is derived from the composite epistemology that combines two epistemologies, abstract process and falsificationism. It is a way to operationalize the assumptions of this epistemology. Several questions arise about the uniqueness and possible limitations of the method.

The first question is the following: Is the alpha–beta method a necessary and sufficient condition for scientific knowledge in economics? Sciences that deal with the social world—hyper complex realities—need to transform the real world into an abstract, much simpler world, through scientific theories. The abstract world takes the form of an abstract process. The use of abstraction, therefore, implies that the scientific theory is in principle false. Falsificationism is then a principle of scientific knowledge.

What is to be submitted to falsification? The scientific theory transforms the real world into an abstract process by making assumptions about exogenous and endogenous variables and about the structure-mechanism elements (alpha propositions) of the process, from which empirical predictions are logically derived (beta propositions). These predictions are falsifiable by construction. The idea of process ensures repetition of the relationships (not an isolated event) and the possibility of empirical regularities, which gives the statistical testing of the theory a logical justification. The application of the alpha–beta method is then sufficient to accept or reject economic theories.

Is it necessary? Given the composite epistemology, the alpha–beta method seems to be the only method that can be logically derived from it. Therefore, the alpha–beta method is not only sufficient, but also necessary in scientific economic research.

In the natural sciences, biology is, like physics, a science, but biology is not a science like physics, as stated by the late biologist Ernst Mayr (1997). The reason is that exogenous variables can be assumed in biology, but not in physics. No exogenous forces can exist to change the trajectory of the physical universe, for there is void outside the universe; hence, everything is endogenous. Therefore, economics is a science like biology, but not like physics. Thus, the alpha–beta method is applicable to biology, but not to physics (Figueroa 2016, Chapter 9).

The second question refers to the relative superiority of the alpha–beta method. The properties of the alpha–beta method are derived from the composite epistemology; hence, the question translates to the relative superiority of the composite epistemology.

In order to answer this question, an analytical distinction needs to be made between methodology and epistemology. *Methodology* refers to the general question of "how" people acquire knowledge. People have their own ways to accept or reject propositions about how the world works. Of course, methodologies vary with space and time, and also with social groups.

In contrast, *epistemology* refers to the most advanced methodology, in which logical errors of previous methodologies have been identified and corrected, and new ways to acquire knowledge have been created. Epistemology is thus the most efficient methodology, the one that minimizes errors in the production of human knowledge, which is developed by the theory of knowledge. Therefore, the use of epistemology leads to knowledge that minimizes errors, to *scientific* knowledge. Science is epistemology.

The concept of methodology is thus very similar to that of technology. The knowledge that people have to produce goods—the *how* to produce goods—is called technology. All human societies have had their particular technologies, otherwise they would have not existed. These technologies differ with time and space. Of course, ancient civilization did not use the modern digital technology, but they had their particular technology to produce goods. The most advanced technology is the one that produces goods at minimum cost in the use of resource inputs, that is, independent of what the relative scarcity (or relative prices) of inputs be. The modern technology is the most efficient and makes previous technologies obsolete.

Similarly, the most advanced methodology—epistemology—is the one that produces human knowledge with the minimum error. Epistemology is the most efficient methodology to produce human knowledge and thus makes previous methodologies obsolete. For example, in light of the composite epistemology, firstly, the risk of errors contained in abstract process and in falsificationism have been corrected in the composite epistemology, which would make those epistemologies to become methodologies now.

Secondly, researchers used to apply and still use deductivism, inductivism, and interpretationism (hermeneutics), but they are not epistemologies any longer, as they lead to significant errors and have thus become obsolete (Figueroa 2016, Chapter 7).

It then follows that epistemology is different from methodology. Methodology refers to what people do, whereas epistemology to what people should do if pursuing scientific knowledge—knowledge with the minimum error.

The concept of epistemology, as said in the introduction of this chapter, is placed in the realm of the formal science of logic. It is the logic of scientific knowledge, and is developed by the theory of knowledge. It is consequently placed outside philosophy, which is the standard view, and where the needs of science for ethical justification are also studied. As purely logical system, the principles of epistemology are valid for any given set of ethical values about scientific knowledge. Once the ethics of scientific knowledge are established, such as what to research on and why, what follows is epistemology, and the results of the research will not depend on the initial ethics of the research question.

A new epistemology that is superior to the composite epistemology will come from progress in the theory of knowledge. This new and superior epistemology would have to contain new assumptions, which would have to be invented. Then the alpha–beta method would have to be abandoned, for it was logically derived from the now relatively less efficient composite epistemology. With the superior epistemology, scientific knowledge will be improved, as it will be error-free knowledge of a higher order. This is the reason to say that a scientific theory is accepted only provisionally, until new data, superior scientific theory, or *new epistemology* is created.

Scientific knowledge is thus the result of Darwinian competition. It has been said repeatedly that science makes progress funeral after funeral of scientific theories. However, the competition does not refer to scientific theories only. This is incomplete. Science makes progress by eliminating through Darwinian completion not only scientific theories, but also datasets, and epistemologies.

Against Deductivism and Inductivism

Deductivism is a methodology, but it is not epistemology, as said above. Theory alone—logic alone—can lead to human knowledge that is subject to the risk of tremendous error, for the theory has not been submitted to the falsification process. Falsification of a theory is not a formality; it is a necessity. The reason is that a theory is an abstract representation of the real world, and as such constitutes a distortion of the real world. Therefore, a theory is in principle false, and falsification is thus a necessity.

However, some researchers even today base their knowledge in this methodology. They *believe or are made to believe* that an economic theory must be true, for it is a system of propositions that is logically correct. Then, the theory itself, the abstract world, not its degree of resemblance with the real world, becomes the criterion of knowledge.

The dogmatic nature of this type of knowledge—economic theory as belief or doctrine—is reflected in the belief that if facts contradict the theory, then the real world must be wrong—not the theory. For example, the economic theory of demand and supply assumes that market prices adjust until markets are cleared. In the case of labor market, this theory predicts that labor markets operate with full employment. This prediction is contradicted by facts, as excess labor supply is a structural feature of capitalism. However, the theory is not rejected, for the dogma is applied to save the theory: There must be something wrong with the real world, which should be corrected, for labor markets *should* work as the theory says.

Deductivism has, in addition, ways to save the economic theory. One is to refer to anecdotic facts, thus avoiding statistical testing. Another is to include unobservable elements in the theory (e.g. people's expectations), the change of which makes the theory a tautology and thus unfalsifiable. By introducing changes in expectations, the theory can always be saved and thus becomes immortal, but useless for understanding the real world.

The methodology of inductivism is not epistemology either. As Einstein said in a letter to Popper, there is no logical route from observations to scientific theory. This is known as the induction problem. Theory is needed to explain reality, and explanation means determining the causality relations—no scientific theory, then no explanation, then no causality. Thus, the why and how questions are given an answer through a scientific theory. No escape on this. Inductivism as epistemology is unacceptable because of the induction problem. If theory is unavailable, it just have to be invented.

However, most of the research work done in economics today is empirical rather than basic. This behavior reveals that inventing and falsifying economic theories—basic research—is not a priority. Empirical research is either theory-free or applied, in which the theory is given, and accepted, not questioned. It uses the methodology of inductivism. From data, and data alone, researchers invoke causality relations. There is no logic that can justify this jump from observation to theory. "The existence of correlation implies causality" is a fallacy, no matter how sophisticated is the statistical or econometric method utilized to determine the correlation. The well-known "Granger causality test" in econometrics is a misnomer.

More recently, "data science" users believe (mistakenly) that the problem with inductivism was incomplete information; so with big data, the problem should disappear. This is epistemologically incorrect. The problem with inductivism is not incomplete data; the problem is that there is no logic procedure to go from data—no matter how big—to scientific theory. Moreover, the statement "the existence of statistical correlation implies causality" is a fallacy, no matter how big the data utilized are, or how sophisticated the econometric method utilized is, as said above.

Statistical correlation is a description of the real world. What big data can do is to improve this description. Nothing more. Even collecting information to represent the reality at the scale 1:1 would not help to derive the knowledge about *what causes what*. Scientific theory would still be needed.

Many researchers expected a breakthrough in the understanding of human behavior with the development of neuroscience. But neuroscience after mapping the entire human brain is unable to say what motivates people's actions—what makes people more selfish or more altruist. No scientific theory can be logically derived from this big data; the progress is in the better description of the brain—what signals appear in the brain when the individual acts as egotist or altruist.

Therefore, there is no such thing as "scientific analysis of data," as is mistakenly said. Data are useful in scientific research to falsify scientific theories, which if unavailable have been invented, and thus need testing! "Data science" is thus a misnomer too.

The other problem is that big data does not imply high quality data. In the social sciences, problems of measurement constitute limits to its progress. First, most theoretical variables are socially constructed, which means that existing data may not correspond to the scientific concept. Usually, data are not collected with the purpose of falsifying theories, of scientific research. Second, most big data are based on people's *opinions*, but science requires data on people's *behavior*—not on what people say but on what they do. Hence, the problem of "garbage in, garbage out" is not eliminated with big data.

The Complexity of Accepting/Rejecting Economic Theories

The rules of the alpha–beta method can be represented by the following diagram and symbols, where α' is the model of an economic theory α (*a* set of assumptions), β' is the derived empirical prediction, and **b** is the empirical data:

$$\alpha' \Rightarrow \beta' \rightarrow \text{given}\,(\tau, \lambda, \eta) : [\beta \approx \mathbf{b}] \qquad (3.5)$$

The economic theory is tested through its beta propositions. If facts (**b**) contradict the empirical prediction (β), then the model of the theory is reject; if not, it is accepted.

However, as the diagram shows, the falsification of the model is mediated by three sets of additional assumptions: the statistical theory assumptions utilized in the testing (τ), measurement assumptions of the variables involved (λ), and epistemology assumptions (η). Although the transit from alpha to beta propositions is logical, the transit to the falsification is operational, which includes additional assumptions, which may introduce distortions in the operation of accepting/rejecting the theoretical model.

It should be remembered that formal sciences are also constructed on sets of assumptions—called axioms or postulates—from which implications are derived by means of theorems. Statistics is a formal science and thus it is founded on a set of assumptions, from which theorems are logically derived. These theorems are utilized in the statistical testing.

Therefore, we need to assume that the dataset utilized in testing was generated in accord with the statistical theory requirements (e.g., from a normally distributed parent population, random sampling).

Measurement of economic variables are also based on assumptions, as most of them are not physical. Mountain Everest altitude is both ontologically objective (physical, not mental) and cognitively objective (positive, not normative). A piece of paper is also both ontologically and cognitively objective. However, the piece of paper as a US dollar bill is ontologically objective (physical) but cognitively subjective (mental), then we say that money belongs to the concept of a *socially constructed fact* (Searle 1995). The same can be said about many other economic variables, such as unemployment, inequality, income, even capitalism and democracy. Then we need to assume that these variables have the same meaning for the social actors whose behavior is under study. In addition, the variables must measure human behavior, not opinions.

Finally, epistemology comes from the theory of knowledge, which as any other theory is based on assumptions as well. Therefore, the confrontation of an economic theory with facts is intermediated by these three sets of assumptions.

Furthermore, the logic of accepting economic theories relies on the principle that scientific knowledge is not about finding the truth, but about minimizing the error in determining the causality relations. Analytically, truth is about the way things are. Epistemologically, scientific knowledge is about what we can consider to be a good approximation to the real world, to the true causality, with the minimum of error. If the empirical prediction of the theory is refuted by facts, then the theoretical model is rejected; if it is not, however, we cannot say that the theoretical model is true, only that it is *consistent* with facts.

For example, if facts show that the diagonals of a figure are unequal, the theory that the figure is a square is rejected; if the diagonals are equal, we cannot say that the true figure is a square (for it could be a rectangle), we can only say that facts are consistent with the theory. In the alpha–beta method, the true theoretical model is unattainable, for there is no one-to-one relation between alpha and beta propositions. The same beta propositions may be derived from different economic theories.

This problem of identification is very much related to the well-known *incompleteness theorem* of mathematician Kurt Gödel, which says that mathematical truth and mathematical proof are not the same thing. Similarly, theoretical truth and theoretical consistency with facts are not the same thing. As said above, if the two diagonals are identical, that fact does not mean that the figure is a square, for the same result can be derived from a rectangle; so whether the figure is a square or a rectangle is *unprovable* with this information. Therefore, we would have two theories that are consistent with facts. This problem is well-known in physics, where the behavior of electrons are consistent with two theories, taken as particles or as waves.

Truth and theoretical explanation are not the same thing. This is another reason why epistemology allow us to accept economic theories but only *provisionally*. Therefore, the procedure to attain a good approximation to scientific truth using the alpha–beta method should include the following rules:

> *Statistical theory*: Large size samples will minimize the error in the decision. Non-parametric statistical theory minimizes error compared to parametric statistical theory, which, by introducing assumptions that are

additional to those of the economic theory, could lead to a rejection of the economic theory, due to the inappropriate assumptions of the statistical theory.

Multiple theories falsification: Accepting a theory in comparison to other theories would also minimize errors in the decision. Economic theories would be subject to a Darwinian competition and wrong theories would be eliminated.

Innovations: New economic theories, new statistical theories, new measurement instruments, new empirical datasets, and new epistemologies, would lead to minimize errors even further. The reason is that the initial decision was taken under various *givens*.

Scientific knowledge based on an economic theory that is accepted only provisionally may sound very limiting human knowledge. This is not the case, however. It is the algorithm in eliminating wrong economic theories—the Darwinian competition—that is conducive to scientific progress. This algorithm is an integral part of the alpha–beta method. Economic theories are not constructed to be protected, but to be destroyed. If an economic theory survives to all the attempts directed to its destruction; if it has survived many battles, then it must be a good theory. Furthermore, accepting an economic theory will *always* be provisional, as scientific knowledge has no end!

The unified theory of capitalism has been submitted to the falsification process, using the alpha–beta method and the procedure it implies; that is, it has been accepted under *givens*. Moreover, the falsification has been based on models, as it is required in the case of economic theories. Two additional traits are worth mentioning here. First, nonparametric statistical testing was used whenever possible.

Second, multiple theories falsification was applied, for the unified theory was systematically compared with the competing economic theories.

As result, the unified theory was shown to be superior to the other economic theories in the epistemological sense: It is able to explain facts that the other theories can also do, but explains facts that the others cannot. In this sense, the unified theory minimizes errors, and qualifies as a scientific economic theory. However, the unified theory was accepted only provisionally, until new datasets or innovations on measurement instruments, new statistical methods, new and superior economic theories, or new epistemologies appeared.

Can economics, which is based on assumptions, produce scientific knowledge? Yes, it does. The use of assumption is sometimes taken as a weakness of economics. Actually, any science is based on assumptions. This is the case of natural sciences. In physics, gravity force in large objects (Newton theory) and stochastic subatomic world (quantum theory) are assumptions; in biology, evolution by natural selection is an assumption too. Even formal sciences are based on assumptions, which are called axioms. This is the case of statistics, as shown above. In mathematics, the assumptions or axioms set down the properties the objects under consideration are to have, such as the set of real numbers or the Euclidean geometry. From then on, truth (scientific knowledge) means simply provable from the axioms, that is, by theorems, in which the use of deductive logic is necessary and sufficient condition.

In factual sciences, however, deductive logic is necessary for the construction of the theory, but it is not sufficient for scientific knowledge. The theory—being an abstract representation of reality—must be confronted against the behavior of the real world. Scientific knowledge in factual sciences depends more intensively on assumptions than in formal sciences. Moreover, given that the social world is much more complex than the physical world, scientific knowledge in economics (and in the social sciences in general) is even more dependent on assumptions than is the case in the other factual sciences, and thus more than in the formal sciences. To explain highly complex real worlds require highly complex sciences too, as shown with economics in this essay.

Biologist Edward Wilson (1998) recognized these differences. He stated, "The social sciences are hyper-complex. They are inherently far more difficult than physics and chemistry, and as a result, they, not physics and chemistry, should be called the hard sciences" (p. 183). Biology is not included in this statement, for biologists consider that biology is a science different from physics. Economics and biology are much alike in that the alpha–beta method is applicable to both sciences, as said earlier.

Conclusions

Economics has the challenge to explain a hyper complex reality: the social world. It has to be a complex science, with sophisticated epistemology and research methods, to fulfill its task, particularly when explaining implies discovering causality relations—what causes what in society. This essay has shown that the alpha–beta method allows economics to comply efficiently with the challenge.

The alpha–beta method is a set of rules for scientific research in economics, that is, for constructing and accepting/rejecting economic theories. It is logically derived from the composite epistemology (a combination of two methodologies: abstract process and falsificationism), and makes it operational.

With this method, the hyper complex social reality is reducible to an abstract social world—in the form of an abstract process, which is simpler to understand—by means of a scientific economic theory. The theory must make assumptions (alpha propositions) about the components of the abstract economic process: the endogenous and exogenous variables and the structure-mechanism elements, through which the exogenous variables affect the endogenous variables, and gives rise to causality relations. Therefore, by construction, the theory generates empirical predictions that are falsifiable (beta propositions), which at the same time show the causality relations.

According to alpha–beta method, an economic theory is a family of models. Therefore, falsification of the theory is made through the models. Causality relations can only be established from a model of a scientific economic theory. Thus, causality in the alpha–beta research method is an analytical concept, derived from a falsified theoretical model, not from statistical relations alone. Causality is not a philosophical or ethical concept either. The alpha–beta method allow us to establish causality relations in both mechanical and evolutionary economic processes. Causality is more involved in evolutionary models.

The alpha–beta method is logically derived from the composite epistemology, and it is the only research method to be derived from it. The composite methodology is superior to other known methodologies in that the risk of errors of those methodologies are eliminated or minimized, making it the current epistemology. Therefore, the use of the alpha–beta method is a necessary and a sufficient condition to attain scientific knowledge in economics *today*.

The alpha–beta method ensures falsification of economic theories by construction. However, the procedure implies some complexities, due to the introduction of additional sets of assumptions—on the statistical theory, on the measurement of variables, and on the epistemological principles. To accept or reject an economic theory is thus under given sets of assumptions, including those of the economic theory, which makes the decision subject to possible errors. However, no method that is superior to alpha–beta in minimizing errors is known so far.

The construction of the unified theory of capitalism is based on the alpha–beta method. It is thus an abstract representation of the capitalist world and it is falsifiable by construction. The procedure to minimize errors included the use of non-parametric statistics (whenever possible), and multiple theories falsification, for the unified theory has been compared to the predictions of competing theories.

Available facts tend to be consistent with the predictions of the models of the unified theory. Therefore, the acceptance of the unified theory as a good approximation of the capitalist system has epistemological justification. It is a scientific theory. In addition, also on epistemological grounds, the unified theory appears to be superior to the other economic theories: It is able to explain facts that the other theories can also do, but explains additional facts about capitalism that the others cannot. Science is epistemology.

References

Figueroa, A. (2016). *Rules for scientific research in economics: The alpha-beta method.* New York, NY: Palgrave Macmillan.

Figueroa, A. (2017). *Economics of the Anthropocene age.* Cham, Switzerland: Palgrave Macmillan.

Georgescu-Roegen, N. (1971). *The entropy law and the economic process.* Cambridge, MA: Harvard University Press.

Mayr, E. (1997). *This is biology.* Cambridge, MA: Harvard University Press.

Popper, K. (1968). *The logic of scientific discovery.* London, UK: Routledge.

Searle, J. (1995). *The construction of social reality.* New York: The Free Press.

Wilson, E. O. (1998). *Consilience: The unity of knowledge.* New York, NY: Alfred Knopf.

CHAPTER 4

Path Dependence and the Economic Process

The unified theory of capitalism assumes that unequal individual endowments in economic and social assets is one of the essential initial conditions to understand the capitalist system. Unequal capital endowments is the very definition of class difference; in addition, people's entitlements to rights and privileges in society are unequally distributed—first and second class citizens—implying that the capitalist system is a socially heterogeneous society.

Where do these initial conditions come from? Assumptions of a scientific theory need no justification. If they did, then this justification would in turn also require another, which in turn would require another, and so on. The method of justification would lead us to the logical problem of infinite regress. Assumptions are established somehow arbitrarily, and provisionally, just as part of an algorithm in the search of the best economic theory. Theory falsification ensures this result.

However, this is not the case for the assumptions about the initial conditions of society in an evolutionary economic process, in which the collapse of the process gives rise to the emergence of another. The final conditions of an economic process thus affects the initial conditions of the next one. Therefore, the initial conditions assumption in an evolutionary process must include the elements that are considered the essential legacies of the previous one.

The unified theory of capitalism assumes that the legacy of the European colonial system is an essential element for understanding the economic process in today's capitalist system. In particular, the unified theory assumes that social heterogeneity under capitalism comes from the legacy of the European colonial system. This essay seeks to elaborate further on this assumption and on its implications.

Some Analytical Distinctions

Colonialism is a system of domination that involves the subjugation of one society to another, the mother country. It also involves the transfer of people to the new territory who remain subject to the mother country. European colonialism in today's Third World countries is the relevant case to examine. Europeans discovered the new world in the sixteenth century and then started colonizing it.

An analytical distinction needs to be made between *European colonies* and *European settlements*. The new world consisted of regions with high density and low density populations. Colonialism was established in the former regions and settlements in the latter.

European colonialism was established in most of today's Third World regions, in different periods, for different durations, and by different colonial powers. Colonization took place roughly from the 1500 until the 1970s, in different periods and for different durations, in Latin America, Asia, and Africa. Mother countries were in some cases pre-capitalist societies, but in others they were already capitalist societies. The major European colonial powers included Spain, Portugal, Great Britain, France, Germany, Italy, Belgium, and Holland. In Africa, colonialism lasted around 350 years, from the 1620s up to the 1970s; in Latin America, around 300 years, from the 1530s up to the 1820s; in Asia, around 180 years, from the 1780s up to the 1960s; and in the Middle East, around 90 years, from the 1880s up to the 1970s (Dalziel 2006; Wesseling 2004).

European settlements were created in regions of relatively low population density. This is the case of non-European countries that are part of today's First World countries, such as the United States, Canada, Australia, and New Zealand.

Some exceptions on this analytical distinction by regions must be pointed out. In Latin America, Argentina and Uruguay were mostly empty lands, in which Spanish colonialism lasted around 30 years only; Chile and Costa Rica were also relatively empty lands and thus subject to weak colonial domination. In these four countries, therefore, the colonial legacy is weak and the nation's formation was through immigrations. Brazil is a case of colonialism, which originated in empty lands, but in order to exploit the extractive industry that was labor intensive, it was rapidly populated with imported slaves from Africa, and lasted 300 years under Portuguese domination.

It follows that in the case of settlements, the problem of colonial power, as defined above, was not present; therefore, settlements will not be part of the analysis presented here. The great majority of today's Third World countries have a European *colonial* legacy. This is the scope of this essay.

Economic Theory of Colonialism: An Outline

Scientific economic theories of colonialism—with epistemology justification included—are not available in the literature. We need an economic theory that is able to explain the functioning of colonialism and its evolution. Only an outline of such theory can be developed in this short essay.

An economic theory of any type of human society needs to make assumptions about the initial conditions—exogenously determined—that define each type of society. Under colonialism, consider the following:

Institutions. The institutions of colonialism include the property of natural resources, capital, and labor (slavery) by the mother country. The objective of the economic process is to supply the mother country with raw materials. The economic surplus is shipped to the mother country. Market institution is limited to local consumption goods only, for trade is monopolized by the mother country. The local government is established by the mother country. Colonialism is a hierarchical society, with the colonizers' supremacy as the main rule.

Initial inequality. Colonialism implies a re-foundational shock of local societies. The invasion implies qualitative changes in the colonized society. The means of production are property of the mother country. The exploitation of natural resources is based on forced labor, local and imported slaves as well. The invaders displace the local power elite and constitute a new power elite. The invaders are of a different race (white) compared to the subjugated people (non-white).

Rationality. The social actors in the colonies are the local power elite, constituted by the whites, who are subordinated to the mother country. They control the production and distribution process. They are also responsible for the economic surplus, which is to be shipped to the mother country. This implies a principal-agent situation, where the local power elite has incentives to circumvent the objectives of the mother country. The labor cost is not real wages, for there is no labor market. Given the direct exploitation of labor as slaves, the labor cost is their subsistence consumption basket.

The initial inequality under European colonialism is thus the result of a re-foundational shock of the precolonial society and involves a new social hierarchy, along class and racial lines. The European whites (the invaders) are endowed by the mother country with economic and social assets, whereas the local people become "indigenous," and slaves of the invaders. Another institution is thus created: *European supremacy*, which means that race and culture are not only different, but have also become hierarchical. Race and culture become the social marks of the hierarchical colonial society.

This social hierarchy leads to an exclusionary society, characterized by segregation. Segregation in turn leads to limited miscegenation. The colonial society thus establishes a racial divide between the European white and the subjugated non-white populations (indigenous and imported slaves), whereas the mestizo lies in between.

This colonial economic theory has thus transformed the colonial real world into an abstract colonial world. The colonial system can be seen as an abstract economic process, with endogenous and exogenous variables and a structure. In order to falsify the theory, models are needed. Static, dynamic, and evolutionary models need to be constructed.

The evolutionary model is the relevant one for the aims of this essay and, again, only an outline is presented.

The evolutionary model assumes that as the economic process is repeated over time, quantitative and qualitative changes takes place in the colonial system. It also assumes that threshold values of social tolerance exist, which set limits to the reproduction of the colonial economic process. The evolutionary model then predicts that colonial systems cannot last forever, for they face limits and thus a collapse period. The principal-agent problem is the mechanism: the interest of the local Europeans to be independent from the mother country rises over time. As British historian Piers Brendon (2008) says, colonies are "children," which, as they grow up, expect to separate from the mother country.

The independence from the mother country now implies a re-foundational shock of the colonized society, as the local elites gain independence from the mother country and thus become the new (independent) power elite—economic and political. The new institutions are those of the mother country—capitalism. These include private property rights of economic resources, market system, and electoral democracy. The new power elite exercise their power through these institutions. Thus, the colonial economic process becomes the capitalist economic process, that is, the colony becomes capitalism endogenously.

The subjugated populations are not the main actors of this social change. The revolution against colonialism could not come from the masses—as in the French Revolution, where it was the people who revolted against the monarchy. The subjugated populations were enslaved and could hardly lead a successful revolution against colonial power, no matter how hard they would try. Hence, the independence from the mother country is the project of the European local elites. Therefore, the subjugated populations will formally be freed from slavery, as labor market institution is introduced, but their low social position of the colonial times will be maintained.

It then follows that independence, and the birth of capitalism, retains the initial European supremacy institution of the colonial times. The economic and social assets are distributed unequally between Europeans and the subjugated people, who become free labor but remain as the lowest class in the social hierarchy, as they maintain their relatively lower endowments of economic and social assets. The subjugated peoples become free workers but second class people in the new capitalist society.

This sketchy evolutionary model of the theory of colonialism is nonetheless able to predict that the capitalism that emerged from the European colonial system (Third World) is qualitatively different from the one that did from European feudalism (First World). The prediction implies that colonial systems are subject to *path dependence or social hysteresis*: once a colonized society disappears to become capitalism, some of its colonial institutions continue—such as the European white supremacy. With the advent of capitalism, the colonial history is not erased.

This simple evolutionary model of the colonial theory is thus able to explain the transformation of colonialism into capitalism. As the economic process of the colonial system is repeated period after period, quantitative and qualitative changes take place. Thresholds values of social tolerance— the ambitions of the European local elite—exist in the colonial economic process, which once reached determine the end of the process and a regime switching, that is, the move to another process—capitalist economic process. This change is endogenous and the new initial conditions of the new process (capitalism) include some colonial institutions, as legacy of the previous process.

Colonial Legacy in the Unified Theory of Capitalism

As an economic theory of capitalism, the unified theory must make assumptions about its initial conditions. The theory assumes that the colonial legacy is an essential trait of the capitalist system; that is, the unified theory of capitalism takes into account the theoretical results about the nature of the social change from colonialism to capitalism, as shown above.

Regarding institutions, the unified theory assumes that private property rights, markets, and electoral democracy constitute the *fundamental* institutions of the capitalist system. This implies that they are not the only institutions. Some colonial institutions are impregnated in the capitalist system and are also part of the institutions, such as the colonial rule of European supremacy, which can now be restated as *Western supremacy*. The latter refers to the supremacy of the First World, now including the Western European countries (ex-colonial powers) and their ex-settlements (Australia, Canada, New Zealand, and the United States), which are also part of the First World.

Concerning the initial individual endowments of assets, the ex-colonial societies have become capitalist societies, in which not only individual capital endowments are unequally distributed, but also social entitlements are unequally distributed, creating first class and second class citizens. This is the rule of Western supremacy, a colonial legacy. This is the main trait of Third World countries. The capitalist system taken as a whole is a class society—unequal capital endowments—and also socially heterogeneous, as it includes first class people (the First World) and second class (the Third World). This is also the rule of Western supremacy, a colonial legacy.

In order to deal with the components of the capitalist system, the unified theory has constructed two abstract societies. *Epsilon societies* are class societies but socially homogeneous. This theoretical construction intends to explain the First World—capitalism that originates from European feudalism and from the European settlements. *Sigma societies* are also class societies but are socially heterogeneous, which means that the initial inequality includes unequal capital endowments and unequal social entitlements, implying first class and second class people—the capitalism that originates from European colonies. This theoretical construction intends to explain the Third World.

Epsilon and sigma abstract societies are thus the partial theories of these two types of capitalism, taken separately, whereas the unified theory seeks to explain the capitalist system taken as a whole. It follows that capitalism taken as a whole is a sigma society as well. It is a socially heterogeneous society, for social entitlements are unequally distributed among the global population—with first class and second class citizens. Western supremacy underlies the existence of differences in social asset endowments. The colonial institution of Western supremacy endures and is impregnated in the functioning of capitalism.

The different origins of capitalism are reflected in the two components of the current capitalist system: the First World and Third World countries. The First World developed from European feudalism and its settlements. The European feudal system was a class society—landlords and peasants—but it was socially homogeneous, from which capitalism emerged, as a new class society—capitalists and workers—but socially homogeneous. The same can be said about the non-European countries that belong to the First

World (Australia, Canada, New Zealand, and the United States). These were settlement territories from which the capitalism that emerged was also class society but socially homogeneous.

Third World capitalism originated from colonial systems, which were socially heterogeneous. European invaders and the subjugated populations (natives and imported slaves) constituted a society in which there were not only class differences, but also social differences. Western supremacy was one of the fundamental institutions of colonial systems. Independence from the mother countries were not the triumph of the subjugated populations revolting against colonialism, not that they did not tried, as the historiographical literature has shown. It was the triumph of the European (white) local elites. Hence, independence from the mother country, from which capitalism was born, retained part of the old social structure, now in the form of first and second class citizens.

The evolutionary model of the unified theory predicts that the economic growth process shows path dependency: the colonial history matters in the growth paths of the First World and the Third World. These two types of capitalism—one richer and less unequal compared to the other—have persisted in the economic growth process. Had capitalism instead emerged as socially homogeneous society everywhere, then the colonial history would have been erased, and today we would not be able to distinguish statistically the First World from the Third World. But empirically this is not the case. This fact is consistent with the prediction of the evolutionary model.

Whatever social hierarchy or social conflicts existed in the precolonial societies, it was also furthered by colonizers, who had the incentives to use it in their own interest as mechanisms of local domination and administration. Hence, the evolutionary model also predicts that colonialism left behind social hierarchies among the subjugated populations, which is consistent with the empirical observation of social conflicts between ethnic groups in the Third World. This *hyper hierarchical* capitalist society is also a legacy of the colonial system.

According to the evolutionary model of the unified theory, the ultimate factor that explains the economic growth process in the capitalist system is the degree of concentration of the power structure. This is the combination of the initial inequality in individual asset endowments and the institutions of capitalism, which include private property rights, markets, electoral democracy and also Western superiority. The power elites exercise their power through these institutions, not only through markets and electoral democracy, but through the rule of Western superiority as well. Therefore, they will have the incentives to maintain them all unchanged and even promote them in the world society.

To be sure, although the economic and political elites have the power to change this hyper hierarchical society, they do not have the incentives to do it. According to unified theory, the power elite exercise their power through the fundamental institutions—market and electoral democracy. Western supremacy also constitutes part of the capitalist institutions and plays the same role. Although the role of this colonial institution is more subtle, the power elites use it to reproduce the power relations; therefore, their incentives are for the endurance of this colonial institution.

Within the sigma society, the descendants of the subjugated people during the colonial times have become free workers but second class citizens, as said above. As result, they are endowed with relatively low quantities of economic assets and with unequal political entitlements. Thus they constitute different people in society, even among workers, and are called the *z-workers* in the sigma society theory. As second class citizens, they are excluded from effective access to some human and economic rights, and public policies of human capital formation discriminate against them. These predictions are consistent with facts, for the poorest within the Third World are the z-workers.

In contrast, in epsilon society all workers are first class citizens. Z-workers do not exist. This prediction is also consistent with the fact that the First World countries do not operate with forms of exclusions among workers, as is the case in the Third World.

Taking the capitalist system as a whole (a sigma society), the power elite—the globalized power elite—also use the Western supremacy rule to exercise its power. Workers of the Third World are seen as different people from those of the First World because of their slavery and colonial background. First World workers are z-workers in the global capitalist system. Third World countries are treated with the Western supremacy rule, as second rate or third rate country. Indeed, the fact is that the First World usually intervenes (through invasions, embargos, and over government elections) in the economic process of Third World countries, but not vice versa. This unilateral intervention is certainly consistent with the rule of the Western supremacy.

Endurance of Colonial Institutions Under Capitalism

According to unified theory, capitalism—taken partially or taken as a whole—operates with power relations. This is reflected in two basic facts of capitalism. First, the persistence of social maladies, which reflect the power of the economic and political elites. As result, capitalism is not a self-regulating system. The high degrees of inequality and of environment degradation are persistent features of capitalism.

Second, the persistence of the power elite itself. The power elite is able to reproduce its privileged social position period after period, not only in the short run, even in the long run economic growth process. The institutions of capitalism are the mechanism that the power elites utilize to exercise and maintain their power. Therefore, they have the incentives to preserve and promote these institutions everywhere in the world society. Indeed, this is what we observe in the real world. First World countries usually justify invasions and intervention upon Third World countries as defense of free markets, democracy, or individual freedom.

Economic elites seek two objectives, hierarchically ordered: firstly, maintenance of the privileged class position and, secondly, maximization of profits. Political elites seek similar motivations: firstly, maintenance of the privileged political position and, secondly, maximization of income by capturing the state. Power elites thus seek to maintain power. This is their priority. Therefore, they act rationally, doing whatever it takes to maintain their privileged position in society, subject to the constraints given mainly by their relative capital endowments—the essential asset under capitalism.

The power elites exercise their power through markets and electoral democracy—the basic institutions of capitalism. They make money, and maintain their power, through these institutions. Moreover, these elites have also the power to manipulate and circumvent the rules imposed by the institutions, as in the cases of corruption behavior and of evasion and elusion behavior regarding taxes. For instance, as is well-known, these elites can choose how much of the taxes not to pay and how much to pay, and to which country to pay, by using the financial market, which the financial globalization has expanded via the offshore banking technology.

Moreover, it is not only matter of motivations, their initial asset endowments give the power elite relative economic advantages to attain their objectives, compared to the rest of society. In particular, high capital endowments give power elites advantages—economies of scale, network relationships—over the rest to make larger investments and have higher capacity to bear the higher risk of losses that highly profitable projects (economic and political) involve. Thus, power elites are able to reproduce their privileged power position.

In the economic growth process, therefore, the initial inequality in capital endowments tends to endure. There is no institutional mechanism that can reduce endogenously the initial inequality; on the contrary, the mechanisms exist for maintaining or increasing the capital concentration endogenously, as shown above. If the capital ownership were redistributed to workers from time to time, the power structure could not be reproduced over time. However, such mechanism does not exist under democratic capitalism, for it goes against the rule of private property rights. Therefore, in the economic growth process of capitalism, there is path dependence; that is, the initial inequality endures, history matters.

According to the evolutionary model, the economic growth does not have mechanisms to eliminate or reduce significantly differences in social asset endowments either. There is technological change, modernization in consumption and life style, but social progress does not occur endogenously. Z-populations may have more real income, but will continue to be second class people. They participate in the electoral democracy, but all the same they continue to be second class citizens.

Power elites have the power but not the will to change this situation because it is in their own interest to maintain it unchanged. They benefit from the rule of Western supremacy, which underlies social assets differences. The unified theory assumes that the power structure is exogenously determined. It can change, but only exogenously.

Facts seem to be consistent with this prediction. Although empirical research on the power elites is scarce (revealing that it has no research priority), the few available studies show very high degrees of concentration in the distribution of capital and financial assets, by countries and in the global capitalism; moreover, this degree of concentration does not tend to diminish in the economic growth process, but to increase, as shown in Chapter 2.

Further empirical implications of the evolutionary model in light of the colonial theory seems in order now. The capitalist system operates with power elites. These elites exercise their power through the fundamental institutions—markets and electoral democracy—to which we can now add the institution of Western supremacy, a legacy of colonialism. Now the evolutionary model predicts that the power elites of the First World exercise their power over the Third World countries through policies (public and private) seeking their own benefits.

This prediction is consistent with facts. The First World indeed influences the economic process of the Third World both directly through episodes of army invasions and the monopolistic behavior of big corporations, and indirectly through more subtle mechanisms, such as influencing the changing of governments. This is done through a discourse, the *freedom discourse*, which is an instrument used for legitimizing interventions, as the defense of markets and democracy, and above all individual freedom. The discourse is however an instrument for obscuring the fact that freedom under capitalism coexists with power relations.

The degree of income inequality in the Third World is higher than in the First World. Unified theory explains this persistent difference by their differences in the initial inequality in individual asset endowments. In particular, the electoral democracy is less redistributive in the Third World than it is in the First World, an indication of the unequal political entitlements, of first and second class citizens in the Third World, which is grounded on the colonial institution of Western supremacy.

This is considering people's thresholds of tolerance for inequality as exogenously determined. However, Western supremacy now implies that the threshold is endogenous: Workers internalize the rule of Western superiority at their subconscious level. The model now predicts that *the threshold of tolerance for inequality is higher in sigma society than in epsilon*. The second class citizens tolerate a degree of inequality that the first class citizens do not.

The observed empirical regularity that income inequality is higher in the Third World than in the First World is, therefore, due not entirely to the difference in the initial inequality; in part, it is due higher tolerance thresholds in the Third World, which is the effect of the colonial legacy. The high degree of inequality in the capitalist system (also a sigma society) is also due, at least in part, to the colonial legacy. The degree of social disorder that inequality generates is weakened in the Third World, and in the global capitalism as well, due to the effect of the Western supremacy institution.

It is a fact that the observed degree of social disorder under capitalism is associated to the income inequality of societies. It is higher in the Third World than in the First World (Figueroa 2015, Vol. I, Chapter 7). However, it is striking to observe the persistence of high degrees of income inequality under capitalism after so many decades of economic growth, modernization, education expansion, democracy expansion, which would indicate that these levels of inequality are not tolerable any more. In other words, there seems to be too little violence in the world for so much inequality.

One could also ask the counter factual question: Could the First World countries tolerate the degree of inequality observed in the Third World? The hypothesis says no, for their threshold of tolerance for inequality is much smaller than in the Third World. The Western supremacy effect—leading to first class and second class citizens in the capitalist system, with different thresholds of tolerance for inequality—would then be part of the explanation.

Another prediction of the unified theory models is that in epsilon societies the only difference between the rich and the poor is that the poor have less money, whereas in sigma societies the difference between the rich and the poor is not money alone, for the poor are different people. These are indeed the factual characteristics of the First World and the Third World countries. However, due to the continuous immigration of people from the Third World—legal and illegal—into the First World, some qualitative changes are taking place: The First World is becoming a sigma society, for the new poor, the illegal immigrants, are now different people. The existence of "different people"—with different social markers—leads to a society with low degree of social integration, which is also the legacy of colonialism.

A theory of colonialism was implicit in one of the assumptions of the unified theory (initial inequality), which has been made explicit here. Because the colonial theory is part of the set of assumptions of the unified theory, it follows that falsifying the unified theory is a way to falsify the colonial theory as well. If the unified theory is accepted, so is the colonial theory; if the unified theory is rejected, however, no conclusions can be drawn about the colonial theory, for the failure of the unified theory may come from the other assumptions. Therefore, the findings that the empirical predictions of the unified theory are consistent with basic facts of capitalism (as shown in Chapter 2) indicate that the unified theory and the colonial theory together can be accepted. The colonial theory proposed here seems to be a good approximation of the European colonial systems.

Explaining the Origin of Western Economic Supremacy

The institution of Western (white) supremacy is not only a colonial legacy under capitalism. Western supremacy is also an economic fact: the persistence of First World and Third World countries under capitalism.

Does this economic superiority have to do with race? Race as skin color is both ontologically and cognitively positive (not subjective, not normative), just as the altitude of a mountain is. However, race as social marker to identify social groups is ontologically subjective (has no material existence) but is cognitively objective (can be recognized); that is, it is a socially constructed category, in the sense of philosopher John Searle. Therefore, people's skin color lies underneath their social marker, just like a piece of paper lies underneath a hundred dollar bill. The social marker comes from history; it is a legacy of the European colonial history.

Recent scientific discoveries are showing that human races (skin colors) are the result of human evolution. Our common ancestor is the man from Africa. As people migrated to other regions of the world their skin color was changing over time to adapt and survive in the new locations. According to a recent study of the University College of London and the Natural History Museum, the first British man had dark skin! People skin color is thus endogenously determined, in the process of human evolution.

Geneticists are also showing that genetic similarity among humans is very high, 99.9%. This means that it is the remaining 0.1% that accounts for human genetic variations, such as skin colors and resistance to diseases, which is mostly the result of human migration and adaptations to different regions of the world in thousands of years. No superior people can be drawn from the human genomes, as migration and adaptations have implied gains and losses of human aptitudes. Humans are different, not unequal. Racism is thus an entirely social phenomenon; moreover, racism is a colonial legacy.

If people's skin color is endogenous, an outcome of regional adaptations over very long periods, then race could hardly be the causal factor of anything, much less of economic differences between human societies. An endogenous factor cannot be a causal factor, for that would imply that it is exogenous too! This is to say that the persistence of the Western economic supremacy—the persistent gap between the First World and the Third World countries—could hardly come from race differences. Race (white) must just be the expression of other significant factors. What seems significant in economics is the social marker, not the skin color. Had the Incas or Aztecs invaded and colonized the Europeans, today's z-populations would have been the white!

What are then the factors explaining the existence and persistence of First World and Third World countries, of Western economic supremacy? This is a big question; yet it still remains unanswered.

Cognitive scientist Stephan Pinker (2018) has suggested that Western supremacy comes from the institutions of liberal democracy, which are the outcome of the Enlightenment values (eighteenth century), such as reason and science. Pinker starts from facts that show social progress in the long run and then attributes these outcomes to the legacy of the Enlightenment values. However, this attribution follows the methodology of interpretationism, which is not an epistemology. No scientific explanation is thus given. Indeed, the arguments of the book cannot be translated into the categories of the alpha–beta method.

On facts, Pinker intends to show that social progress has been continuous in the world, that is, economic growth has not been accompanied by social maladies, but by social progress. However, income inequality and environment degradation are simply dismissed as social maladies. The first has no consequences on social wellbeing—only poverty does—and the second will be solved endogenously with science.

Biologist Jared Diamond (1999) has proposed the theory that geography explains the origin of Western economic supremacy. The endowments of natural resources and the geographic position of Europe led these societies to have economic advantage over the rest of the world, as they were able to produce goods with significant *economic surplus*, which led to urbanizing and the developing of science and technological innovations—due possibly, one may add, to the Enlightenment ideals of reason and science. Geography explains why the Spanish—equipped with guns, steel, germs, and written language—conquered the Incas and Aztecs, and why it did not happen the other way around.

Employing the alpha–beta method, Diamond theory can be represented as a dynamic economic process, in which geography is a structure element of the process, through which the causality relations between endogenous and exogenous variables operate. Societies with different qualities of geography will show different beta propositions and thus different causality relations in the economic process. Therefore, the growth frontier curve—showing the trajectory of an endogenous variable output per worker—of societies located at the higher quality geography will lie above the curve from a lower quality geography, even though both curves had the same growth rate over time. This initial difference has led to path dependency.

According to Diamond's theory, therefore, differences in natural resource endowments—including climate, distribution of wild plants and animal species, soils, topography tied to geographic locations—have had an essential role upon the social phenomena of the Western economic supremacy. The observed correlation between skin color and the First World and Third World countries is thus spurious; invoking causality to this relation would fall into the fallacy known as *Cum hoc, ergo propter hoc* (simultaneously with that, then because of that). Geography—not skin color—is the causal factor of the persistence of First World and Third World countries. Furthermore, European colonialism was an endogenous outcome in the world economic process.

Diamond's theory so put could not mean geographic determinism, for non-geographic factors are also present in the economic process. Western economic supremacy is not destiny either. It can be changed. The laws of the social world are not like the laws of the physical world. Indeed, the unified theory predicts that changes in the current power structure will lead to the elimination or reduction of the Western economic supremacy.

Path Dependence and Institutions

The question of whether Darwinian competition does apply to institutions has not produced a scientific explanation in the field of institutional economics—with the required epistemological justification, that is. However, according to Hodgson (2003), Darwinism is returning and the Veblenian research project on "natural selection of institutions" is coming back to the agenda.

In absence of scientific knowledge on this topic in the literature, a brief history of institutional changes are presented now. The idea is just to outline the theoretical proposition developed above, which says that social institutions are subject to path dependence, when power relations are significant in society. In this context, Darwinian competition could hardly apply to institutional changes.

On a horizontal timeline, consider a brief and highly stylized history of institutions in today's First World and Third World regions of the world. Before 1500, there were the European feudalism in the first region and primitive and independent civilizations in the second. Let the institutional rules under which these societies were functioning be labeled by the letters A and M.

Consider now the period covering the sixteen to nineteenth centuries, a period of European feudalism and the beginning and development of colonialism. European empires conquered the New World and subjugate them.

Europe imposed its feudal institutions (A) to its colonies, but new rules appeared, those referring to colonial domination (B)—European supremacy. Hence Europe operated with rules A and B. The colonized societies operated with rule B, which was supposed to displace rule M, the institutions of precolonial societies. However, rule M was not displaced totally, for the colonized did not accept the new rules passively. As studies on colonialism have shown, this struggle is reflected in "the varying mixtures of resistance, rejection, collaboration, attempted assimilation or even mimicry with which colonized people reacted to colonial rules and their culture" (Howe 2006, p. 75). Then the colonies operated with a mix of rules: M, A, and B.

From the beginning of the nineteenth century, Western Europe changed toward capitalism. It also made its appearance the capitalism of the European settlements in United States and Canada, and then in Australia and New Zealand. The new capitalist rules included private property rights, markets, and electoral democracy, call it rule C, which displaced rule A, but retained the colonial rule B, as the colonial system continued its expansion in this period.

The colonial system came to an end in Latin America in the first decades of 1800, and in Africa and Asia, between the end of the WWII and the 1970s. The end of the colonial system implied for the European capitalist countries to operate with rule C alone. These are the *epsilon societies*, as defined in the unified theory. For the colonies, independence from the mother country implied adopting capitalist rules (C), which did not displace the existing colonial rules; hence, societies that started capitalist development out of colonial domination operate with a mix of rules: M, A, B, and C. These are the *sigma societies*, as defined in the unified theory.

The current capitalist system taken as a whole includes the workings of the First World and the Third World taken separately, but also their interactions. In these interactions, rule B is present—as the institution of Western supremacy. Therefore, the capitalist system as a whole operates with the mix of rules of the entire system, which are just the rules of the sigma society ($C; A, B, M$). The capitalist system taken as a whole is thus a sigma society.

Table 4.1 summarizes the changes in institutional rules in today's capitalist countries. The institutional changes that took place in the transition of the ex-communist-socialist societies to become capitalist societies in the 1990s are not included in the table.

According to this table, it is notable the endurance of institutions in the history of today's capitalist societies. There exists in each case a predominant or fundamental institutions, which are separated by a semi-colon from the others; that is, not all rules have the same significance. In particular, it is remarkable the endurance of the colonial rule (B). The rule of Western supremacy is present in today's capitalism, considering that colonialism ended many years ago. This is a case of social hysteresis.

Colonial institutions are impregnated even in market relations. The assumption that market exchange requires first class citizenship everywhere has been ignored in standard economics. Given the imperfect information that characterizes market exchange, trust and honesty are required among buyers and sellers, otherwise market exchange will be overwhelmed with transaction costs, as Adam Smith (1976 [1759]) argued long ago, in his *Moral sentiments*. A society with low degrees of trust and honesty, where opportunism—the worst of human traits—dominates will be a society with high transaction costs, a low quality society.

Table 4.1 Formation of capitalist institutions

	First world		
System	Feudalism	Feudalism and colonialism	Capitalism and colonialism	Capitalism
Rules	A	A, B	C, B	C; B
			Third world	
System	Primitive	Colonies	……	Capitalism
Rules	M	A, B; M		C; A, B, M

Source Author's elaboration

In addition, market exchange is voluntary and thus assumes exchange as free choice, which in turn assumes not only individual freedom, but equal people. Market exchange in a society with first class and second class citizens implies transactions costs that are hierarchical. Second class people are—more frequently than relative to first class people—subject to opportunistic behavior and market power abuse, for they are different people, having unequal rights before the law.

The unified theory indeed predicts that the market system operates differently in the Third World compared to the First World. The abuse of market power and the consequent transaction costs will be relatively higher in the Third World. The practice of importing First World regulatory institutions of market behavior into the Third World assumes that markets operate in the same way everywhere, that is, citizenship of first class everywhere. What we observe is, however, that regulatory laws of markets will tend to fail more significantly in the Third World. The rule of law does not operate in a vacuum; its degree of enforcement is endogenous, as it depends upon the degree of citizenship of individuals and the power of money. Not all are equal before the law.

The feudal rules (A) that disappeared long ago in the West are still present in the Third World, such as practices of serfdom that are impregnated in the labor relations, even in labor market relations, such as low labor standards, but accompanied by some forms of redistribution and social protection practices of the employer.

Even the capitalist's philanthropic behavior can be seen as a modern version of the feudal rule. Under the feudal system, landlords had to follow the redistributive rule in favor of the serfs, which served the purpose of legitimizing the feudal system through the magnanimous landlords' behavior.

Today, philanthropy—including here corporate social responsibility—also serves the purpose of legitimizing the capitalist system through the magnanimous capitalists' behavior, particularly in the Third World. (See Chapter 7 below).

Finally, the persistence of precolonial institutions (M) in the Third World is even more striking. For instance, we observe the persistence of ancient rules of reciprocity in the peasant communities of today and its coexistence with market rules of exchange.

Table 4.1 indicates that institutions are not the outcome of a kind of Darwinian competition—the survival of the fittest. Why is this so? The unified theory would explain the observed path dependence as follows: The power elites have incentives to maintain the capitalist institutions, as they exercise their power through these institutions; hence, they would have incentives in preserving and defending those institutions. Some colonial institutions are part of the set of capitalist institutions and are thus maintained. The existence of a concentrated power structure blocks any possibility of significant endogenous changes in institutions—a Darwinian competition. Minor institutional changes may certainly occur.

Conclusions

The unified theory of capitalism incorporates implicitly as one of its assumptions the legacy of the European colonialism. This essay has made it explicit.

The colonial economic theory outlined here has assumed that European colonial powers introduced new institutions into their colonies, including the rule of Western supremacy. The implication is that capitalist societies have had different origins. First World capitalism originated from feudalism or from settlements, in any case, from socially homogeneous pre-capitalist societies—not that capitalism firstly had to transform socially heterogeneous societies into homogeneous.

Third World capitalism originated from colonialism. The end of colonialism did not imply the end of the colonial institutions—a case of social hysteresis or path dependence. Therefore, the Third World operates with capitalist institutions, markets and democracy as the fundamental ones, in which colonial institutions are impregnated, particularly the rule of Western supremacy. As to the capitalist system taken as a whole, changes in institutions from pre-capitalist to capitalist societies have led to a current capitalist system in which the predominant rule includes markets and electoral democracy, but together with the endurance of an institution that corresponds to colonialism: Western supremacy.

The persistence of differences in income levels and equality degrees between the First World and the Third World can then be explained by their positions in the European colonial history—and in the very long run by geography. In particular the initial inequality under capitalism, an essential factor in the economic growth process, is a legacy of this colonialism.

The persistence of the First World and the Third World is usually attributed to the latter's larger dowry of mineral resources. This is called the "mineral resources curse." Facts refute this hypothesis: Several First World countries are also well endowed with mineral resources (Australia, Canada, and the United States). According to unified theory, the colonial legacy is the real curse, much more significant than the mineral curse.

In the transit from colonialism to capitalism, the colonial history has not been erased. There is institutional path dependency or institutional hysteresis: colonialism ended but its institution of Western supremacy has endured in the capitalist system that followed. The reason is that power elites do benefit from it.

In order to legitimize their social position, the power elites utilize the freedom discourse, according to which private property rights, markets, and democracy are institutions of a free society. Freedom of choice is thus guaranteed to all in society. The discourse obscures the fact that markets are controlled by the economic elites and that democracy is electoral and thus controlled by the political elites. Capitalist institutions include markets and electoral democracy—called in the unified theory the *fundamental institutions of capitalism*—but also includes some colonial rules of domination (Western supremacy), which is also obfuscated by the discourse.

If Table 4.1 shown above reflects well the institutional history of capitalism, then the predictions of the unified theory as to the endurance of old institutions under capitalism—particularly the colonial institutions—would be consistent with facts. The table would also be consistent with the other prediction of the unified theory that the First World and the Third World are qualitatively different capitalist societies. They operate differently. The Third World has *not* become First World endogenously in two centuries of capitalist development. In all this time period, Japan—never a European colony—is the only new member of the First World club, of 23 countries, whereas the nearly 150 countries of the Third World—the large majority with colonial legacy—remain in this category.

In the process of capitalist development, history matters. There seems that institutions are not the outcome of a kind of Darwinian competition—the survival of the fittest.

The unified theory explains the observed path dependence as follows: capitalism operates with a power elite, and this elite has the incentives to maintain these institutions, including old colonial institutions, because they exercise their power though them.

The main conclusion of this essay, that colonial institutions matter in capitalist development, is in accord with the empirical literature on institutional economics, as reviewed by Maseland (2018). (The difference is that it is presented as part of an economic theory—the unified theory of capitalism.) It is interesting that Maseland also seeks to challenge the standard view by showing that the colonial legacy effect is declining in Africa and that precolonial institutions and geography are instead taking more relevance over time. This is also in accord with the hypothesis of this essay. As shown in Table 4.1, Third World countries operates with a mix of institutions coming from their colonial and precolonial history.

References

Brendon, P. (2008). *The decline and fall of the British Empire 1781–1997*. New York, NY: Alfred Knopf.

Dalziel, N. (2006). *Historical Atlas of the British Empire*. London: Penguin Books.

Diamond, J. (1999). *Guns, germs, and steel: The fate of human societies*. New York, NY: W. W. Norton.

Figueroa, A. (2015). *Growth, employment, inequality, and the environment: Unity of knowledge in economics*. New York, NY: Palgrave Macmillan.

Hodgson, G. (2003). Darwinism and institutional economics. *Journal of Economic Issues, 37*(1), 85–97.

Howe, S. (2006). Colonialism. In D. Clark (Ed.), *The Elgar companion to development studies*. Northampton, MA: Edward Elgar.

Maseland, R. (2018). Is colonialism history? The declining impact of colonial legacy on African institutional and economic development. *Journal of Institutional Economics, 14*(2), 259–287.

Pinker, S. (2018). *Enlightenment now: The case for reason, science, humanism, and progress.* New York: Penguin Random House.

Smith, A. (1976 [1759]). *The theory of moral sentiments.* Oxford, UK: Oxford University Press.

Wesseling, H. L. (2004). *The European Colonial Empires 1815–1919.* London, UK: Pearson.

CHAPTER 5

Population and the Quality of Society

Population has played different roles in the unified theory of capitalism, depending on the particular theoretical models. In the static models, the population *size* is exogenously determined; in the dynamic models, the relevant variable is population *growth rate*, which is also exogenously determined; finally, in the evolutionary model, population *growth rate* is endogenous.

This essay seeks to elaborate further on the role of population in the Anthropocene age and thus in the quality of society. The population growth rate effect is distinguished from the population size or density effect, which is the relevant variable in a finite ecosystem.

A Dynamic Model with Exogenous Population

Consider an economic growth process, seen as a dynamic process, and analyzed through a dynamic model. Firstly, take the case of an epsilon society (Figueroa 2015, Vol. II and Chapter 3). The dynamic equilibrium implies that the endogenous variable output per worker (y^*) will move along a given trajectory, which is called the *growth frontier curve*. This is a rising curve over time. The level of the curve varies among capitalist societies, whereas the slope is similar everywhere, for it depends on the growth rate of technological progress (g), which is exogenously determined in the capitalist system. The level of the curve depends positively upon investment rate (e) and the average level of education of workers (E), and negatively upon the population growth rate (n).

The investment rate (e) refers to physical capital and is assumed to be constant and independent of the individual society's saving, in a world of free capital movements. The assumption of a constant level in years of education (E) implies that the rate of investment in education (as proportion of total output) falls over time. The reason is the following: Given the unit cost per graduate and the enrollment rate, then the required investment in education (equal to the total cost) to maintain the same education level would have to grow at a rate that is equal to the population growth rate, which in the growth process is lower than that of total output. Investment in education has a similar behavior of the Engel curve in household consumption goods.

Assuming the standard aggregate production function of the Cobb-Douglas type $Y = K^\alpha [AL]^{1-\alpha}$, in which total output (Y) depends on two groups of factors: physical capital (K) and labor in efficiency units (AL), which includes workers (L) and technology (A). Then it follows that output per worker is a geometric average of capital per worker and technology levels, which implies that the growth rate of output per worker is a linear combination of the growth rates of the latter two.

Dynamic equilibrium (along the growth frontier curve) conditions require that the growth rate of capital per worker be equal to the growth rate of technology, which—given the linear relation indicated above—implies that output per worker will grow at that rate too. (It is assumed that the equilibrium is stable; hence, if the growth rate of output per worker were higher than its steady value, then it will tend to diminish spontaneously to reach the equilibrium value; if lower, then the adjustment would go in the other direction.)

Consider the following example of dynamic equilibrium. The growth rate of total output (say, 5% per year) is equal to the growth rate of capital (5%) and also equal to the sum of the growth rates of population (2%) and technology (3%). The growth rate of the labor supply is equal to the growth rate of population; that is, the unemployment rate remains fixed. The growth rate of output per worker or output per capita (3%) is therefore equal to the growth rate of capital per worker (3%) and to technological change (3%).

The effect of changes in the population growth rate can now be analyzed. The effect upon the growth frontier curve is a level effect (just upon the intercept) and is negative: The lower the former the higher the latter. The reason is simple: Investment in physical capital is needed to equip workers with machines in order to make them more productive. When the population *size* is constant, a given amount of investment fund will be allocated totally to increase capital per worker, which is called *capital deepening*; then, output per worker—labor productivity—will rise. If the population size increases at the growth rate n, then the same amount of investment fund will partly be allocated (at the rate n) to maintain the same capital per labor, which is called *capital-widening*; hence, less investment will be available for capital deepening.

In the dynamic equilibrium, the amount of investment is allocated to both needs, which makes possible the equality between the growth rate of capital per worker and the growth rate of technology. This equality in turn allows a steady growth in output per worker over time, at the growth rate of technological progress.

If the population growth rate declines, then a lower fraction of the total amount of investment will be needed to maintain the same capital per worker; hence, this lower capital widening requirement makes possible to increase capital deepening. Thus capital per worker will rise and lead to a higher level of output per worker. The growth frontier curve will shift upwards, maintaining the same slope, meaning that the per capita income of society is placed at higher level. The society becomes richer. Note that population has a *level effect*, that is, upon the level of the growth frontier curve—not a *growth effect*, not upon the slope.

The growth frontier curve along which the equilibrium value of output per worker (y^*) travels over time can then be written as follows:

$$y^*(t) = F(t; y_0^*, g), F_j > 0 \tag{5.1}$$

$$y_0^* = f(n, e, E), f_1 < 0, f_j > 0 \tag{5.2}$$

$$y^*(t) = F(t; n, e, E; g); F_2 < 0, F_j > 0 \tag{5.3}$$

$$\Delta y^*/y^* = g \tag{5.4}$$

Given the values of the exogenous variables, output per worker will move along a particular trajectory, just due to the passage of time (t). This trajectory is the growth frontier curve. The level of the curve (its intercept y_0^*) is determined by the exogenous variables (n, e and E), whereas its slope is determined by the growth rate of the supply of new technologies (g). Equation (5.3) constitutes the reduced form equation of the dynamic model. It shows that the effect of population growth rate (n) is negative. Equation (5.4) just states that the growth rate of output per worker along the growth frontier is equal to the growth rate of technological change.

From its given initial output per worker (y_o), the epsilon society will move towards the growth frontier curve, which will take time and then describe a trajectory for the output per worker (y). This trajectory is called *transition dynamics*. This trajectory can be written as follows:

$$y(t) = F\left(t; y_0^*/y_0\right) = F(t; n, e, E; y_0),$$
$$\text{where } F_2 < 0 \text{ and } F_j > 0, \text{ for } y_0 < y_0^* \tag{5.5}$$

$$\Delta y/y = G\left(y_0^*/y_0, g\right) = G(n, e, E, y_0; g) > g,$$
$$\text{where } G_1 < 0, G_4 < 0, G_j > 0, \text{ for } y_0 < y_0^*; \tag{5.6}$$

$$\text{if } y_0 = y_0^*, \text{ then } \Delta y/y = g$$

Equation (5.5) says that, given the values of the exogenous variables (n, e, and E), and given the initial income, the output per worker in epsilon society will move along the transition dynamics curve until it reaches the growth frontier curve. It shows that the effect of population growth rate (n) is negative.

Equation (5.6) says that income per worker will move from the initial income to the growth frontier curve, at a growth rate that is *necessarily* higher than the *assumed* growth rate of the frontier curve (g); moreover, the higher the distance between the initial income from the intercept of the growth frontier curve (which is observable, determined by n, e, E, as said above), the higher the growth rate needed to catch up with the frontier will be. It also shows that the effect of population growth rate is negative.

It follows that the growth frontier curve is unobservable, for the value of technological change growth rate (g) is unobservable, whereas the transition dynamics is observable. Therefore, Eqs. (5.5) and (5.6) are observable and testable. Given that they are derived from the growth frontier curve, these equations constitute beta propositions of the dynamic model.

The unified theory assumes two types of capitalist societies: regarding initial endowments of labor and physical capital, epsilon society is underpopulated and sigma society is overpopulated. Epsilon (intended to explain the First World) is a full capitalist society, whereas sigma society (intended to explain the Third World) operates with a capitalist sector and subsistence sectors as well, due to its overpopulation. The model presented above represents the case of the epsilon society. However, the growth frontier of sigma society can also be represented by equations of the type (5.3) and (5.4), shown above, for the economic growth process takes place in its capitalist sector only. The subsistence sector is residual.

In sigma society output per worker is equal to the aggregation of the corresponding values in capitalist and subsistence sectors. Under the assumption that the subsistence sector is residual, and that the engine of growth lies in the capitalist sector, then the growth frontier curve refers to that of the capitalist sector, the determinants of which are just the same factors shown above. The transition dynamics within the capitalist sector is derived in similar fashion as done above. However, there exists an aggregate transition dynamics that starts from the aggregate initial income, which is the average income of the capitalist and subsistence sectors incomes, but all the same its trajectory moves spontaneously towards the growth frontier curve (Figueroa 2015, Vol. II and Chapter 5).

In sum, if similar equations to (5.3) and (5.4) represent the growth frontier of sigma society, then similar equations to (5.5) and (5.6) also represent the transition dynamics. Furthermore, as in the case of epsilon society, the effect of population growth in sigma society is negative in all the equations. These reasonings would also be applied when dealing with the capitalist system taken as a whole. The dynamic model predicts in any type of capitalist society the same effect of changes in the population growth rate (n) over the economic growth process. A fall in the population growth rate will shift upward the growth frontier curve, which would imply another trajectory for the transition dynamics, now growing at a higher rate in order to catch up with a more distant frontier. It then follows that the change in the growth rate of total output is undetermined.

If the values of the other exogenous variables were the same everywhere, the model would predict that capitalist societies where population growth rate is smaller will tend to be richer. This is indeed consistent with facts. The First World is richer than the Third World and indeed its population growth rate is smaller. Actually, the investment rate and the level of education—the other exogenous variables—are both empirically higher in the First World, so they just tend to reinforce the effect of the lower population growth rate on the observed income differences between the First World and the Third World. (The growth rate of technological change is unobservable, but the assumption of the dynamic model is that the rate of technological adoption—from the same technological frontier—is similar between these two groups of capitalist countries.)

Dynamic Model with Endogenous Population

Some economic theories assume that population is endogenously determined. Four standard theories are summarized here.

The first theory assumes that households see children as if they were consumption goods, just like any other good that enters into the consumption basket of households. The price of this good is the opportunity cost of income (income forgone) that implies raising children. As real income of households increase, the opportunity cost will also increase and thus households will tend to reduce the number of children. Therefore, the theory predicts that higher real incomes that come with the economic growth have the effect of lowering birth rates or fertility rates.

The second theory assumes that households see children as if they were economic assets, just as bank deposits, bonds, company shares, or houses. This assumption is connected to the old-age security that parents pursue. The introduction of new assets that offer the same old-age security, such as private pension schemes and financial instruments, are substitutes to children as asset. Hence, the theory predicts that, given social protection policies in society, financial innovations will lead to a fall in birth and fertility rates. Given that the process of economic growth has been accompanied by the development of financial innovations, then the theory predicts a fall on birth rates and fertility rates along increasing income levels of countries.

The third theory assumes that fertility rate depends upon the degree of women empowerment to decide on the number of children. The prediction is the more empowered women are, the lower the fertility rate. Indeed, this negative relation has been corroborated in most empirical microeconomic studies (Upadhyay et al. 2014). The economic growth process leads to qualitative changes in society, including changes in the gender roles in society, associated to rising in both education levels and labor market participation of women. Hence, fertility rates should decline in the economic growth process due to this effect.

The previous theories are incomplete, as they have no mechanisms for making the number of children a viable choice. Thus, the fourth theory assumes that contraception technology innovations are conducive to changes in fertility rates. (Abortion is thus the old technology.) The new technologies of birth control should then reduce birth rates and fertility rates. The new technologies of birth control appeared around 1960. From then on, the theory predicts that fertility rate should have declined.

In sum, the growth rate of population (n) depends negatively upon the income level (y), shown above by the first theory. At any given income level in society, both the birth rate and the death rate will remain unchanged, so will the population growth rate (the difference between birth and death rates); as the income level rises in society, birth rates will fall and thus the population growth rate will decline. Rising income levels is the outcome of economic growth. The other theories are also related to the economic growth process, such as financial innovations, social changes in the gender roles, and technological modernization. Therefore, the economic growth process is conducive to falling population growth rates.

Another relationship between economic growth and population growth rates has recently been suggested by biologists: qualitative factors play a role in reproductive biology. Thus, infertility increases with the modern lifestyle. Empirical studies tend to corroborate this hypothesis (Sharma et al. 2013). Economic growth is accompanied by qualitative changes in lifestyle as well, which imply overweight, alcohol drinking, and stress, which in men tend to reduce the quality of sperms, whereas in women implies to postpone maternity (beyond 40 years of age) causing lower quality of ovules for gestation.

All these theories appear to be complementary. They predict that, in the economic growth process, when income per worker is rising (accompanied by new financial institutions, women empowerment, new contraceptive technologies, and changes in life style), population growth rates will tend to decline endogenously.

The growth model with endogenous population growth rate now shows a different process. Given the initial population growth rate, there exists a given growth frontier curve; as income levels increase along the transition dynamics toward the curve, the value of population growth rate will decline, and the growth frontier curve will be shifted upward, leading to higher income levels, which in turn will induce a further decline in the population growth rate, and so on. As a result, the growth frontier curve will continuously be shifted upwards over time. The curve joining the average values of each period will describe a new trajectory, which may be called the *grand growth frontier curve*. This curve will be steeper—grow at a faster rate—than the initial growth frontier curve.

In the new dynamic model, the reduced form equations are:

$$y^*(t) = G(t; e, E; g); G_j > 0 \qquad (5.7)$$

$$n^*(t) = H(t; e, E; g); H_j < 0 \qquad (5.8)$$

Equation (5.7) shows the grand growth frontier curve, in which the population growth rate is decreasing along the curve. The slope of the grand growth frontier is of a higher value (say, g', such that $g'>g$), as it cuts from below successive growth frontier curves, all with slope equal to g. Equation (5.8) shows the trajectory of population growth rate as an endogenous outcome of the economic growth process. In sum, output per worker and the population growth rate are both endogenous outcomes of the economic growth process.

The corresponding transition dynamics will show a trajectory of output per capita growing at higher rates (say, g'', such that $g''>g'$), as it has to catch up with the grand growth frontier curve now. What happens to the growth rate of total output is undetermined, as the growth rates of population and output per worker change in opposite directions, for given values of the exogenous variables (e and E).

The effect of increases in either of these exogenous variables will be to shift the grand growth frontier curve upwards. Consequently, the growth rate of total output along the transition dynamics path will also increase.

Consider a final step in the construction of this dynamic model. Assume that the exogenous variables (e and E) depend upon the initial inequality of society (δ), for they influence investment decisions in physical and human capital (Figueroa 2015, Vol. II and Chapter 6). Therefore, the grand growth frontier—Eq. (5.7)—now depends upon δ and g, where the former determines its intercept and the second its slope. The grand growth frontier curve of the First World is thus placed above of the corresponding curve of the Third World, given their differences in the values of δ. Therefore, the corresponding transition dynamics trajectory—Eq. (5.8)—is directed to each frontier separately.

The exogenous variable of the model is the initial inequality. As long as the relative degrees of initial inequality prevail, the two curves will maintain their differences in levels.

It then follows that this model predicts conditional convergence (to each separate frontier), but not absolute convergence (to the unique frontier of the First World), that is, economic growth is not conducive to income equalization between the First World and the Third World. This is an empirical prediction of the model. The other prediction is that the population growth rate (endogenous) is higher in the Third World than in the First World; therefore, the initial differences of under-population and overpopulation with respect to capital stocks will remain. These predictions together imply that, in the economic growth process, a sigma society does not become endogenously epsilon society.

What do available data show? The capitalist system is characterized by continuous increase in per capita income, which has been very rapid since World War II. According to the data for 1960–2016 published by the World Bank (2017), GDP per capita (measured in real values, at 2010 US$) has increased continuously almost everywhere, in both the First World and in the Third World. However, the gap between these two regions remains, which is consistent with the prediction of the dynamic model.

On the other prediction, the population growth rate has declined continuously in the capitalist system in the same period (1960–2016), both in the First World and in the Third World. The region of Sub-Sahara Africa showed a much higher rate and also a much later decline in this rate: the population growth rate was 2.4% per year in 1960, raised to its peak of 2.9% in 1982, and from then on declined to reach 2.7% in 2016; moreover, the increase in GDP per capita in this region has only been 1.5 times in the period, compared to 4.5 times in the rest of the Third World. Therefore, available data seem to support the predictions of the dynamic model with endogenous population.

We should remember that the definition of the capitalist system—First World and Third World—utilized in the unified theory excludes non-capitalist countries, that is, countries where market and electoral democracy are not the basic institutions. This category includes countries that in the Cold War era were called "Second World," or countries under a communist-socialist regime, some of which have become capitalists since the 1990s, such as the ex-Soviet Union (possibly having a different economic theory), and some that continue under this regime, such as China, Cuba, and North Korea (definitely having a different theory). Today China is the most significant non-capitalist country—given its relative size, 20% of the world population and producing 15% of the world output in 2016.

A comment on data for the entire world scale is thus in order. The same data set of the World Bank shows that GDP per capita has increased continuously whereas population growth rates have declined since 1970. Critical figures on population growth rates are as follows: from 1.3% per year in 1960, went up to reach the peak of 2.1% in 1970, and then declined to reach 1.2% in 2016. In this decline, the effect of China is significant (due to its explicit population control policy), which went from 2.7% in 1970 down to 0.5% in 2016. The fastest rate of population growth occurred in the period 1950–1970, nearly at 2% per year, a rate that has never, before or after, been surpassed or approached even closely (Piketty 2014, Table II.3 and Figure II.2).

Researchers usually state that the negative association between fertility rates and income levels is one of the most solidly established empirical regularities of the world society since the mid-1970s (Myrskyla et al. 2009). Then, today more than half of the world population lives in countries with below-replacement fertility (less than 2.1 children per woman). Rapid population aging have now become a social concern. Although empirical data show trends towards fertility rate reversals in few advanced capitalist countries, the global fertility rate decline is a global empirical regularity of the last decades.

Economic Growth as Entropic Process

According to unified theory of capitalism, the economic process is entropic. Production of goods are subject to the laws of Mother Nature, particularly the physical laws of thermodynamics, which deal with the relations between matter and energy. Hence, production of goods implies waste of matter and energy and also pollution of the atmosphere; that is, depletion and pollution of the environment. The theory assumes that production of goods in society has a negative effect upon the environment, then there is the feedback effect upon society. The economic process is not an isolated system. The mechanisms operate as follows.

As a helpful logical artifice in the analysis, initially consider a static model, in which population size, capital stock, and total output are all fixed. As the *same level* of total output is repeated for another period, the pollution flow will also be repeated and then the accumulated pollution in the atmosphere will rise. Thus, a static society, with a given population size, producing a *given* total output rate (say 100 ton per year), will accumulate the same flow of pollution (proportional to 100) period after period; hence, the pollution concentration in the atmosphere will also increase period after period.

There will also be an indirect effect upon the environment, which refers to the pollution effect upon the ecological system, in particular to its biodiversity, which is repeated period after period as well. This effect upon biodiversity is also negative.

There is then the feedback effect upon human society. The first effect is negative for human wellbeing, as human health tolerance for pollution is limited. On the second effect, the recent literature shows that the human health status depends upon biodiversity (Chivian and Bernstein 2008). We humans need nature to survive. We need insects, bacteria, fungi, plankton, plants and other biological species to survive. In sum, on both accounts, the feedback effect upon human wellbeing is negative. The quality of society and the quality of the environment both degrade over time.

The population size is constant, and total output flow is constant, and yet the biophysical and the social environment will both tend to degrade over time. The reason is that the same output is *repeated* period after period, which leads to pollution emissions that are also repeated period after period, which accumulates into the atmosphere also period after period, damages the biodiversity period after period, and the negative effect upon society is repeated period after period as well. The revelation is that in an entropic economic process, *static economic equilibrium is a mirage*, for it cannot be repeated forever.

In the economic growth process, total output increases continuously over time, along a dynamic equilibrium, and population growth rates declining along that trajectory, as shown in the second dynamic model above. The increase in total output over time leads to the increase in pollution emissions over time, which will have a negative feedback effect upon human health; moreover, pollution effect upon biodiversity will be negative, the feedback effect of which upon human health will be negative.

Increasing total output in the economic growth process implies increasing output per person as well, the effect of which is to increase consumption per person. Therefore, human health should be improving over time. There are two effects on different directions upon human health. What would be the net effect? Unified theory predicts that at the initial stages of economic growth the positive effect will prevail, but at later stated the negative effect will ultimately dominate. Facts suggest that we are already on the latter stage.

Along the total output trajectory showing dynamic equilibrium, therefore, both the environment and human health continuously degrade. Economic growth cannot go on forever. At some point, the process will breakdown. Dynamic equilibrium is only temporary. Again, the revelation is that in an entropic economic process, *dynamic economic equilibrium is a mirage*, for it cannot be repeated forever. Economic growth can only be seen as an evolutionary process.

The interactions between the economic process and the environment do not end here. Changes in human health should have also a feedback effect upon total output. The treatment of human health would increase the maintenance cost of human capital—similar to depreciation cost in the case of physical capital. Then more gross output will be needed, which will increase pollution emissions, and so on. For the sake of simplicity, assumes that these additional effects are small and can be ignored. There are no more relevant interactions to consider and thus the conclusion stated above follows.

Population Density Effect

Population growth rates fall continuously along the total output trajectory showing *temporary* dynamic equilibrium. This of course means that the absolute size of population is *rising* over time. Indeed, the world population size was one billion people in 1850, which has jumped to around 7.7 billion in 2010, and is projected to reach 10 billion in 2100. This increase in population size has certainly implied higher population density in our planet.

Given the finite size of the Earth and of the ecosystem, population density increases just with the rise in population size. In 1980, the world population density was 33 persons/km^2, which jumped to 50 in year 2000, when world population was nearly six billion people. Even though the world population growth rate is declining, the absolute size will keep increasing. Thus, the expected population size is nine billion in year 2050 (50% higher), which also implies 50% increase in population density, that is, 75 persons/km^2. Population density increases in proportion to the *absolute increase* in population size, not in proportion to the *growth rate*.

Population density cannot increase forever without affecting the ecosystem. Agricultural or Ricardian land is the catching net for rainfall and sun energy, where the net is fixed. Fertility of land was at some point considered as original and indestructible, but this is not the case. Agricultural land fertility has been increased by the introduction of new technologies, whereas continuous cultivation tends to exhaust land fertility. In the long run, the second effect will tend to dominate, as soil is a non-renewable natural resource. Water resources are also non-renewable.

The food supply coming from the Ricardian land is thus limited. We humans are just left with the inter-generational choice between population sizes and for how long. The higher the former, the lower the latter.

The ecosystem is also a catching net. Natural capital is not the same as Ricardian land, but they share some traits. Natural capital is also limited by the size of the planet and its "fertility"—the capital services—is not original nor indestructible, but subject to destruction, particularly by the expansion of the human species, which by displacing other biological species disturb the ecological equilibrium.

The higher population density reduces the areas for forestry and biodiversity, which in turn affects the natural capital of the ecosystem. The occupation of more areas of agricultural land and urban land implies reducing the areas for the wild life. The higher biomass of the human species affects other species sharing the same ecological system.

Consider the following conceptual experiment. Suppose total output grows by 5% per year. Two alternative scenarios are possible: 5% increase in the per capita income level, maintaining the same population size, or 5% increase in population size, increasing its density, maintaining fixed the income level. Which alternative would lead to a higher environmental degradation? The increase in pollution emissions will be similar, as total output increase is the same in both cases; hence, it would seem that pollution emissions will also increase proportional to total output (5%) in both cases.

This result assumes that there is no density effect. However, the second alternative implies rising the population density, the effect of which is to increase further the environment degradation, as more people will affect directly the natural capital of the ecosystem, its biodiversity, which human health status is dependent upon. This additional and more direct environment degradation could be defined analytically as the *population density effect*. Then there is the feedback effect upon society. Degradation of biodiversity has a negative effect upon human health.

The population problem can be defined as its *density effect* over the finite ecosystem. The problem is overpopulation of the human species relative to the ecosystem. This notion of overpopulation should be distinguished from the one that refers to capital per worker: too much population for the given capital stock of society. Whereas the latter concept of overpopulation refers to the Third World alone, the former refers to the world society.

Facts are consistent with the population density effect. According to a recent WWF Report 2018, only 25% of world's land area is now free from the impact of human activity and thus Earth is losing biodiversity at a rate seen only during mass extinctions. This Report also presents the population density of 2018 by regions: the First World countries show lower density than the Third World, with Asia and Africa having the highest density. However, population density increases everywhere. The fact that wildfires are causing high mortality of people even in the First World indicate that this is the case.

The overpopulation of the Third World relative to the First World now refers not only to physical capital but also to natural capital. The process of economic growth has not changed this situation: overpopulation differences persist. This is consistent with the predictions of the unified theory of capitalism—sigma societies do not become epsilon endogenously.

Population density has a negative effect upon human health, a feedback effect of its influence upon biodiversity, as said above. This is not the only effect, however. Given the limited size of the planet, higher population density leads to higher degrees of social conflict due to the stronger competition for natural resources. Thus, the scarcity of urban land is a source of social conflict, through invasions that are increasingly violent. The same can be said about the struggle for agricultural land and water resources. Land saving new technologies are often harmful for human health, as they use more chemicals that are toxic, aggravated by new seed varieties that are transgenic.

Higher population density of cities lead to increasing struggle over the available infrastructure, waste management, and public services. In addition it is harmful as the risk for communicable diseases increases and life is increasingly stressful.

In sum, higher population density leads to stronger social conflicts, as more people have to compete for the same natural resources or declining quantities of natural resources. This in turn leads to stressful life, decline in human health, and, in short, a lower quality of society. At some population density level, threshold values for social tolerance of those conflicts will be reached. Social disorder could then become uncontrollable, and it may be the factor setting limits to the economic process and causing its collapse.

Conclusions

The evolutionary model of the unified theory in which population growth rate is endogenously determined generates predictions that are more consistent with facts that under the alternative assumption of exogenous population. In the outcome of economic growth with social maladies, therefore, population is not a cause but a consequence.

The relations between population, the environment, and the quality of society (all endogenous variables) are thus part of the structural equations of the evolutionary model. Along the total output trajectory showing temporary dynamic equilibrium the environment degrades, population growth rate declines, but the absolute population size increases over time.

Population density increases over time endogenously. In the structural relations, population density leads to environment degradation, as population displaces other species that are needed for human survival, the feedback effect of which upon society is negative. Competition for natural resources become stronger and leads to more acute social conflicts. Along the total output trajectory, therefore, population density increases and human health declines, so does the quality of society.

Population change, environment degradation, and quality of society falling are all outcomes (endogenous) of the economic growth process. As a result of the economic growth process, we humans have changed the Earth's behavior from the Holocene to the Anthropocene age. The causal factor, the ultimate factor of this process is given by the power structure. Changes in the power structure will change the way the growth process works.

In the Anthropocene age, the population density is rising, leading to overpopulation of the human species relative to the finite ecosystem. The population density effect destroys the natural capital, which in turn affects not only the productive capacity of the system, but affect negatively human health and human survival. The observed decline in the population growth rate implies a population increase in absolute size over time, and thus the increase in population density also over time. In order to reduce the current population density, a *negative* population growth rate would have to occur.

The relation between population and the environment presented in this essay is of a different nature compared to the standard debates. In the classic Malthusian view, population was checked by food production, which in turn was constrained by available natural resources. One could then think of an equilibrium population size, which would be determined where the curves of food demand (increasing with population, proportionally) and food supply (increasing with population, but at diminishing returns) are met at that population size. Technological change would shift the supply curve and thus the equilibrium population size could be higher. Population size is thus self-regulated. Standard economics has argued that population growth rate is endogenous, but ignores that the production system is also endogenous.

In the evolutionary model of the unified theory of capitalism, the production process is entropic. Food demand and supply curves are not independent. Higher population size increases demand but it also affects the degradation of land resources; hence, the supply curve will change to a lower level. In the long run, the population size is not self-regulated.

Given the global nature of the environment degradation problem, it follows that First World countries are suffering today the impact of climate change, such as extreme weather, flooding, droughts, wildfires, hurricanes, which, in part, are originated from the overpopulation in the Third World. The environmental problem has ended the illusion that the First World wellbeing could grow independently of whatever may happen in the Third World, trying to ignore that they both constitute just one single society, living in the same ecosystem. It takes theoretical economics to discover these connections.

References

Chivian, E., & Bernstein, A. (Eds.). (2008). *Sustaining life: How human health depends on biodiversity*. New York, NY: Oxford University Press.

Figueroa, A. (2015). *Growth, employment, inequality, and the environment: Unity of knowledge in economics*. New York, NY: Palgrave Macmillan.

Myrskyla, M., Kholer, H.-P., & Billari, F. (2009). Advances in development reversal fertility decline. *Nature, 460*(7256), 741–743.

Piketty, T. (2014). *Capital in the twenty first century.* Cambridge, MA: Harvard University Press.

Sharma, K., et al. (2013). Lifestyle factors and reproductive health: Taking control of your fertility. *Reproductive Biology and Endocrinology, 11*(66), 1–15.

Upadhyay, U., et al. (2014, August). Women empowerment and fertility: A review of the literature. *Social Science and Medicine, 115*, 111–120.

DATA SOURCE

World Bank. (2017). *Population growth (annual %) 1960–2016.* http://data.worldbank.org/indicator/SP.POP.GROW. Accessed August 25, 2017.

CHAPTER 6

Unified Theory of Capitalism and Bio-Economics

The scope of the science of economics is the study of the principles that govern the production of goods and its distribution among social groups in human societies. Economics is a social science. It seeks to explain the social world, which is a more complex world than the physical world. As to method, therefore, the production of scientific knowledge in economics is more intensive in epistemology justification than in the natural sciences.

Since its foundation (with Adam Smith's *The wealth of nations* published in 1776), the main scope of economics has been the study of a particular type of human society: capitalism. In addition, economics has assumed for a long time that the economic process is an isolated process, independent of the ecosystem, the home of the human species. This holds true in standard economics (neoclassical and Keynesian economic theories).

Analytically, three levels of interaction between the economic process and the biophysical environment may be distinguished. First, the role of the environment in the economic process; second, the feedback effect of the economic process upon the environment; and third, the feedback effect of the environment upon the economic process. Standard economics has taken into account the first relation only, in which some elements of nature are included in the economic process as exogenous variables, such as land resources and fossil energy.

The second relation has been taken into account as a new sub-discipline of standard economics, called *environmental economics*. Its scope is to apply neoclassical theory to formulate public policies to remedy environmental damages that result—as market failures—from the economic process. Environmental economics is just the application of neoclassical theory.

Economics has ignored the third analytical relation for a long time, which refers to the *interactions* between man and nature. Problems of pollution and climate change affecting human life have triggered this question in recent times. The scope of standard economics would have to be radically changed to cope with this question. Human society must be viewed as a particular biological species, and thus subject to evolution and to risks of survival. It is not a matter of just applying standard economics to seek solutions to problems of environment degradation that accompany the economic process, which is the view of environmental economics.

Ecological economics is another new field that seeks to integrate the ecosystem with the economic process, that is, ecological science and economics—which one, standard economics? It intends to be interdisciplinary. But then it faces the usual challenge of whether creating unity of knowledge under such framework is viable.

A new field has been developed to tackle the third analytical problem. It involves a different approach from standard economics and thus has given rise to the development of a new school of economics, called *bio-economics*. Georgescu-Roegen (1975) introduced this term and the relevant analytics, and is considered the founder of this school (Bonaiuti 2011). It reflects the evolution of the science of economics, a response to the new environmental and social problems of our time. Bio-economics is intended to replace standard economics in the explanation of today's economic process. However, its foundations to become a scientific economic theory are still pending. Bio-economics has been criticized for analyzing the economic process as entropic in a social vacuum (Sweezy 2017).

The aim of this essay is to propose—or to make it explicit—the foundations of bio-economics. To give bio-economics an epistemological justification. Science is epistemology. The alpha–beta method will be applied to undertake this task. The primary assumptions (alpha propositions) of the bio-economic theory is thus formulated. Then, the empirically falsifiable predictions of the theory through an oversimplified model (beta propositions) are derived, which are confronted against basic facts. The essay ends with some reflections about the place of bio-economics in the evolution of the science of economics and about its relation with the unified theory of capitalism.

Foundations of Bio-Economics

In order to study the interrelations between human species and the rest of biological species, we need to construct an abstract world in which people act under two environments at the same time: social and biophysical. How do human societies operate under this context? This will be the scope of the theory of bio-economics.

The ecological system or ecosystem is assumed to consist of biological and physical elements. It is a biophysical environment.

Species are biological organisms living in an ecosystem. The ecosystem then takes the form of biodiversity. The stock of biological resources (plants and animals) constitute the *natural capital* of the ecosystem. It is "capital" in the sense that it is a stock that supplies the services needed for the production of goods (bees pollinizing); it is "natural" in that the stock depends upon sunlight energy alone, not on human activity to produce and maintain it. These stocks are *renewable* (fisheries and forestry) in the economic process.

The ecosystem also includes the stocks of mineral resources on the Earth's crust, which take two forms: fossil fuels (carbon, gas, oil) and material minerals (gold, silver, copper, lead, and iron). These stocks are *nonrenewable* in the economic process, as they enter as material inputs (not as services) in the production of goods and are thus subject to depletion. In sum, the ecosystem is populated by the human species together with other biological species; it also contains mineral resources; it is a biophysical environment.

For analytical convenience, consider firstly the biophysical environment in which the presence of the modern man (*Homo sapiens*) is ignored. Consider the following assumptions:

Alpha 1: The ecological system of the Earth is endowed with a biodiversity of species. Species need matter and energy to survive. The Earth is an open ecosystem regarding energy in that it receives energy from the exterior (sunlight), but it is closed regarding matter.

Alpha 2: Each species is in turn an open ecosystem, as it needs to exchange matter and energy with the surroundings. Species are not autonomous, but interdependent.

Their interactions are conducive to a general equilibrium situation regarding the quantities of species and the biodiversity, which is established by adaptations, by trial and error.

Alpha 3: The ecological system is hyper complex, as interactions among the species are full of feedbacks and critical thresholds. However, the hyper complex ecological reality can be transformed into an abstract process. The exogenous variables of the abstract ecological process include the flow of sunlight and the initial endowments of biological species and mineral resources. The endogenous variables include the biodiversity. The structure elements of the ecological process include the Earth, taken as land, as the catching net of sunlight. The mechanisms by which exogenous variables affect the endogenous variables include two laws of nature: photosynthesis and thermodynamics, which govern the exchange of matter and energy among species.

These assumptions seek to transform the hyper complex ecological real world into an abstract ecological world, which is simpler to understand. The ecological system can then be analyzed under the justification of the abstract process epistemology.

Analytically, consider the ecological system as a static process. Given the initial endowments of species (plants and animals), the ecosystem is just reproduced, period after period. This is the general equilibrium of the ecological system. It means that, given the initial ecosystem, call it E, each species seeks to adapt to it; these adaptations will in the aggregate generate an ecosystem E'. If E' is equal to E, then the initial E is the equilibrium ecosystem. If E' is different from E, then again each species will seek to adapt to the new ecosystem E', and these adaptations will in the aggregate generate another ecosystem E''. If E'' is equal to E', then E' is the equilibrium ecosystem. If E'' is different from E', then another round of adaptations will take place, and so on. Thus, by trial and error, the general equilibrium quantities of the ecological system is attained. This outcome assumes that such equilibrium exists and is stable.

As biologist Edward Wilson (1998) stated: "Each species is a master piece of evolution because it is so thoroughly adapted to the environment in which it lives. Species alive today are thousands of years old. Their genes, having been tested by adversity over so many generations, engineer a staggeringly complex array of biochemical devices to aid the survival and reproduction of the organisms carrying them" (p. 295).

Once in static equilibrium, the biophysical environment will be repeated period after period. If for any reason the environment is outside equilibrium, it will be brought spontaneously to restore equilibrium. Its biodiversity operates as the assets of a financial portfolio: biodiversity reduces the risk of total collapse and gives stability to the environment.

Now introduce in the abstract ecological system so constructed the human species as integral part of it. Consider the following assumption:

> *Alpha 4*: Human society constitutes a species of the ecological system. As any other species, it needs matter and energy to survive, which is exchanged with the ecological system. And, as any other species, humans can survive in a particular ecological niche only, with a particular range of values of oxygen, humidity, and temperature in the Earth's atmosphere.

This set of assumptions constitute the primary assumptions, the foundations of bio-economics. The set is non-observable, non-tautological, and constitutes a logical system, in that the assumptions do not contradict each other. These are the epistemological requirements for a scientific theory.

Capitalist Model of Bio-Economics

The economic theory of bio-economics is the abstract world constructed by a set of primary assumptions (alpha propositions) about what is essential and what is not in the ecological process; hence, the use of abstraction implies a distortion of the real world. Therefore, the theory is in principle false. It then needs to be submitted to empirical testing, to falsification. The epistemology of falsificationism will then justify the decision to accept or reject the theory.

Beta propositions must then be generated from the alpha propositions. However, as any economic theory, the primary assumptions of bio-economic theory are too general to generate the needed beta propositions; hence, falsification goes through the method of using models of the theory. A particular theoretical model of bio-economics, with a particular social situation as context, indicating particular constraints, is then needed to derive beta propositions.

Consider a particular social context in which the bio-economic process takes place: *capitalism*. Then bio-economics will not operate in a social void, but in a particular social context—and we can take care of the criticism of Paul Sweezy (2017) to Georgescu-Roegen in a letter of 1974, which has been discovered only recently. Bio-economics is now a social science. Its general scope is the study of the interrelations between the human economic activity—production and distribution of goods—and the biophysical environment. The model seeks to answer the question, how do these interactions operate under a capitalist society?

In order to construct the particular model of bio-economics, in which society is organized as capitalism, the consistent economic process to be considered is the evolutionary process. The economic process is entropic, which is conducive to an evolutionary process.

An evolutionary model of capitalism—dealing with the economic growth process—is the relevant model of bio-economics. A set of auxiliary assumption are needed to construct this model, such that the assumptions do not contradict the alpha propositions of bio-economics. The assumptions of the neoclassical theory could not be used as the needed auxiliary assumptions, for they contradict the primary assumptions of bio-economics; neoclassical theory assumes that the economic process is independent of the ecological system, and its models can only be mechanical, not evolutionary.

The assumptions of the unified theory of capitalism do not contradict the primary assumptions of bio-economics and these will then be utilized as the auxiliary assumptions. Considering the capitalists system as a whole, they are:

A1: Institutional context: Private property rights, markets, and electoral democracy constitute the institutional rules of capitalist society.

A2: Initial conditions: (1) Capitalist society is endowed with a stock of labor and a stock of exosomatic instruments of production in the form of machines; it is also endowed with stocks of natural resources, renewable and nonrenewable. (2) Individuals are endowed with *unequal* quantities of economic and social assets. This is called the initial inequality (δ), which together with the institutions imply a concentrated power structure in society.

A3: Economic rationality: Consistent with the institutional context, individuals act guided by self-interest.

A4: The capitalist society produces one single good. Labor is homogeneous.

Bio-economics seeks to integrate the economic process and the ecosystem. The relations between matter and energy are then part of the process of production and distribution. The treatment of physical relations require some analytical distinctions. First, the dimensionality distinction, the stock-flow distinction. This refers to the characteristic of flows (water flowing in rivers), which can be accumulated into stocks (the lake). Thus, stocks are amenable to accumulation, decumulation, and depletion.

Second, the flow-fund distinction. Some stocks enter into the economic process as fund of services, such as workers and machines. Natural capital—the stock of animals and plants in the ecosystem—should also be included as fund of services. These stocks can also be accumulated and decumulated, but these changes are not symmetrical on time, as decumulation is not physical, but economic, which takes time—different from depletion. These types of stocks are called *funds*. They enter into *and* come out from the economic process intact and thus make its repetition viable. Then we have those elements that are part of the physical transformation, which includes those materials that enter into (cotton) *or* come out from the economic process (shirts). These are called *flows*—dimensionally, they are indeed flows.

Table 6.1 shows the capitalist model of bio-economics. The taxonomy includes four categories of elements in the economic process: stocks, funds, flows, and social categories.

Table 6.1 Bio-economic process: growth and the environment

Categories	Input	Output
Stocks		
Non-renewable natural resources	N_0	$N_0 - n = N(T)\downarrow$
Pollution concentrations	Π_0	$\Pi_0 + \pi = \Pi(T)\uparrow$
Funds		
Machines	K_0	$K_0 + I = K(T)\uparrow$
Workers	L_0	$L_0 + p = L(T)\uparrow$
Renewable natural resources	R_0	$R_0 - r' - f(\pi) = R(T)\downarrow$
Assets inequality	δ	δ
Flows		
Materials from N	n	
Materials (net) from R	r'	
Total output		$Y(T)\uparrow$
Output per capita		$y(T)\uparrow$
Income inequality		$D(T)\uparrow$
Waste		$\pi = f(Y)\uparrow$
Mechanisms		

Institutions: markets and electoral democracy
Laws of nature: photosynthesis and thermodynamics

As the economic growth process is repeated, the two stocks go through changes: the stock of mineral resources is depleted and the stock of pollution in the atmosphere is accumulated. As fund factors, the table includes machines and workers; it also includes renewable natural resources (the ecosystem, the natural capital), for it supplies services for the production process. As flow factors, the table includes materials inputs coming from the biophysical environment (as matter and energy), and the material output of goods; it also includes waste as an irrevocable outcome of the economic process.

Finally, the model includes two social category: the initial inequality in the individual endowments of economic and political assets—which together with the institutions determine a concentrated power structure in society—and the distribution of the flow of total output of goods among social groups.

In terms of the components of an abstract economic process, we can now distinguish the exogenous and endogenous variables of the process and the structure-mechanisms as follows:

Exogenous variables: The initial endowments of capital, labor, natural resources (renewable and nonrenewable), and the initial inequality in individual endowments of economic and political assets.
Endogenous variables: Total output, output per capita, and income distribution, waste and pollution.

The elements of the structure-mechanisms through which the exogenous variables affect the endogenous variables include: institutions of capitalism (market and electoral democracy), preferences, and technology, and the laws of nature (photosynthesis and thermodynamics).

From Table 6.1, we can write the structural relations between factors and the output flow (Y), not as a production function, but as a production system, consisting of a system of equations. They are:

$$Y = F(K, AL) \tag{6.1}$$

$$n = \tau Y, \text{ then } \Sigma n_j = \Sigma \tau Y_j \leq N_0, j = 1, 2, \ldots, T''' \tag{6.2}$$

$$r = \lambda Y, \text{ then } \Sigma r_j = \Sigma \lambda Y_j \leq R^*, j = 1, 2, \ldots, T'' \tag{6.3}$$

$$\pi = \gamma Y \tag{6.4}$$

$$\Pi = \Pi_0 + \pi = \Pi_0 + \Sigma \gamma Y_j \leq \Pi^*, j = 1, 2, \ldots, T' \tag{6.5}$$

$$R = R_0 - r' - f(\pi) \leq R^* \tag{6.6}$$

Equation (6.1) shows *net* output of the single good being produced (Y), which is dependent upon the quantities of capital (K) and labor (L), whereas A is the productivity level, which reflects the current technology level. Equations (6.2) and (6.3) refer to nonrenewable (N) and renewable (R) natural resources used as inputs of matter and energy, and in fixed coefficients per unit of output (τ, λ). Initially, natural resources are redundant factors of production.

The remaining equations represent the entropic nature of the economic process. Equation (6.4) indicates that production of goods imply production of waste as well; hence, the rate of pollution emissions is an outcome of the economic process and is proportional to total output. This flow of pollution is added in each period to the stock of pollution in the atmosphere, which is indicated in Eq. (6.5). Finally, Eq. (6.6) says that renewable resources—the natural capital—decline in each period due to effect of pollution upon biodiversity.

The Workings of the Model

The economic process implies repetition of production period after period. For the sake of exposition, firstly, consider that the output level Y is exogenously fixed at $Y = Y'$. Also let the quantities of K' and L', and the value of A', are sufficient to produce that output level. As production is repeated, K' and L' will remain unchanged over time—through depreciation of capital and subsistence income of workers, which implies that Y' is net output. Equilibrium in the first period will then be Y', which could be repeated period after period, as long as natural resources continue to be redundant factors of production.

This *appears* to be a static process, but it is not. The flow of material inputs coming from the nonrenewable natural resources—minerals as matter (copper) and as energy (oil)—will be repeated in each period and thus the initial stock (N_0) will decrease over time (at the rate of n). At period $T = T'''$, the initial stock will be completely depleted, as shown in Eq. (6.2).

The same thing happens with renewable resources: the flow of material inputs—wood as matter and energy—will be repeated in each period (at the rate of r) and, assuming that this flow rate is equal to its rate of regeneration ($r°$), the stock of R_0 would remain constant; however, assume that this rate is smaller, then the initial natural capital (R_0) will decrease over time by the difference (at the rate $r' = r - r°$)—Eqs. (6.3) and (6.6). The same flow of pollution is also repeated period after period, but the concentration of pollution in the atmosphere accumulates. In addition, pollution degrades the biodiversity and contributes to the decrease in R_0—Eq. (6.6).

In the production of Y', natural capital plays a fundamental role, as provider of productive services, such as biomass, temperature, humidity, climate in general, detoxifying soils, regulating droughts and floods, pollination, photosynthetic capture of the sun's energy, purifying air and water, and so on. Natural capital is a fund of these services.

The production of Y is therefore a complex process, beyond the simple machine and labor combinations, due to the interactions with the ecological system. Labor productivity and its variations depend upon the services of natural capital: "The more species that live in an ecosystem, the higher its productivity, and the greater the ability to withstand droughts and other kinds of environmental stress" (Wilson 1998, p. 294). Thus, a biodiversity decline decreases the productivity of the economic process and increases risk.

The production system assumes implicitly an initial stock of natural capital and its biodiversity—as dowry, a natural gift to man. This dowry provides services to man—gratis—and make the production of Y viable. Note that this is in addition to the role of renewable resources as material inputs (r) in the production system.

The production of the given level of output is subject to the laws of thermodynamics and thus generates waste and environment degradation *irrevocably*. The waste takes the form of matter waste (plastics) and energy waste (carbon dioxide, CO_2, and other greenhouse gases), the dictum of the first law of thermodynamics. This waste is dumped into the atmosphere at zero cost of disposal. Due to the second law of thermodynamics (entropy law), this waste ends in pollution of the atmosphere, leading to the qualitative degradation of the biophysical environment. The greenhouse gases then originate climate change.

As the process is repeated at the same scale of output, the stocks of both renewable and nonrenewable resources, which started as redundant factors, will decline in each period;

thus, they will eventually become the limiting factors in the economic process. Pollution emissions will increase in each period and accumulate in the atmosphere. If human health tolerance for pollution is limited, then it might become the limiting factor of the process.

Which of these factors do determine the limit of the number of periods (T^*) that the process can be repeated? Certainly, not K or L, for their reproduction, depreciation and subsistence consumption, ultimately uses natural resources. The limits imposed by the three relevant factors can be distinguished easily, as they are represented in the production system by the numbers of repetitions of letter j in the summation sign.

The stock of nonrenewable resources is depleted at period T''', when the stock of mineral resources has been completely depleted; whereas the stock of renewables can be repeated up to period T'', when the threshold value of natural capital that provides the ecological services needed to maintain the human species survival (R^*) is reached; finally, pollution concentration can be repeated up to period T', when the threshold value (Π^*) of human health tolerance for pollution is reached, which is still compatible with the ecological niche that human survival requires— oxygen 21%, nitrogen 78%, and 1% other gases, as CO_2, in the composition of dry air in the atmosphere, and average temperature of 15 °C on the Earth surface.

The limit of periods of repetition of $T = T'$ will be determined by one of these three factors, whichever comes first. The smallest value of $T = T^*$ depends upon the technological coefficients τ, λ, and γ, and the threshold values N_0, R^*, and Π^*.

The capitalist model (based on the unified theory) assumes that the pollution constraint will come first; that is, in the production system showed above, the relation is $T < T' < T'''$; therefore $T^* = T$. The reason is that the effect of pollution upon human health is a problem of the public goods, for clean-skies is a problem of the commons. Similarly, the natural capital degradation due to pollution is also a problem of the commons. Power elites have no incentives to solve these problems, for they are problems of public goods and long term problems.

All biological species have adapted themselves to live in particular ecological niches with particular values of oxygen and temperatures, which are changed with the pollution accumulation. Therefore, sooner or later, the threshold values of human health tolerance for pollution will be reached. As the process is repeated, ecological equilibrium is disrupted due to the continuous and irrevocable increase in pollution; then biodiversity cannot remain unchanged. The initial ecosystem (E) will be affected with degradation. Thus, human society affects E, which becomes E'. At this situation, species will seek to adapt to the new situation, some will succeed some will not, but biodiversity will be reduced. There will then be a feedback effect of the ecosystem E' upon the human society.

Initially, therefore, ecological equilibrium implies the reproduction of the initial ecological human niche. As pollution accumulates, as in the case of the other species, the ecological niche of the human species is degraded, due to the degradation in the oxygen-nitrogen component of the atmosphere and the rise of the mean temperature of the Earth's surface (climate change). Human health depends upon the degree of biodiversity and the degree of cleanness of basic elements, such as air, water, and soil. Thus the cost of reposition of labor will increase over time, but eventually human society, as we know it, will be unviable.

Increasing pollution concentrations also degrades natural capital (a disruption of the biodiversity), which is needed to produce goods for human survival at level Y'. The cost of reposition of machines—and other capital goods, such as seeds and livestock—will increase as well. The degradation of the natural capital reduces the productive capacity of human society.

In sum, as output level (Y') is repeated period after period, the human ecological niche will also tend to degrade over time. It follows that in the entropic economic process, not even the static process can be repeated forever. *Static economic equilibrium is thus a mirage.*

Suppose that the level of output, exogenously determined, had been set at a higher level, say $Y'' > Y'$. Then, it follows that the degradation of the ecosystem would have occurred at a higher rate; moreover, the end period of the process (T^*) would have been shorter, whichever the relevant constraint was. The collapse of the bio-economic process would have occurred sooner.

Consider the process of economic growth, in which total output increases continuously over time, and increases endogenously. It is now very ease to figure out the consequences of economic growth on the degradation of the ecosystem and upon the survival of the human species. The following relation can be established: *The higher the growth rate of total output, the shorter the collapse period (T^*) will be.*

Which constraint will determine the limit in the repetition of the bio-economic process? The answer cannot come from the laws of nature only, for these laws do not operate in a social void, but they operate in a particular social context: capitalism. The way capitalism operates will also have an influence. Then, given the incentives of the power elite, who run the capitalist society, the limiting factor will still be the pollution concentration in the atmosphere, as shown above.

Therefore, the capitalist model of the bio-economic theory assumes that capitalist societies will have a particular trajectory of output per worker. This is the dynamic equilibrium, which is called the growth frontier curve. Along this curve, the bio-economic process goes through qualitative changes in the environment, which makes the process evolutionary, for the dynamic equilibrium will only be temporary. The economic growth process cannot go on forever. *Dynamic economic equilibrium is also a mirage.*

As the level of total output rises over time, it follows that the interactions between human society and the ecosystem will underlie the growth frontier curve. Human economic activity affects the ecosystem, the ecosystem has a feedback effect upon human society, which in turn affect the ecosystem, and so on.

Among the reactions of society, new technologies would appear to increase productivity and compensate the negative effects of environment degradation. Technological innovations that save mineral resources as energy source—and use more solar energy—will be endogenously generated by the power elite.

As the economic growth process is repeated over time, including the economic activities of technological innovations (also subject to the laws of thermodynamics), degradation of the environment will continue operating irrevocably. The economic growth process can hardly go on forever. A higher scale of total output implies more waste and pollution been dumped into the environment, even in the face of technological innovations. Technologies that save mineral resources will reduce the coefficient of pollution per unit of output, but total output will be higher; thus, the *total* flow of pollution will tend to increase as well.

Power elites have mixed incentives to innovate in mineral saving technologies, for the industry of mineral exploitation (mineral producing corporations) will oppose those innovations. However, power elites have general incentives for investing in new technologies that are labor saving, as higher profits would be realized for all. Land saving innovations, such as new seeds in agriculture or new machinery, will be endogenous; moreover, these will tend to be more mineral intensive and energy intensive. Therefore, the increasing scale of total output implies a higher flow of waste and pollution.

Economic growth implies modernization not only in productive technology, but also in consumption goods and ways of lifestyle. Hence, economic growth implies more consumption of exosomatic gadgets—produced with material inputs. This adds to more pollution and the destruction of the ecosystem.

The relations between the ecosystem and human society in the economic growth process is indeed a complex process, for the bio-economic process is a process full of feedbacks and threshold values. The stocks of capital and labor are reproduced in expanded form in each period. The stocks of minerals and the stock of renewable resources are however decreased over time; that is, the ecosystem itself or the size of the natural capital is endogenous. Therefore, the production system presented above—Eqs. (6.1) to (6.6)—constitute a very abstract representation of the production process, namely, the basic structural relations only.

Beta Propositions

So far, we know the structural relations of the model. The bio-economic process is certainly too complex a process to be represented by mathematics and come up with the reduce form of the system, which is needed to derive the beta propositions and the causality relations of the model. It is not only the problem of feedback relations, which also exist in neoclassical economics, such as the well-known supply-demand theory. The problem is the qualitative changes that accompany the feedbacks. The bio-economic process is not a mechanical process, but an evolutionary one. This poses difficult problems to derive falsifiable empirical predictions from a bio-economic model.

Epistemology—the logic of scientific knowledge—is needed to circumvent this problem. We may use the logical artifice that the evolutionary process can be approximated in the form of a dynamic model with a *temporary* dynamic equilibrium. Structural equations will then be explicit in this type of model, the solution of which will give us the reduced form equation.

As in any theoretical model, the solution of the structural equations is just assumed, not proved. Indeed, this is what we also find in the ultra-familiar supply-demand models, where the market model assumes that the market system operates like a big computer and thus solves the system of equations, which are the structural equations, from which the reduced form equations—leading to the beta propositions—are derived. Whether the assumption of the computer is appropriate or not will be seen in the confrontation between the data and the empirical predictions of the model.

Similarly, the assumption about the particular solution of the structural equations in the capitalist model of bio-economics is that one of the outcomes of the economic growth process is the continuous degradation of the biophysical environment, which eventually ends in a breakdown of the process. The first part of the prediction is testable. The prediction of collapse is not, for it is about the future (unobservable).

In sum, the interactions between the human society and the biophysical environment constitute an evolutionary process, in which quantitative repetitions and quantitative changes are accompanied by qualitative changes in both society and the ecosystem. The bio-economic process is not mechanical, which can be repeated forever; it is evolutionary. However, for analytical convenience, the evolutionary process can be analyzed with a temporary dynamic model, which is mechanical, just as a logical artifice, to allow the falsification of the evolutionary capitalist model. It should be kept in mind that, in this logical artifice, dynamic equilibrium is still a mirage, for it is *temporary* only. Certainly, if the dynamic model fails, then the corresponding evolutionary model does too, for the dynamic trajectory of the quantitative endogenous variables could not reach the breakdown situation that the evolutionary model predicts.

From the structural equations of the capitalist model, the reduced form relations are logically derived, which in turn determines both the beta propositions and the causality relations. This model is based on the evolutionary model of the unified theory of capitalism; hence, the beta propositions will just be similar to those derived in that evolutionary model (Figueroa 2015, Vol. II and Chapter 6). Only some of these causality relations and beta propositions are now highlighted.

> *Beta 1*: The ecosystem tends to degrade continuously and irrevocably in the economic process, and more forcefully in the economic growth process.

As we know, the economic process in the beginning of the age of the modern man was based on hunting and gathering. The production instruments were basically endosomatic. The goods produced were basically food and shelter in natural forms. The energy source was basically sunlight. Man's behavior was just similar to that of the other biological species in the ecological system and could hardly disrupt the ecological system equilibrium. The effects of the laws of thermodynamics were also there, but they were negligible.

The evolution of human societies implied qualitative changes in the goods produced and in the technology utilized. In the primitive societies, man had simple needs that could be satisfied, just as other wild animals; however, in modern times human necessities have increased continuously, not as biological needs, but mostly as social needs. Goods have become more and more processed, and the instruments of production more and more exosomatic. Human society has become increasingly dependent upon exosomatic instruments—*addicted to*, as Georgescu-Roegen would say. The implication has been a more and more energy intensive technology in human life. Fossil fuel has entered into the process and mineral resources have been exploited more intensively.

The process of economic growth has implied qualitative changes in the human society and in the ecological system of which is part. Biological species need energy, but in the human economic growth process this requirement has increased tremendously and endogenously. The laws of thermodynamics that govern the economic process have led to the growth of waste of matter and energy as well. Increasing pollution of the atmosphere and depletion of natural resources have taken place.

Increasing pollution has disrupted the ecological system, as the greenhouse gases have increased its share in the air of the atmosphere, which has led to climate change. Increasing waste of matter, such as plastics, has also disrupted the biodiversity of the ecological system and thus reduced the natural capital.

At the same time, another more direct disruption in the ecological system has also occurred as economic growth has been accompanied by human population growth, which has affected the stock of renewable resources, such as forestry (the density effect of population), the reduction of which has implied less land space for the biodiversity of the ecological system equilibrium. In sum, the economic growth process has brought with it more pollution, more depletion, and less biodiversity.

The Holocene age (*recent age*) is known as the age of the modern man, together with the plants and animals that we know today, which began around 10 thousand years ago. In this age, the economic process could be repeated period after period at the similar scale, for the natural resources were redundant factors.

The human history of the last two hundred years has been characterized by the predominance of capitalism together with economic growth. The growth of output has accelerated since the World War II, to rates never seen before. The consequence is that natural resources have rapidly become scarce, cease to be redundant. Economic growth process is repeated period after period, but each time it is repeated, the biophysical environment is degraded at increasing rates too. Hence, the Holocene age has been changed to another age, the Anthropocene. The name Anthropocene is implicitly justified by a biologist as follows: "We [humans] are the first species to become a geo-physical force, altering Earth's climate, a role previously reserved for tectonics, sun flares, and glacial cycles" (Wilson 1998, p. 277).

In the Anthropocene age human actions constitute the major force changing the Earth's behavior. According to Earth science studies, these changes include not only the well-known climate change, but also new ecological markers on the earth surface, such as waste accumulation of plastic and concrete particles, nitrogen and phosphorus in soils, and wild life being pushed into an ever-smaller areas—leading to a biodiversity reduction.

From the perspective of the science of climate physics, climate change is a fact. The UN Report *Climate Change Science Compendium 2009* concludes that in terms of some key environment parameters, the Earth's system has moved well outside the range of natural variability exhibited over the last half million years at least (McMullen 2009).

The beta proposition derived from the model is thus consistent with facts. Observed measures of the ecological disruption or changes in the behavior of Earth include:

- Increase in the greenhouse gases (CO_2 and others) in the atmosphere.
- Increase in the earth's surface temperature.
- Extreme weather variations.
- Biological diversity reduction.
- Glacier/glacial surface decline, a source of fresh water.
- Natural capital that can be regenerated in one year has been consumed in nearly half of the year, so humans are already eating up the stock of natural capital (Global Footprint Network, August 2017).

Beta 2: Human health tends to deteriorate with economic growth.

Earth is the only known planet in the solar system with an atmosphere that can sustain human life. This is so because the air has some particular parameters of oxygen and nitrogen and the average surface temperature also has some parameters that make Earth the particular niche of human life. Since the World War II these parameters have been changing. Because the human species has adapted to this ecological niche with those parameters, an adaptation that has taken many years, changes in the parameters would imply—sooner or later—a collapse of the human species, as we know it.

Empirical studies have shown that indeed human health depends upon the biodiversity of ecosystems. We humans need nature to survive. We need insects, bacteria, fungi, plankton, plants, and other species to survive; our health depends upon the health of the other species and the natural functioning of ecosystems of the natural world (Chivian and Bernstein 2008).

Capitalism has induced economic growth, with the degradation of the biophysical environment as a side effect. Both have occurred more significantly since World War II. Therefore, in this period of seven decades, we should observe the health situation of humans have shown a change, either still improving but at diminishing rates, stopping to improve, or declining. This is indeed the change that recent studies show: global health datasets collected since 1990 indicate that people live longer but a sicker life, so social progress measured by *healthy* life expectancy is not as impressive as life expectancy taken alone (IHME 2016). In addition, pollution is now among the top ten killers in the world (World Bank and IHME 2016). These facts are consistent with the capitalist model of bio-economics.

Beta 3: Man needs nature, but nature does not need man.

Bio-economics assumes that the ecosystem is prior to the appearance of the modern man. Human species is the pinnacle of biological evolution and the last element in the food chain. We indeed observe that ecosystems exist where no man lives there; at the same time, humans exist only in ecosystems, where other species exist. Then this empirical prediction seems also consistent with facts.

Man as the last chain in the biological evolution is a special species. Man needs inputs from nature for survival, but nature does not need inputs from human species to survive. Man needs ants, but ants do not need man, as biologists like to say. Man is no prey of any other species. Human parasites are not specific to man. Thus, if human species disappeared overnight, the effect upon the ecosystem equilibrium would not be a collapse.

If nature had also needed inputs from man, then man and nature would have created the ecosystem equilibrium together. Then man would not have had the freedom to destroy nature. The ecosystem could have been a self-regulating system, as shown earlier, which is not the case now. The feedback effects upon man come from the rebound of the effect of man's action upon nature, from the laws of photosynthesis and thermodynamics, not from a game of two players exchanging goods. Then the common statement that "man *exchanges* matter and energy with nature" is an incomplete description of reality. Man, guided by greedy motivations, with growing needs that go beyond biological needs, is able to set the terms of the exchange. Man's actions are the exogenous variable; the response of nature is endogenous. Man is thus the agent of change of Earth. The Anthropocene age is man-made.

In seeking his own interest, man acts in ways that include the exploitation of natural resources gratis. Mother Nature has no cashier. Pollution and climate change is just the vengeance of Mother Nature. Hence, man has the power to set the rate of destruction of nature, according to his interest. However, the social actor in the bio-economic process is not man in the abstract. It is the power elite, who actually runs the capitalist society.

In sum, the consistency between the predictions of the capitalist model of the bio-economics theory and the basic facts allow us to accept the model. Therefore, the set of assumptions of this model are appropriate. The abstract world constructed with these assumptions is a good approximation of the real capitalist world. Bio-economics seeks to explain the role of natural resources in the evolution of human societies. In a long run perspective, economics has become bio-economics. Economics is an evolutionary social science too.

Comparing the Unified Theory of Capitalism and Bio-Economics

The unified theory of capitalism was developed to explain the First World and the Third World, taken separately, through partial theories, and then the capitalist system taken as a whole, through a unified theory. In order to falsify the unified theory, static and dynamic models were initially developed (for the short run and long run), in which the role of nature was ignored. Then an evolutionary model was developed (for the very long run), in which natural resources and the laws of nature (photosynthesis and thermodynamics) were introduced into the economic process; that is, the assumptions of bio-economics were introduced into the unified theory as auxiliary assumptions. Hence, bio-economics was a kind of model of the unified theory.

In this essay, the relationship has been turned around. The bio-economic theory is autonomous and seeks to explain the interactions of man and nature in the economic process. It is an evolutionary theory. To be falsifiable, bio-economics also needs models. It needs to introduce particular social relations under which those interactions operate. One of its models refers to the capitalist model, which has been constructed including as auxiliary assumptions those of the evolutionary model of the unified theory. The unified theory of capitalism is now a kind of model of the bio-economic theory.

Are these theoretical constructions equivalent? Yes, they are. The equivalence can be shown as follows. Let α_1 and α_2 indicate the set of alpha-propositions of the unified theory of capitalism and bio-economics, respectively. Let α'_1 indicate the evolutionary model of the unified theory. Then, by definition, it is equal to the set of alpha propositions of the unified theory (α_1) plus the set of auxiliary assumptions of the evolutionary model, written as $A_1(ep, \alpha_2)$, which may be separated between those that refer to the evolutionary process proper (ep) and to the thermodynamic laws, which in turn correspond to the alpha propositions of bio-economics (α_2). Thus,

$$\alpha'_1 = \alpha_1 + A_1(ep, \alpha_2) = \alpha_1 + A_1(ep) + \alpha_2 \qquad (6.7)$$

Now let α'_2 indicate the capitalist model of the bio-economic theory. Then, by definition, it is equal to the set α_2 plus the set of auxiliary assumptions $A_2(\alpha'_1)$, which refer to the evolutionary model of the unified theory of capitalism. Hence,

$$\alpha'_2 = \alpha_2 + A_2(\alpha'_2) = \alpha_2 + \alpha_1 + A_1(ep) \qquad (6.8)$$

As can be seen, the two models are equivalent. They contain the same set of assumptions. Therefore, in operational sense, they contain the same endogenous and exogenous variables, the same structural equations, which generate the same set of beta propositions (and causality relations), which are by construction falsifiable. Moreover, testing one has implications for the testing of the other. So far the evolutionary model of the unified theory has been accepted, for its predictions have not been refuted by the available facts; therefore, the equivalent model can also be accepted, as shown above.

The assumptions of the unified theory of capitalism do not contradict the assumptions of bio-economics. Hence, and as shown above, the unified theory can be seen as a particular model of the bio-economic theory; similarly, bio-economics can be seen as a particular model of the unified theory.

Epistemologically, either theoretical model seems to be justified. However, these economic theories are quite different. Because the interactions between man and nature evolve over time, bio-economics can be seen as the *grand economic theory* of evolution. It can explain the functioning of the economic process in the Holocene and also in the Anthropocene age; it can also explain the transit from one age to the other. In order to do this, bio-economics needs to construct models, assuming capitalist and non-capitalist human societies, and thus give social content to human and ecological problems.

These theoretical models of bio-economics may be seen as partial theories, explaining man-nature relations over historical time. Then bio-economics can explain the ecological world of species—human and non-human—taken as a whole, as a grand economic theory of evolution. Unity of knowledge would thus be attained.

One of the predictions of bio-economics theory is that the economic growth process is ecologically unsustainable—even the no-growth society is unsustainable, the only difference is that process will last longer. Had we discovered bio-economics long ago, we would have been more aware that we humans were heading to the dismal Anthropocene age. Such are the promising features of bio-economics, which this essay has intended to show. Its realization will depend upon the development of scientific research—that is, with epistemology justification.

On the other hand, the unified theory of capitalism is able to produce, in addition to models for the very long run, models for the short run and the long run, something that bio-economics cannot. Therefore, if one is interested in understanding the capitalist system at different runs, and attain unity of knowledge, the unified theory of capitalism is the relevant theory. If one is interested in understanding the interactions between the human societies and the ecosystem in the very long run, under capitalist or non-capitalist societies, then bio-economics is the relevant theory.

Conclusions

Bio-economics is a new school of economics. Bio-economics assumes that human societies are biological species too. The economic process is thus integrated into the ecological system, which becomes the bio-economic process. There exists an ecological context in addition to a social context in which the economic process takes place.

This essay has proposed a set of assumptions that constitute the foundations of bio-economics. Then bio-economics now lies in realm of the social sciences, as the entropic economic process is not studied in a social void; at the same time, social relations cemented by goods can be studied, but now the role of the ecosystem is not ignored either. Its scope is still to explain the economic process of production and distribution in human societies in the long run.

According to bio-economics, human society interacts with nature in a complex way, including feedbacks and thresholds.

Human society, as any other species, needs matter and energy to survive. It takes matter and energy from nature, which is returned to nature in the form of waste, which affects nature; nature in turn affects the quality of human society. The repetition of the economic process degrades the ecosystem and the biophysical environment. Human society and nature evolve together. Thus, advanced capitalism and the Anthropocene age have come together. Both capitalism and the ecosystem are not what they were hundred years ago. Moreover, degradation of the ecosystem is endogenous and sets limits to the survival of the human society—as we know it. Man has designed its own collapse.

In addition, the economic process is not mechanical, but entropic. Therefore, the economic growth process has limits; it cannot be repeated forever. At some point in time, it will collapse. In the bio-economic process, not only the static process is a mirage; also the dynamic process is a mirage, for it can have only a temporary dynamic equilibrium.

The entropic process implies evolutionary process, but not vice versa. The limiting threshold values leading to the collapse of the evolutionary process may come from the entropic process, such as the limited social tolerance for pollution, but they could also come from the limited social tolerance for unjust situations, such as inequality degree (as Marxian theory proposes).

To be sure, bio-economics is not a multi-disciplinary field, in which some knowledge of economics, biology, and physics, are combined. Bio-economics can be constructed on its own foundations. As a scientific economic theory, its foundations are constituted by a set of primary assumptions by which the social and ecological real worlds are transformed into a single and abstract world. If the empirical predictions of the theory were refuted by facts, then the assumptions would prove to be wrong; if they were not refuted, then the assumption would be good. The theory of bio-economics thus has epistemological justification. Science is epistemology.

In contrast to bio-economics, standard economics assumes that the economic process is an isolated system, independent from nature. Human society can affect the ecosystem but the feedback of the ecosystem is small and can safely be ignored. Only social relations matter. Human society can be studied in an ecological void. This view of the economic process corresponds to the Holocene age, when natural resources were redundant factors of production. However, it fails in the Anthropocene age, for natural resources are not redundant any more, but have become scarce.

The history of human societies is the history of social changes. Human societies have gone through social changes over time. The economic process of primitive societies had possibly nil effects upon nature. The same can be said about European feudalism. European capitalism has begun around two hundred years ago. Then it became the First World, while their colonies became the Third World, which together constitute the capitalist system. The economic process of the capitalist system has had little effects upon nature in most of these two centuries. However, the rapid economic growth that took place since the World War II has implied a significant effect upon nature and the consequent interactions between society and nature. As result, the Holocene age has been replaced by the Anthropocene age.

Standard economics correspond to the old age, the Holocene, whereas bio-economics deals with the current Anthropocene age. Standard economics is old economics, whereas bio-economics is the new one. Standard economics could not explain the interactions of human society and nature, for it assumes a mechanical economic process, which can be repeated forever. The assumptions of standard economics lead to empirical predictions—such as sustainable economic growth—that are refuted by facts. Thus the assumptions are proved to be inappropriate.

The set of assumptions of bio-economics and that of the evolutionary model of the unified theory of capitalism does not contradict each other. They are complementary. Moreover, they are able to generate models that are equivalent: the evolutionary model of the unified theory of capitalism includes the assumptions of bio-economics, whereas the capitalist model of bio-economics includes the assumptions of the evolutionary model of the unified theory of capitalism. Therefore, testing one model is just testing the other. Since the former model has already been accepted as empirically valid, then the latter model can too.

Bio-economics assumes that humans are just another species of the ecosystem. Production and distribution of goods and the ecosystem are interdependent. Bio-economics can explain the passage of the Holocene age to the current Anthropocene. The observed evolution of the real world has induced the corresponding evolution in the science of economics.

References

Bonaiuti, M. (Ed.). (2011). *From bio-economics to degrowth: Georgescu-Roegen new economics in eight essays.* London: Routledge.

Chivian, E., & Bernstein, A. (Eds.). (2008). *Sustaining life: How human health depends on biodiversity.* New York, NY: Oxford University Press.

Figueroa, A. (2015). *Growth, employment, inequality, and the environment: Unity of knowledge in economics.* New York, NY: Palgrave Macmillan.

Georgescu-Roegen, N. (1975). Energy and economic myths. *Southern Economic Journal, XLI,* 347–381.

McMullen, C. P. (Ed.). (2009). *Climate change science compendium 2009.* New York: UNEP.
Sweezy, P. (2017). A letter to Nicholas Georgescu-Roegen, July 31, 1974. *Monthly Review, 68*(9), 56–57.
Wilson, E. (1998). *Consilience: The unity of knowledge.* New York, NY: Alfred Knopf.
World Bank & IHME. (2016). *The cost of air pollution: Strengthening the economic case for action.* Washington, DC: The World Bank.

Data Sources

Global Footprint Network. (2017). www.footprintnetwork.org.
Institute for Health Metrics and Evaluation (IHME). (2016). *Global burden of disease.* http://www.healthdata.org/gbd.

CHAPTER 7

Individualism in the Anthropocene Age

What is the relationships between individual behavior and the social outcome or, alternatively, between individual freedom and the common good? This may be considered the fundamental question that economics and the social sciences in general need to explain.

Adam Smith (1937 [1776]) gave an answer to this question, which has become famous: Individuals acting guided by self-interest are led, as by an *invisible hand*, to the common good. Later on, the invisible hand proposition became a theorem in neoclassical economics to determine the logical assumptions under which it was true. However, this proposition constitutes even today the core of neoclassical models and their policy prescriptions. In addition, liberal doctrine, together with its corresponding *freedom discourse*, takes this proposition as its foundation.

Unified theory of capitalism has shown just the opposite result. The theory predicts that individual freedom is conducive to economic growth with social maladies, which is consistent with the basic facts of capitalism. This essay summarizes the nature of the economic growth process as developed by unified theory and then discusses its implications for the role of individualism in the Anthropocene age.

The Nature of Economic Growth Under Capitalism

According to unified theory, economic growth under capitalism is an evolutionary process. Then it is studied using an evolutionary model: Quantitative changes are accompanied by qualitative changes, which have threshold values of social tolerance, leading eventually to the breakdown of the process and to its replacement by another process.

As a logical artifice, the evolutionary model includes a dynamic model, the dynamic equilibrium of which is *temporary* only. The quantitative endogenous variable of the dynamic model is output per worker (or output per capita). It moves along a rising trajectory over time, showing the temporary dynamic equilibrium, called the growth frontier curve, given the exogenous variables (initial inequality in individual asset endowments) and the structure elements (market and electoral democracy, as institutions) of the abstract economic process.

From particular situations in society, the initial output per worker will move spontaneously to the growth frontier curve, along the transition dynamics curve. Therefore, changes in the growth frontier curve will change the transition dynamics curve.

For the following analysis, consider the capitalist society as a whole, which theoretically is a sigma society. Qualitative changes will take place in the economic growth process. Along the growth frontier curve, each point will mark increasing income inequality and increasing environment degradation, measured by pollution concentration in the atmosphere. These qualitative changes imply increasing social conflicts, social disorder, and human health deterioration, that is, social maladies.

Can this situation qualify as dynamic equilibrium? Can the growth process be repeated along the growth frontier curve, and the corresponding transition dynamics curve, even if temporarily only? This is truly a dynamic equilibrium as defined in economics: Along the growth frontier no social actor has the power and the incentive to change the trajectory. This is the case here.

Unified theory assumes initial inequality in the individual distribution of economic and social assets. The initial inequality leads to the existence of elites, who are then able to use the institutions of capitalism, market and electoral democracy, to exercise power; thus, a concentrated power structure is created, in which the power elites (economic and political) run the society seeking their own interests.

Economic elites have the power to change the growth process but not the incentive, for they are maximizing profits and maintaining their privileged position in society, as capitalists. Similarly, political elites have the power but not the incentive to change the process, for they are maximizing incomes from their capture of the state and maintaining their privileged position in society as well.

The power elites have no incentives to change the institutions either, for they exercise their power through markets and electoral democracy. It may seem a paradox that social maladies is an outcome under democratic capitalism. The paradox is explained easily because democracy takes the particular form of electoral democracy, which means a transfer of people's political power granted by the principle of democracy into the hands of the political elite, who are then able to capture the state and use it in their own benefit. Electoral democracy is business too.

Technological change is endogenous in the economic growth process. The power elites invest in technological innovations, which are guided by their own interests. These innovations are profit driven, and can hardly lead to social problem solving.

Workers act guided by self-interest too. This motivation leads them to free-riding behavior on collective problems, such as social disorder (public good) and pollution (problem of the commons). Therefore, they do not have neither the power nor the incentives to change the process.

In sum, the economic growth process can be repeated period after period because no social actor has both the power and the will to change the process. The dynamic equilibrium is temporary, but all the same it reproduces over time economic growth with social maladies. Individuals acting freely and guided by self-interest are led, as by an invisible hand, to economic growth with social maladies. Individual freedom does not lead to the common good.

The economic growth process been evolutionary will ultimately come to a collapse. The thresholds of social tolerance to inequality and pollution, whichever comes first, will put an end to this process. The evolutionary model predicts that the threshold value of pollution will come first. Therefore, the economic growth process puts into risk the very survival of the human society, as we know it.

Human Behavior Evolution

From biology, we know that human behavior is the result of nature (genes) and nurture (social influence). This theory implies that human behavior can be controlled and changed. We also know that man is genetically endowed with two drives: individual and social, and that the relative strength of these two drives are not fixed by inheritance alone but also by the influence of society.

According to unified theory, indeed, the power elites are able to control and change the behavior of workers (Figueroa 2017, Chapters 3–5). They have the power, the incentives, and the means.

In particular, it is in the power elite's interest to raise the relative strength of individualism over altruism drives of workers. Workers would then be more inclined to accept the institutions of capitalism. They would then be induced to become closer partners of capitalists in the firms and of politicians in the political parties. Workers would be induced to enjoy the outcomes of economic growth, such as new goods and the modernization of lifestyle. Higher degree of individualism would raise the power of the elites ("divide and conquer"), as collective actions would be reduced. In sum, workers would be induce to like the system and accept less reluctantly to play by its rules, which would legitimize the power of the elite.

The means include all forms of behavioral engineering techniques, upon which power elites are willing to invest. These techniques can then be used in business and electoral processes, as forms of advertisement; it can also be used in the media, which the power elites also control, to promote the value of capitalist institutions: private property rights, market relations, and electoral democracy. Workers would be indoctrinated in the liberal doctrine through its individual freedom discourse.

The individual freedom discourse thus constitutes another mechanism that power elites use to exercise their power. As any discourse, it is less visible and more subtle, but very effective in delivering the capitalist ethos and aligning all social actors around it. The discourse proclaims that capitalism is the land of individual freedom. Like in the case of advertisement, the discourse is directed to the subconscious level of workers.

Another prediction of the evolutionary model can therefore be stated as follows: In the economic growth process, the behavior of workers become endogenously more individualistic. This prediction is consistent with the basic facts of capitalism, such as modernization and consumerism. Declining trend in the significance of collective action among workers is another. Declining in the significance of civic engagement is yet another (Figueroa, idem.).

Another prediction on changes in economic behavior of workers include is increasing significance of illegal behavior over legal. Workers seek to close the gap between their basket of consumption and that of the consumption frontier, that is, they seek the objective of "keeping up with the Joneses." The power elites push workers even further, towards exacerbated consumerism. This objective will eventually place workers beyond their means. The adjustments may include reducing savings, higher credit demand, but may also include more illegal activities as part of their economic choice.

In all cases, the adjustments imply rising stress and vulnerability in the life of workers. On the other hand, in the aggregate, illegal activities (together with the violence that is involves) will rise endogenously in the economic growth process, which implies higher degree of social disorder. Thus, the quality of society would tend to decline.

Facts are consistent with these predictions too. Illegal activities and the degree of violence associated (drug trafficking, illegal immigration, street criminality) increase over time. Diseases associated to a more stressful life are also in the increase (Figueroa, idem.).

In sum, along the growth frontier curve three qualitative changes take place, all rising over time: income inequality, environment degradation, and higher relative strength of egotism over altruism, which lead to social maladies: more hazardous human life, more stressful, more vulnerable, and more social disorder with violence. Given that the outcome of the economic growth process is higher income levels accompanied by social maladies; and given that the growth process will ultimately collapse, and thus put human survival into risk, it follows that individual freedom under capitalism does not lead to the common good.

THE MYTH OF COMPETITION

Adam Smith is considered the founder of economics. He is cited over and over again as saying that individual self-interest is conducive to the common good, that is, individuals acting guided by self-interest are led as by an invisible hand to the common good. The invisible hand refers to the workings of the market system.

According to some historians, Smith developed this proposition in the context of the British colonialism, as supporting the idea that protectionism (colonial system) was less profitable than free trade; that the monopolist order of the colonial system should be replaced by free markets, by competitive mechanisms (Brendon 2008, p. 13). It was an argument against colonialism. However, Smith's proposition has become part of the freedom discourse in the modern capitalist system.

Later on, theoretical economics developed Smith's invisible hand proposition as a theorem. Under what conditions the invisible hand proposition would be *logically* true?

If logically true, would this theory be able to explain the real world?

Science is epistemology. According to composite epistemology, a set of propositions that is logically correct can be empirically false. The assumptions of a theory are arbitrary! There is no other way to construct an abstract society, to apply an algorithm to create new ones, searching for the best theory. Then theories need to go through the falsification process.

The conditions under which the invisible hand proposition is logically true have been established. These include *absence* of public goods, of oligopolistic and monopolistic markets, of externalities, of imperfect information, and certainly absence of power elites.

The mechanisms that the invisible hand principle assume are essentially the following. First, people know better than the state what is good for them; thus, people behavior could hardly be irrational, as they do what they want, given their resource constraints. Second, the best institution is the market system, because the exchange of goods is based on people's voluntary choices, which in turn are based on selfish motivations; moreover, markets constitute a very efficient mechanism to reveal what people's wants and needs are. Third, individual egotism is transformed into the common good through market competition.

It follows that the market mechanism constitutes the invisible hand. The existence of negative externalities and public goods is the only possible justification for state intervention in the economy. Collective choice is needed for that. Furthermore, the best institution for that is electoral democracy, for it also leads to competition among political parties—similar to market competition among firms—to be elected as government and thus attain the best public choices. Individual egotism of politicians are transformed into the common good through electoral competition. Markets and electoral democracy are thus the fundamental institutions of capitalism, and constitute the mechanisms of the invisible hand, through which egotism is turned into the common good.

The fact that the outcome of the economic growth process is increasing income levels accompanied by social maladies refutes the invisible hand proposition. The assumptions underlying the proposition are then proved to be inappropriate; it leaves aside elements that are essential in the economic growth process. The invisible hand proposition has thus become mostly a belief, a liberal doctrine, and thus part of the individual freedom discourse. Given that the invisible hand principle constitutes the core of the neoclassical models, this conclusion also leads to reject these neoclassical models on epistemological grounds.

In contrast, the unified theory predicts that individual freedom is not conducive to the common good, but to economic growth with social maladies, and is thus able to explain the workings of the real capitalist world. The unified theory assumes that markets and electoral democracy are the fundamental institutions of capitalism, as neoclassical theory does, but they are operated differently by the power elites.

The unified theory, in brief, assumes that capitalism operates with power relations. The economic and political elites exercise their power through markets and electoral democracy. The power elites have the incentives to promote growth policies, for they are the main beneficiaries, as they can maintain their income positions and their privileged social position. As a result, economic growth is conducive to higher degree of income inequality and higher environment degradation as side effects, that is, to social maladies. Therefore, the power elites have perverse incentives for attaining the common good.

In particular, why does competition under power relations fail? In light of the unified theory, two sources can be distinguished. First, there is the problem of incentives. People do compete, but about what? People compete in the economic process game seeking to make private gains, such as profits, market shares, jobs. People do not compete seeking directly collective goods, such as public goods, social order, clean skies. Power elites have induced workers to become more egotists and less altruists.

Second, people do compete, but with what? Competition may be a game among equals, in which participants have similar endowments of assets—economic and social. This would be a kind of fair competition, based on meritocracy, and the outcome would certainly tend to be efficient—just as in Olympic Games. If competition is among non-equals, where inequality in asset endowments and the consequent power elites exist, then these elites would be able to set the games in such a way that they would be the winners. Therefore, the game would be unfair, and the competition need not lead to the common good, but rather to attain the private interests of the power elites.

Analytically, therefore, competition is a much more elaborated concept. We need to make a distinction between *first order competition* (competition for the asset endowments) and *second order competition* (competition through markets and electoral democracy once the asset endowments have been solved). *Given* the unequal endowments and the corresponding existence of the power elite, the outcome of the competition through markets and electoral democracy is the result of the *second order competition*; however, the *first order competition* is lacking because these unequal endowments were not the result of competition, but were exogenously determined. The Darwinian type of competition may apply to the second order competition only: the survival of the fittest, where the fittest is the wealthiest. However, there is no Darwinian competition in the first order competition, which may be seen as the *meta-competition*.

To be sure, the current capitalist class is not the group that won the competition among all people in society to become the capitalists. The mechanism for this kind of first order or meta-competition does not exist. So we do not know whether the society's capital stock is in the hands of the most talented people—from the set of all possible alternatives—to produce goods at the least cost and seeking to serve best people's needs. Actually, this was Vilfredo Pareto's concern, about the elites' formation, about the first order competition—the *elite circulation* problem, as he called it. However, Pareto has become known in standard economics for his normative criterion—Pareto optimality—that refers only to the second order competition.

Although empirical studies on the power elites are scarce, the available evidence corroborates the hypothesis that economic elites do not circulate, that they are not the outcome of a first order competition. International consulting financial firms now publish regularly the wealth of the group of billionaires of the world. For example, according to the Forbes Report *Billionaires of the World* 2017, there are only 2200 families in the world, mostly from the First World, who are billionaires—having accumulated wealth for one billion dollars or more—having an average value of 4.1 billion dollars.

Placed in the world perspective, this group certainly qualifies as the world economic elite: very small and very wealthy.

The same source reveals that the majority of this group, around two-thirds, are the heirs of wealthy parents, not the self-made capitalist (Bagchi and Sweynar 2016); moreover, the degree of circulation of this economic elite is very low (Figueroa and Rentería 2016).

In addition, this world economic elite do not compete or they compete as much as they cooperate. Recent studies have shown the development of social networks among this group, which in turn is leading to the formation of the international capitalist class amid globalization (Carroll 2010). Therefore, competition applies mostly to the powerless, the thousands and millions of people running small enterprises and job seeking workers in local labor markets.

The same analytical question applies to the political class. Certainly, the political class is not the outcome of a competition among all people in society to become the political elite, for the mechanism for this meta-competition does not exist either. So we do not know whether the government is in the hands of the most talented, ethical, and knowledgeable people—from the set of all the possible alternatives—to run the state.

The freedom discourse preaches free markets and free elections, but markets and electoral democracy are not free. The power of money have intruded them—market relations are business, but electoral democracy is business too. The power elites exercise their power through these institutions, and thus run the society. The fact that the economic and political elites show endurance does not mean they are the most efficient social actors for running the society. *Any* power elite—once established—will be able to reproduce its social position. Therefore, competition among non-equals, competition under power relations, could hardly lead to the common good.

The Freedom Discourse

Discourse is the usual mechanism utilized to indoctrinate people on a particular dogma. Religion teachings and precepts—*heaven discourse*—deal about the outer world. Similarly, capitalism teachings and precepts—the *freedom discourse*—deal with life in the capitalist system. The freedom discourse is dominant in the capitalist system. In both cases, the precepts tell people what to belief in to attain individual success, in the outer world or in this. The belief in the doctrine will also shape human behavior.

According to unified theory of capitalism, the power elite runs the society. The power is exercise through the fundamental institutions of capitalism, markets and electoral democracy. Moreover, the power elite use also the freedom discourse to obtain social legitimacy. Capitalism is thus a system of governance and domination. The freedom discourse can then give social viability to the inequality with which the system operates.

The freedom discourse preaches the value of individual freedom in doing choices, both in the market and in the electoral democracy. However, these choices are given in different feasible sets, depending on the asset endowments of people. The rich and the poor have the freedom to choose, but the options to choose from are different. The discourse just seeks to obscure income inequality in society.

The power elites indeed have the incentives, the power, and the instruments to control, manipulate, and change the behavior of workers. Therefore, the choices made by workers do not reflect their autonomy, but the preferences they have been induced to assimilate. People's preference systems are endogenous and internalize the particular value systems, and particular ethos of capitalism.

Individual behavior therefore cannot be taken as something to be respected or to be seen as sacred. The reason is that the underlying motivations of workers are subject to manipulations and are thus endogenously determined. Human behavior does not reflect who people are, but who they have become. Therefore, there is no such thing as people's autonomy; moreover, society cannot be seen as just a set of independent and autonomous individuals. The doctrine of individualism has shaky grounds.

The observed increasing egotism of workers is not the outcome of his or her individual nature (genes); it is not exogenous to the economic process; it is endogenous. It is a social imposition by the power elite; certainly, not by force, which would be the mechanism of capitalism under dictatorships, but by the incentives created by markets and electoral democracy. These institutions of capitalism allow the exercise of power by the economic and political elites. The equilibrium with social maladies is the reflection of the existence of that power. It includes the freedom discourse and the supply of many kinds of "soma" (as in the Huxley's world)—through the entertainment industry—that seek to make workers even feel happy.

Individual freedom under capitalism is therefore limited. Not only limited by the initial inequality in the asset endowments, which makes freedom of choice unequally distributed, but limited in the sense of autonomy as well. Workers thus have limited freedom of choice in both senses. The power elite is able to manipulate human behavior, according to their own interest. They exercise this power through the institutions of capitalism, market and electoral democracy, and through the freedom discourse.

The invisible hand proposition constitutes the foundation of the individual freedom discourse. The invisible hand works through the market system because market competition transforms egotism into the common good. Hence, the discourse calls for free markets, that is, without state intrusion. However, the so-called free markets clearly include all types of market structures, including monopoly, oligopoly, and imperfect competition, that is, the discourse hides the intrusion of the power elites in the working of markets. The invisible hand also works through electoral democracy, as political competition transforms egotism into the common good. The discourse call for free elections, in which the intrusion of the power elites' money to buy votes is hidden.

The freedom discourse is based on the neoclassical theory. This theory disregards power relations among the essential factors in the economic process. The discourse chooses the assumptions that are needed for the dogma. The freedom discourse is thus based on the wrong theory. Given that the objective of the discourse is to legitimize the capitalist system, and its power elite, this failure does not matter. The discourse is presented as doctrine: something to be believed in, which is just another indication of the existence of the power elite.

In sum, under capitalism individual freedom and freedom to choose goods (in the market system) and governments (in the electoral democracy) are not conducive to the common good because those choices are made under power relations. The discourse intends to present the coexistence of individual freedom with power relations as a logical impossibility. The unified theory has shown that this coexistence is not only logically correct, but it is also empirically consistent with facts. The unified theory has thus unraveled the freedom discourse as the fallacy of "competition", "free markets" and "free elections," which has been created and is utilized to manipulate and obscure the fact that capitalism is run by a power elite.

Individual Freedom and Social Responsibility

According to unified theory, the relative strengths of human drives change endogenously in the economic growth process. The egotist drive of people tends to become increasingly dominant over the altruist.

Egotism implies that people do not care about the consequences of their actions upon others. Thus, the problem of negative externalities is commonly observed in the real world capitalism. Opportunistic behavior is also common. Free riding behavior in the production of public goods—or solving the problem of the commons—is another feature of the real world capitalism. It follows that egotism implies lack of social responsibility. Therefore, lack of social responsibility is increasing over time.

Capitalists, for example, can decide to open or close firms according to the profitability criterion. However, they take no responsibility for aggravating the unemployment problem that these decisions may create. Employment constitute the means for profits; it is not their social responsibility. Similarly, seeking high returns and low risk for their investment projects, capitalists can invest in countries run by dictatorships, or buy bonds of these type of governments, which give economic viability to the dictatorships. They take no social responsibility for the consequences upon human rights violations that come with dictatorships.

Elected governments also take actions disregarding their social consequences. This paradox is not hard to understand. Electoral democracy is also business, in which political elites act guided by their own interests, which lead them to seek to capture the state for their private interests. Thus, electoral democracy generates a perverse incentive system.

Workers do not take social responsibility for their actions either. They seek their own interest in both market exchange and the electoral democratic process, subject to the unequal individual endowments of economic and political assets, and the power structure that this inequality implies. Their incentives are thus for neglecting negative externalities regarding private goods, and free-riding behavior regarding public goods, and adopting opportunistic behavior as well.

In sum, no social actor under capitalism seeks to take social responsibility for their own actions. This is just the result of selfish-motivated individual behavior with which capitalism operates, and a motivation that capitalism promotes.

Social actors do not seek to take social responsibility for the actions of others either, seeking to correct them. In particular, concerning the environment degradation—the fundamental problem of the commons of our time—social actors are free-riders. More significantly, the power elites, who run the capitalist system, do not seek to take social responsibility for their own actions or the actions of the rest in society. The power elites are not the entrepreneurs of social progress, but the entrepreneurs of their own interests. They act just following their own interests, which lead them, for example, to promote economic growth policies, disregarding its social and environmental consequences. According to the current discourse, capitalism is a free society, which makes capitalism a superior society. However, the discourse hides the fact that this freedom implies *freedom from social responsibility*.

Some clarifications are now in order to take account of the beliefs contained in the current discourse, which, in light of the unified theory, are just fallacies. The more significant fallacies are the following.

Corporate Social Responsibility (CSR)

Capitalists appear to be socially and environmentally responsible because they allocate resources to these objectives However, it can be shown that this behavior is just part of the selfish motivation. CSR behavior, for example, can be predicted from a profit maximization behavior. Corporates face risks in their investment projects; therefore, they seek to maximize profits subject to bearable risks. Reduction of risk is then pursued. In a very unequal society, profits face the risk of legitimacy. Investing in CSR is a means to gain that legitimacy.

However, CSR is usually presented as philanthropic behavior. This is just another form of obtaining legitimacy, not only on the profits, but also as economic elite. Although these elites have power in society, all the same, it helps them to have legitimacy. To be reproduced, the power must be socially viable. It follows that CSR is an investment that is expected to have a private return, increasing or maintaining the profit of the firm or the market value of the firm, reducing risk, and attaining social legitimacy. The motivation underlying CSR behavior is self-interest. It is business. The empirical prediction of this assumption is that investment in CSR will be propagandized. It will be charity with big trumpets, which is far from the motivation of altruism. CSR is thus profit seeking with guile.

Another prediction is that firms would prefer to allocate funds to CSR instead of paying taxes, for the former generates higher economic returns. Taxes are paid anonymously, whereas CSR contributions are visible, can be propagandized to get social recognition, and are thus conducive to economic returns.

Facts seem to be consistent with this prediction. The First World countries are, relative to the Third World countries, more egalitarian societies. Hence, social control on the government behavior is stronger, which makes the state and democracy also stronger. The law enforcement capacity is then higher. Hence, firms must pay the taxes they owe to the state. In the Third World, states are weaker and then firms have the choice of paying taxes or spending on CSR. The incentives for the latter are higher. CSR is used in projects that seek to help the poor, given the extent of poverty and the limited reach of public policies (which might include the crowding out effect).

Conflicts with z-populations about the exploitation of natural resources that are located in their territories are also managed with the instrument of CSR. Because the z-populations constitute the poorest groups in these societies, CSR appears as altruism, which is not. Therefore, the fact that CSR is mostly applied in the Third World—and relatively less in the First World—is consistent with the prediction. It follows that most of the so-called philanthropy is business with guile.

Crime Responsibility

The rule of law assumes that any crime is the result of individual decisions. The individual is held responsible and must be punished to protect the wellbeing of society. This is what neoclassical economics would also say, for it assumes that people have exogenously given preferences and motivations that guide their actions. Therefore, it is the individual perpetrator who commits the crime, whereas society, the capitalism system, is innocent.

If motivations are endogenous, then the view will be different. The unified theory takes from biology the assumption that individual behavior is the result of nature (genes) and also of nurture, which refers to the influence of society. Therefore, the society is also responsible for individual behavior, including individual crimes. A long run general equilibrium with excess income inequality is conducive to social disorder. General equilibrium with unemployment and underemployment, income gaps that limit workers to "keep up with the Joneses," where the Joneses are consuming more modern goods continuously push people to react and seek to find the needed additional money, even by illegal means (robberies, drug trafficking, corruption practices, and so on). Illegal behavior is thus endogenous. Illegal behavior is the outcome of a social imposition.

People are not criminals, they have become so. However, society takes no responsibility upon the bad behavior of the individual, who is society's child.

According to unified theory, power elites are able to manipulate individual behavior in direction of their own interests by using behavioral engineering techniques. Thus, in the economic growth process, workers are induced to consumerism, which goes beyond their means; then they would consider ways of making additional money, including illegal activities. Although human drives include self-interest and the desire for private goods, consumerism is a social imposition, and so is the induced individual crime.

In the economic growth process, workers are induced to become more egotists. The relative strength of egotism becomes increasingly dominant over altruism, which have significant implications for the workings of society. Competition becomes dominant over cooperation. Consumerism is promoted. Economic incentives prevail over social incentives. In particular, egotistic motivation implies that the individual's will is above the law: Economic returns—benefits net of costs—is the main criterion to obey or not to obey the law, given the individual's degree of shame. The net economic returns tend to increase in the economic growth process because the degree of egotism increases, which in turn leads to declining individual shame.

To be sure, illegal behavior is predicted by any theory that assumes strong selfish human drive. Illegal behavior is just matter of economic choice. If benefits are above costs of illegality, then the illegal activity will be undertaken; if it is not, illegal activity will not be chosen. Illegal behavior is rational behavior! The legal or illegal behavior of people is endogenous; it depends upon the benefit-costs relations only. In this choice, the individual preferences for social prestige and honor are given. According to unified theory, however, in the economic growth process, preferences are induced to change the significance of shame; thus, shame becomes less of a constraint over time.

In the aggregate, society tolerates higher levels of shame and corruption over time. Economic incentives tend to dominate social incentives in the behavior of people, for the social cost of shame declines. The consequence is higher degree of individual freedom to make economic choices free of social responsibility.

In sum, the unified theory predicts that social responsibility of social actors tend to decline in the economic growth process. People may act with apparent altruism, but it is ultimately guided by self-interest. Behavior toward the common good, in which the individual reward sought is social not economic, tends to decline.

This prediction tends to be consistent with observed facts. Crime rates are in the increasing in the capitalist system. Robberies, drug trafficking, human trafficking, arms trafficking, wood trafficking, corruption practices are all part of the social maladies and all are in the rising. Social incentives are in decay, which is the same as saying that social responsibility of the social actors are declining over time.

Corruption, especially the grand corruption of public personalities in the political and economic sphere, is in the increase. The usual impunity of this behavior is not only legal, but it is also social, as they tend to continue as part of the elites.

In contrast, standard economics assumes that people's preferences are exogenously given. Preferences can change, but only exogenously. Human preferences can change, but only due to external shocks. Hence, lack of social responsibility is embedded in people's preferences, namely, it is embedded in people's freedom, which should then be respected. Moreover, it is the state intervention—considered an intrusion into individual freedom—what creates incentives for bad behavior. Illegal behavior is just seen as the vengeance of the market: "Take away the state and illegal behavior would disappear". This hypothesis is refuted by facts: compared to the First World, illegal behavior is relatively more significant in the Third World, where the state size is relatively smaller.

Individualism Question in the Anthropocene Age

According to bio-economics, man has disrupted the ecological equilibrium. However, the ecosystem is also inflicting damages to man. Man cannot sustain economic growth forever because natural capital and the portfolio of biodiversity have been degraded rapidly in the economic growth process; moreover, the ecological niche, the only known niche, in which man lives is consequently being changed. The ecological niche for human life is very specific, and this—the only known human niche, to repeat—is being degraded.

The human species, as any other species, has limited tolerance to changes in its niche; hence, by pursuing economic growth, the human species inflicts itself a damage—a more hazardous life—and also commits a collective suicide.

Man is destroying the planet and at the same time destroying himself. This is the action of the Homo sapiens, the species that is endowed with superior intelligence compared to the rest of the species of the ecosystem. This behavior is certainly a paradox and needs a scientific explanation.

What bio-economics shows is that the common belief that human species exists apart from the ecological system and holds domination over it is a dream (Wilson 1998, pp. 277–292). Human species is not exempt from the iron laws of ecology that binds other species. We depend upon the natural world. Man needs nature. Man actions can indeed change the ecosystem, but cannot choose the directions of change. The only power man has is to disrupt the ecological system, but not upon the feedback effects.

The dream of man freed from the ecosystem has been subject to biological experiments. The results have failed. The life supporting services that the ecological system provides the human species, and for free, has no substitutes, as biologists have reported (Wilson 1998, pp. 277–292). According to bio-economics theory, this dream is just that—a dream.

As we know from biology, human behavior is the result of both nature and nurture influences, that is, from genes and from society influences as well. We also know that man has two drives, egotism and altruism, and the mix depends upon the influence of society. The evolution of human society towards capitalism has developed the egotist drive more than the social drive. This means that the relative superior intelligence of the Homo sapiens is individual intelligence, not social, a result of the evolution of society under capitalism.

Why has this type of evolution occurred? Why has capitalism not promoted the social drive of humans? Is this a problem of capitalism or of the type of capitalism that we have? According to unified theory, the current capitalism operates with power relations. Capitalism is run by a power elite.

It might come as a surprise to some readers to know that humans—the Homo sapiens, the pinnacle of biological evolution of species—are vulnerable to social influence and to manipulation. Humans are endowed with genes that give them capacity to learn, but also to be influenced in that process by social actors—capitalists, politicians, religion leaders, teachers, and even peers. The fact that the Homo sapiens is the result of evolution does not mean it is perfect, just that has evolved, as biologist like to say.

Capitalism has become the dominant system in the world society. Communist societies of Eastern Europe failed. They were defeated by the relative success of capitalism regarding economic growth. The engine of economic growth is technological innovations, but the economic incentives for innovations, compared to capitalism, were relatively low in the command economy of Eastern Europe (Eichengreen 2006). These countries have made a transit to the capitalist system since the 1990s.

Communist China is the only relevant case of resistance to capitalist expansion so far—although the market institution has already been adopted and adapted there. With the new mix of institutions, communist China has become a case of international success in terms of economic growth. Even with the rapid economic growth experienced in the past decades, China represents around 20% of the world population and produces nearly 15% of the world output. Hence, the point is that capitalism—run by power elites—dominates the world economy today.

According to unified theory, the power elites seek income and power and this motivation underlies their behavior of promoting pro-growth policies. The evolution towards selfish and greedy motivations is endogenous, and is consistent with the norms and rules of capitalism, with their institutions. The elites and the rest of society are thus prisoners of their individual ambitions, which is induced by the rules of capitalism, and exacerbated by their leaders, the elites.

The degradation of the biophysical environment could not be seen as a case of "human collective suicidal," as many have called the risk of the human species collapse. It is rather the result of the power elite's behavior—of the rapid economic growth objective—that is leading the human species to its collapse. Thus, rapid environment degradation is an endogenous outcome of the rapid economic growth process; the exogenous variable is the power structure of society. The system operates in such a way that the power elites impose their private interests to the rest of Homo sapiens, and markets and electoral democracy—the fundamental institutions of capitalism—are the mechanisms for that. Thus, unified theory is able to explain the paradox of the Homo sapiens.

It follows that the power elite does not take any social responsibility for this outcome of the economic process. The incentive system under capitalism is against that: Individuals have no incentives to take social responsibility for their actions, much less the power elite. Moreover, the elites' incentives are to insist on pro-growth policies, so as to maintain their social position of privilege. Indeed, the current discourse is pro-growth.

To be sure, the environment degradation is not something that the power elite seeks as their main objective. The unified theory is not a conspiracy theory. The power elite seek their own interests—money and power. This motivation is inescapable under the capitalist institutions—private property rights, markets, and electoral democracy.

The collective outcome of individual actions is the most fundamental question in the social sciences. Adam Smith called the mechanism transforming individual actions taken separately into collective outcome the "invisible hand." Smith was right on this point, for assuming that such mechanism must exist. However, his particular assumption (included in neoclassical theory) that the collective outcome of market exchange is the common good turned out to be empirically wrong. If it were true, then the state would hardly exist. The state would endogenously have disappeared.

In contrast, the unified theory assumes a capitalist system that is not run by the state, but it is run by a power elite and predicts that the invisible hand mechanism under capitalism (markets and electoral democracy) works in the opposite direction: The money and power pursued by the economic and political elites lead society to economic growth with social maladies, which include social disorder and degradation of the biophysical environment.

The power elites are able to control and change the behavior of workers in the directions of their own interests. Individualism and consumerism—egotistic human drive in general—are promoted by the power elites. The capitalist ethos of money is disseminated through the individual freedom discourse. Workers are thus induced to seek money (even illegally) and allocate their time more to private endeavors than to civic engagements or duties. Economic incentives tend to prevail over social incentives. Social control and social shame become less important. The common good is displaced as priority.

Is this form of democratic capitalism destiny? The laws of the social world are different from those of the physical world. Contrary to atoms in the physical world, human behavior is controllable and changeable. Indeed, this is what happens in the economic growth process. Could human drives be reversed, from predominant egotism to predominant altruism? In principle, yes. However, it does not mean it is an easy task.

The environment degradation constitutes the fundamental problem of our time. It is a problem of the commons. It is the outcome of the selfish, greedy, opportunistic behavior of all social actors under capitalism, including here the economic and political elites and workers as well, which is an outcome of the economic growth process. Therefore, the solution cannot come from the continuation of the way the current capitalism operates.

To cope with the problem of the commons the human drive of altruism would need to be strengthen over egotism. Social incentives would need to dominate economic incentives. Individual freedom *with* social responsibility would have to replace irresponsible individual freedom. It calls for evolution of human behavior on reverse. The arrival of the Anthropocene age, marking another context for the economic process, would possibly—and somehow—lead to the end of individualism, both as human behavior and as doctrine.

How to solve the problem of the commons is a major challenge for the human society, the magnitude and urgency of which has never been confronted before. History will be of no help. This is the problem of an evolutionary process (not of a mechanical process), in which time moves in one direction only, so history is not repeated. The needed help could come from a good scientific economic theory. The unified theory is confronted against this challenge.

According to unified theory, human society is now confronted to social maladies that are collective in nature.

Economic growth with excess income inequality is conducive to weak social order, which is a public good; economic growth is also conducive to biophysical degradation, which constitutes a problem of the commons. Better quality society—where social maladies are reduced or minimized—implies a collective, not individual, human drive. For sure, it involves the fate of human society. This includes the inequality within the current generation and between generations.

In contrast, the current discourse preaches individualism as the basis for solving social maladies, which is a flagrant contradiction in terms, for social maladies arouse out of individualism (and selfishness) in the first place. This is another reason for abandoning the standard social welfare criteria. Pareto optimality is individualistic, for it is based on the individual utility function.

According to unified theory, the current power structure has no incentives to follow those policies; their own interests go in the opposite direction: pro-growth policies. Moreover, the power elite cannot change endogenously in the economic growth process; it can change, but only exogenously. Therefore, changing the power relations that prevails in the capitalist system would imply introducing redistribution of the concentration of physical and social assets and institutional changes in the system, such as replacing the current electoral democracy for another superior form of democracy.

This re-foundation of capitalism is something that egotism cannot produce. No mechanism of invisible hand exist to make it happen. It is a collective endeavor. It calls for individual freedom but *with* social responsibility. This transformation could be attained by using the well-known techniques of social engineering—currently in the hands of the power elite, in the wrong hands that is—but now in the hands of the social reformers of the new democracy, who by design would have the social incentives to seek the common good over generations.

According to unified theory of capitalism, individualism has led society—as by an invisible hand—not to the common good, but to social maladies. Therefore, it cannot be defended as normative theory. This is what the unified theory has discovered. Hence, the unified theory calls for changes in the standard economics concept of individual freedom as the sacred principle. Individual freedom under power relations implies basically the freedom of the elites to manipulate the behavior of workers; to run the society according to their interests; to distort the reality through the discourse and the media. Individual freedom is thus limited.

Reducing or eliminating the power structure would then imply a higher degree of individual freedom. The power structure can be changed by reducing the inequality in individual endowments of physical and social capital or by institutional changes, such as replacing the electoral democracy by another form of democracy. Certainly, in an equal society where physical and social assets are evenly distributed and democracy is not plutocracy (as is the case under electoral democracy), individuals will enjoy a higher degree of freedom compared to that in the current democratic capitalism.

Unequal asset endowments lead to power relations because the capitalist class is able to exercise its power through markets and electoral democracy. The capitalist class is able to capture the market and the state; hence, capitalism becomes a system of domination and oppression.

This "old freedom" is becoming unviable in the Anthropocene age. The new individual freedom now implies freedom from the power elite domination. It also implies individual freedom subject to the common good, with social responsibility. Not only economic growth is unsustainable, but also the egotism that it promotes as the main human drive is too. The entropic economic process will collapse in a finite future and thus put an end to them both.

Individualism and Quality of Society

The arrival of the Anthropocene age has also marked the end of the economic growth age. If society cannot produce more goods, then we are left with the alternative of improving the quality of society. Actually, there is much to improve in quality of society, given the existence and persistence of social maladies. This implies more of a social life than an individual one.

The unified theory has shown that capitalism leads to a mediocre society. Anything that is massive becomes mediocre because the demand comes from workers, who have been made mediocre by the system, as described above. Most Third World workers have limited capacity in literacy and numeracy. This is a factor that facilitates the power elite's incentives to manipulate workers' behavior. Thus, workers in general live a sub-human life.

A higher quality society implies not only the reduction of income inequality, but of inequality in all its dimensions. It implies that workers are relatively well-educated, well-read, and well-spoken, in sum, have proficiency to participate in market exchange and democracy. Today the gaps are tremendous.

Workers are manipulated to consume private goods through the media, which makes them prisoners of consumerism—addicts of exosomatic gadgets. The media are not used to educate workers to enjoy the art that human talents have created. Workers are not educated to enjoy beauty.

The fact that we have reached the end of the economic growth age—where production of exosomatic gadgets will have to be limited—might be, after all, good news for opens the possibility of constructing a new, higher quality society.

According to unified theory, the economic growth process has led to a lower quality of society. The individual human drive has been promoted and the social human drive discouraged. As a result, the society now operates with higher degrees of egotism, opportunism, and greediness. Therefore, shame has declined in society. Compared to economic incentives, social incentives have become weaker. People tend to act based on economic gains only, on economic benefits net of costs, where shame is becoming less and less significant. Illegal behavior has thus augmented tremendously.

The exacerbation of individualism goes in the opposite direction of what is needed to function as society in the Anthropocene age. The environment problem is the problem of the commons, the solution of which requires collective action, social responsibility, cooperation, and altruism, that is, requires more of the social human drive. Individual freedom but with social responsibility would imply reversing the current trend.

Can the increasing egotism be reversed? Social control over people's behavior assumes a high quality of society, where most people can have shame. This is not the case today. In a society of shameless people, social incentives cannot control individual bad behavior, such as externalities, opportunism, and free riding; even worst, it cannot control crime either; ostracism cannot be a mechanism to penalize these anti-social actions, for the ethics have been devalued. Legal sanction has become the relevant concern, which is subject to impunity, for justice can be bought and sold. The ethos of capitalism has changed endogenously with the economic growth process to favor the value of money over almost everything else. To expect the *spontaneous* reversal of this trend would certainly imply wishful thinking and voluntarism.

Not only has the end of the economic growth age arrived, but also has the end of individualism—individual freedom without social responsibility. The science-based policies derived from the unified theory also call for competition, but for new types of competition: finding institutional innovations to solve the commons problem, which implies a structural change in the current capitalist system, its re-foundation. The unified theory can be seen as the new economics for the new Anthropocene age.

Conclusions

The relation between individual freedom and the common good is a complex one. It is one of the fundamental social problems that economics and the social sciences in general need to explain. According to neoclassical economics, individual egotism is conducive to the common good, which is included in the current freedom discourse. In contrast, according to unified theory, egotism is not conducive to the common good.

The difference is, of course, due to their different assumptions. According to neoclassical theory, egotistic behavior under capitalism is transformed into the common good via market competition and electoral democracy competition. According to unified theory, the existence of the concentrated power structure implies competition of different nature and the outcome of the economic process is economic growth with social maladies; that is, under these conditions egotistic behavior is not conducive to the common good. The reason is that the power elite runs the capitalist society, for the economic and political elites exercise their power through the capitalist institutions of markets and electoral democracy. Under power relations, competition is just a myth. Neoclassical economics disregards the existence of power structure. Facts refute the predictions of the neoclassical theory, but are consistent with the predictions of the unified theory.

As long as the concentrated power structure remains unchanged, the evolutionary economic process of growth with social maladies will continue over time, leading ultimately to its breakdown. This economic process will not be changed with more state regulations, as they seek to attack the symptoms (social disorder and pollution) not the cause of the maladies; nor will it come from endogenous changes in human behavior, a voluntarist view, given the evolution of human behavior towards strengthening its egotistic drive over the altruist. The science-based public policies that are derived from the unified theory says that profound changes in the structure of capitalism are needed.

References

Bagchi, S., & Sweynar, J. (2016). Does wealth distribution and the sources of wealth matter for economic growth? In K. Basu & J. Stiglitz (Eds.), *Inequality and growth: Patterns and policy* (Vol. II, Chapter 5, pp. 163–188). New York, NY: Palgrave Macmillan.

Brendon, P. (2008). *The decline and fall of the British Empire 1781–1997*. New York, NY: Alfred Knopf.

Carroll, W. (2010). *The making of a transnational capitalist class: Corporate power in the 21st century*. London, UK: Zed Books.

Eichengreen, B. (2006). *The European economy since 1945*. Princeton, NJ: Princeton University Press.

Figueroa, A. (2017). *Economics of the Anthropocene age*. Sham, Switzerland: Palgrave Macmillan.

Figueroa, A., & Rentería, J. M. (2016). On the world economic elite. *Economía, 39*(77), 9–32.

Smith, A. (1937 [1776]). *An enquiry into the nature and causes of the wealth of nations*. New York, NY: Random House.

Wilson, E. (1998). *Consilience: The unity of knowledge*. New York, NY: Alfred Knopf.

CHAPTER 8

Science-Based Public Policies

Unified theory of capitalism is a scientific economic theory. From this, therefore, science-based public policies can logically be derived. However, public policies cannot directly follow from a scientific theory. Normative theories are needed to give policy choices an ethical justification. This essay seeks to establish the logical relations between positive and normative economics, and then discusses further these relations in the light of the unified theory.

POSITIVE AND NORMATIVE PROPOSITIONS

An analytical distinction is usually made between positive and normative economics. The first is about what the *world is*, whereas the second is about what the *world ought to be*. This distinction could hardly emerge in the natural sciences, for the laws of the physical world are unchangeable by man. What follows from scientific knowledge in the natural science is engineering, just the application of scientific knowledge. In economics, the distinction assumes implicitly that the laws of the social world are changeable by man through public policies, the content of which requires ethical values.

The next analytical question is whether the propositions of positive and normative economics are independent or not. Consider, firstly, the logical sequence going from positive science to normative science. A *good* scientific, positive economic theory is the one that is able to explain the functioning of a particular type of society; it is able to show how the world is. This means that its beta propositions have been established and have been corroborated by facts. These beta proposition contain the causality relations, the effects of the exogenous variables and structure elements upon the endogenous variables. Then public policies can be derived from the theory.

When several endogenous variables are involved, the valuations about their priorities would require ethical principles. Similarly, ethical valuations may be involved in the choice of the exogenous variables or structure elements as policy instruments. Then, normative principles are needed to derive science-based public policies. Normative principles require in turn a normative economic theory.

A normative theory deals with the problem of how the world ought to be. As any theory, it is also a set of assumptions that constitute a logical system. It follows that the assumptions of the normative theory could not be independent from those of the positive theory; consistency is required. Then, and only then, the endogenous variables would constitute the policy objectives and the exogenous variables and structure elements the policy instruments for such transformation. The positive and the normative theories together would then allow man to transform the world from what it is into what ought to be.

Could the sequence go the other way around: normative theory first and then positive theory? No, it could not.

Normative theory could not establish how a society ought to be without knowing how this type of society actually operates, which requires positive theory. This sequence is then logically unviable, for there is no causality relations on which to base the policies because there is no positive theory. In this case, public policies would just be wishful thinking propositions.

Positive and normative theories are inter-dependent. This is not difficult to prove. Scientific knowledge starts from a research question. However, any research question is value laden. It has an ethical content. If one wished to give a purely logical justification to a scientific research question, a logical principle would be needed, the justification of which would in turn need another logical principle, and so on. We would fall into the logical problem of infinity regress. The same problem would appear if one wished to give a research question a purely empirical justification. Hence, the scientific research question cannot be logically or empirically justified; it needs an ethical justification, which could be explicit or implicit.

Public policies therefore require the interactions between positive and normative theories. The sequence positive-normative shown above is just part of this interaction. Because normative theories come from ethics (a formal science) and positive theory refers to the real social world; and because epistemology also comes from logic (another formal science), it follows that formal and factual sciences interact to explain and act upon the real social world.

In the case of economics, the logical ordering of the interactions of positive and normative theories can be established using the alpha–beta method. The logical derivation of science-based public policies from a scientific economic theory can be established as the following set of rules.

Rules for Science-Based Public Policies

1. Research question is justified by a normative theory **N**, which sets the assumptions, as a logical system, about the relevant and problematic endogenous variables of society (Y), which needs to be explained.
2. From positive theory **P**, the alpha propositions: Set of assumptions, as a logical system, which is intended to explain the set of endogenous variables (Y).
3. Model of **P**: Particular social situation under which the economic process takes place. If a static process is assumed, then the structural relations constitute an implicit function $H(Y, X; S) = 0$, where X are the set of exogenous variables of the model, for a given set of structure elements S.
4. Beta propositions: Reduced form equations of the model, $Y = F(X)$, showing causality relations as well, which are testable by construction.
5. Falsification: Dataset **b** is statistically consistent with the beta propositions, which implies that the model of the theory can be accepted.
6. Science-based policies: From normative theory **N**, priorities are established by the social welfare function $W(Y)$, which is sought to be maximized, subject to $Y = F(X)$.

The rules ordering can be explained as follows. Step (1) just indicates that a research question about what is considered the fundamental problems of society comes from a normative theory. Steps (2)–(5) constitute the epistemological justification for accepting the model of the theory as a good approximation of what the real social world is. Then step (6) shows that the derived science-based public policies must be consistent with both the normative theory and the corroborated positive theory, where $W(Y)$ is the preference ordering of the endogenous variables (Y) according to the normative theory, which is sought to be maximized, subject to the causality relations shown in function F. Given the causality relations, the science-based policies consist in determining the values that the exogenous variables and structure elements should take in order to attain the socially desired values of the endogenous variables.

Therefore, the logical sequence (1)–(6) goes from a normative theory to positive theory, and then back to the normative theory to derive science-based public policies. Then, and only then, the propositions about public policies will be consistent with the normative theory and with the causality relations of the positive theory. However, once the scientific research question has been established (step 1), what follows in steps (2–5) is epistemology, not ethics. The ethics implicit in the research question will play no role upon the results of the scientific research.

These conclusions also apply to dynamic and evolutionary processes. However, some additional analytical distinctions must be made. In the case of dynamic models, the structural equations include inter-temporal relation among the endogenous variables, which results in reduced form equations—function F—that should include the variable time (t), as mechanical time. Then, the beta propositions and the causality relations are obtained from the reduced form, and shown by the corresponding transition dynamics function.

Analytically, evolutionary models operate through dynamic models, where dynamic equilibrium is a logical artifice, for it is only temporary. The reduced form will include the variable Time (T), as historical time, and the threshold values of the endogenous variables, which indicate that indeed the dynamic equilibrium is only temporary, as the process will collapse when the threshold values are reached. The property of the transition dynamics also apply in this case. The beta propositions and the causality relations refer to the effect of changes in the exogenous variables upon the trajectories of the endogenous variables and upon the collapse period are shown in the transition dynamics functions, which are observable and testable.

The static model is also known as short run model, the dynamic as long run, and the evolutionary as very long run. The concept of *run* utilized here is analytical, not chronological. There are more *givens* in the short run than in the longer run.

The static or short run model of the unified theory, when dealing with the capitalist system taken as a whole, assume the following givens: factor endowments, stock of natural resources, and initial inequality among exogenous variables, and preferences, technological knowledge, and institutions among structure elements. Changes in any of these will change the values of the endogenous variables, total output and degree of income inequality. The dynamic or long run model, dealing with the economic growth process, assumes that factor endowments are now endogenous; thus changes in the remaining givens will shift the trajectories of the endogenous variables.

Finally, the evolutionary or very long run model in turn assumes that preferences and technological knowledge change endogenously in the economic growth process; also introduces the stock of natural resources as exogenous. A new endogenous variables is the amount of waste. Therefore, the remaining givens are just the initial inequality and the institutions, which together constitute the power structure, the changes of which will shift the trajectories of the endogenous variables and change the collapse period of the process.

This is a summary of the causality relations to be found in the unified theory. Causality relations are equivalent to beta propositions. Beta propositions are not always equal to the reduced form of the model, except in the short run model. In the long run and very long model, beta propositions are provided by the transition dynamics functions. Public policies can be derived from each of these theoretical models.

The Case of Neoclassical Economics

The research question of neoclassical economics is the following: How efficient is the use of the scarce resources in the capitalist society? This question is justified by a normative theory, which assumes that human societies face scarcity of resources to produce goods with which to satisfy their needs. Therefore, the normative proposition is the following: Human societies should organize the economic activity so as to use their scarce resources in the most efficient way. The ethical concern is with the efficiency in the allocation of scarce resources. The corresponding scope of economics is then the study of the principle under which a capitalist society allocates its scarce resources to alternative ends.

Neoclassical positive theory then seeks to answer the research question by transforming the real world capitalism into an abstract capitalist society. In terms of the alpha–beta method, the positive theory is able to make this transformation by using a set of assumptions about the abstract society (alpha propositions), from which empirical predictions are logically derived (beta propositions), which is turn can be submitted to the falsification process. The theory is falsified through models. If the set of empirical predictions are not refuted by facts, the theory is accepted, otherwise it is rejected.

Consider the simple static neoclassical model. Given the factor endowments of society, the initial individual resource endowments, and also given individual preferences, individuals seek to maximize their individual utility function, subject to their individual resource constraints. The market system is the mechanism to allocate scarce resources, through supply and demand. The static general equilibrium exists and would lead to a particular solution in the allocation of the scarce resources. The outcome of the economic process is the set of prices and quantities that clear all markets. Then this is the answer to the question of how the real world is.

The normative question that logically follows is whether this solution is efficient. The normative criterion utilized is Pareto optimality, which is consistent with the assumptions of the positive theory. Utility function is individual. It is not cardinally measureable, it is only ordinal, it is not observable, which makes interpersonal comparison of utility unviable. Hence, the solution is said to be Pareto optimum if no one can be made better off without making some else worse off. This is logically consistent with the normative theory, which values efficiency, and the Pareto optimality is the criterion of economic efficiency. The model conclusion is that individual selfish behavior leads society—through the market system, the invisible hand—to Pareto optimum situation.

In the dynamic process, society's factor endowments change endogenously; technology also changes over time; thus, the economic growth process takes place: per capita income increases over time. Moreover, economic growth has no limits and thus can go on forever. Pareto optimality can also be applied to this dynamic outcome. The market mechanism is conducive to dynamic efficiency as well (the turnpike theorem). In addition, as per capita income grows for everyone, the Pareto optimality is improved: individuals gain with economic growth, that is, they are richer and are thus in higher utility curves, and no one is worst off.

Therefore, general equilibrium, static or dynamic models, is Pareto optimum. The standard neoclassical model assumes perfect competition in markets, but the usual argument is that even if cases of imperfect competition existed, which would then lead to deviations from Pareto optimality, the model assumes that their effect on the outcome is small and can thus be ignored. Other cases known as "market failure," such as externalities, public goods, imperfect information are said to exist and have an effect on the optimal solution, but, again, the usual argument is that these effects are not significant, and thus they can be ignored.

As to allocation of public goods, the standard neoclassical model assumes electoral democracy, in which political parties compete to win elections. Voters choose the best proposal. Hence, political competition also leads to efficiency in the allocation of scarce resources. Again, any failure will be small in magnitude and can be ignored. In sum, the abstract society constructed with the set of assumptions of the model is intended to be a good approximation of the real capitalist world.

Income inequality and environment degradation are also outcomes of the economic process. The assumption is that general equilibrium can be attained with any value of these outcomes; that is, too much income inequality has no consequences upon the existence and reproduction of equilibrium; even if it has, its magnitude is assumed to be very small, and can be ignored. The same can be said about environment degradation.

Now consider the following theorem that is consistent with the Rules of science-based policies given above:

Theorem 8.1 Science-Based Public Policies in Neoclassical Theory

If

1. Neoclassical theory explains how the capitalist society is;
2. Society's wellbeing is improved if the individual gain in utility is not at the cost of the losses in utility of other individuals (Pareto optimality).

Then, public policies ought to

A. Promote economic growth.
B. Income redistribution ought to be avoided.
C. Promote competition in markets and electoral democracy.
D. Avoid state intrusion in individual freedom.

Premises (1) and (2) refer to the neoclassical positive and normative theories; they indeed constitute a logical system for they do not contradict each other. These premises lead to conclusions about how the capitalist world ought to be and the corresponding public policies. Therefore, public policies should be pro-growth, which implies real income rise for everyone, and thus leads to Pareto optimality. The Pareto principle implies that income redistribution does not improve society's wellbeing, therefore it ought to be avoided. Market and electoral competition is to be promoted. Finally, state intrusion into the individual's freedom of choice and egotism is to be avoided, for egotistic behavior leads in the aggregate to Pareto optimality.

Submitted to the falsification process, however, basic facts refute the predictions of both the static and the dynamic models. The factual outcome of the economic growth process is indeed growth in income levels, but accompanied by social maladies. The capitalist system operates with excess labor supply, income inequality, environment degradation, and the consequent social disorder and hazardous human health and human life. Therefore, on epistemological grounds, we could say that neoclassical theory fails to explain how the real capitalist world works.

Given that the positive neoclassical theory is refuted by facts, then assumption (1) in Theorem 8.1 fails. Therefore, the derived Pareto optimality criterion becomes irrelevant for science-based public policies.

The Case of Unified Theory of Capitalism

The research question of the unified theory of capitalism is about the determinants of production and distribution of goods in the capitalist society. This question is justified by a normative principle that makes the following assumptions:

- Society is confronted with scarcity of resources.
- People's tolerance for inequality is limited.
- Man and nature interact in the economic activity.
- People's health tolerance for pollution of the atmosphere is limited.

Therefore, the normative proposition is the following: Society should organized itself to use scarce resources efficiently so as to attain the highest quality of society, which is a combination of high levels of consumption of goods with reduced income inequality and reduced concentration of pollution. The ethical concern is with the quality of society in which people live, including the future generations.

The corresponding scope of economics is then the study of the principles under which a capitalist society allocates its scarce resources to alternative ends and how total output is distributed among social groups in the Anthropocene age, when natural resources are not redundant but scarce factors of production.

The positive unified theory constructs an abstract capitalist society to represent the real capitalist society by establishing a set of assumptions (alpha propositions). Then, from the set of assumptions, empirical predictions of the theory are derived (beta propositions), which are testable by construction. The theory is falsified through models. If the set of empirical predictions are not refuted by facts, the model is accepted, otherwise it is rejected.

Consider an evolutionary model, dealing with economic growth. In the economic growth process, per capita income increases endogenously over time. This quantitative change in the economic process is accompanied by qualitative changes: increase in income inequality and in the concentration of pollution in the atmosphere. These qualitative outcomes imply a more intense social conflict, higher degree of social disorder, and more hazardous human life, that is, social maladies. Because there exists in society thresholds of social tolerance to inequality and health tolerance to pollution, the economic growth process cannot go on forever, but is led to its collapse in a finite period. Therefore, the economic growth process is not a mechanical process but an evolutionary process, in which dynamic equilibrium is just temporary. The outcome of the economic growth process is higher income levels over time but with social maladies.

The normative criterion to value this outcome is quality of society. The quality of society is improved with the rising income levels, leading to higher consumption levels, but it is diminished by the social maladies. The net effect will be positive in the initial stages of economic growth, but eventually the negative effect will dominate. The quality of society depicts a U-inverse curve over time. The downward side of this curve has already been reached, which corresponds to the new Anthropocene age. Capitalism is increasingly a low quality society. This proposition follows even if capitalism were efficient in the allocation of its scarce resources.

The policy implication of the unified theory can be presented as a theorem, which takes into account the Rules of science-based policies given above. Then

Theorem 8.2 Science-Based Public Policies in the Unified Theory

If

1. The unified theory explains how the capitalist society is;
2. The capitalist society's wellbeing is improved when the quality of society is improved.
3. The common good prevails over the individual interest

Then, public policies ought to

A. Avoid promoting economic growth.
B. Promote income redistribution.
C. Promote efficiency in the use of scarce resources, particularly non-renewable natural resources.
D. Avoid promoting egotism.
E. Promote the change (reduction) of the current power structure.

The premises (1)–(3) are logically consistent to each other. Premise (2) says that the normative criterion is quality of society—rather than individualistic interests. Premise (3) is the normative criterion in the particular Anthropocene age, when the quality of society is in the downward stage and the survival of the human species is at risk. It says that *in situations of collective risk, society is better off when the common good is pursued rather than the individual interest.* This is the *common good principle.*

Facts are consistent with the predictions of the evolutionary model. In the last decades, healthy life expectancy has shown a tendency to increase, then level off, and then to start falling (Figueroa 2017, Chapter 6). Therefore, the current situation is already indicating the beginning of the down-slopping side of the quality of society curve. This is analytically consistent with the emergence of the Anthropocene Age, the new ecological context in which the economic growth process takes place now. Thus, premise (1) of the theorem is complied. Theorem 8.2 then follows.

The three premises lead to the propositions about how the capitalist world ought to be and thus what the public policies should be. The main policy objective is to shift upward and continuously the quality of society curve, so as to postpone continuously the collapse period. Therefore, public policies should promote a no-growth society, which in turn would reduce social maladies: stopping the increase in the degree of income inequality and reducing the rate of pollution emissions.

The wellbeing of future generations are taken into account in the no-growth policy. Future generations will inherit a bio-physical environment with lower degree of degradation. No-growth policies are thus in favor of current and future generations via the environment effect. There are no inter-generational tradeoffs, as is the case with the current pro-growth policies.

Redistribution policies should also be promoted, not to congeal the current level in the degree of income inequality.

This would improve the degree of social order. Innovations of mineral saving technologies should also be promoted, both as energy and material inputs in the production function, so as to reduce pollution flows. Egotism in the Anthropocene age is not to be promoted, instead freedom with social responsibility should. The environment problem is a problem of the commons, the solution of which requires collective action.

The evolutionary model of the unified theory explains how the capitalist system operates in the long run. The normative question now refers to what can be done to transform the way capitalist society *is* towards what it *ought to be*. Therefore, the policies in the theorem presented above now apply as *science-based policies*.

Who would carry out these policies? The current power elites run the capitalist society. These elites exercise their power through markets and the electoral democracy, the fundamental institutions of capitalism. They have captured markets and the state. Therefore, they would not have the incentives to give up their power. Instead, they have the incentives to carry out the public policies derived from neoclassical theory, even if this theory fails to explain the reality.

The choice of public policies is not a matter of scientific knowledge, but of incentives and power. The set of public policies depends on who runs society; it is endogenous. The fact that the pro-growth policies are maintain in the Anthropocene age just reflects the interests of the power elites. They are the main beneficiaries of economic growth, not only in terms of maintaining the high income position, but also, and more fundamentally, in maintaining their privileged social position.

According to unified theory, public policies are endogenous. This discovery shows that public policies can be explained. This is contrary to the usual view of exogenous public policies, which leads people to propose policies that are just a set of wishful thinking propositions.

The evolutionary model predicts that the quality of society curve will move along its current trajectory as long as the power structure remains unchanged. This is the ultimate factor determining the evolutionary process. The current power elites have no incentives to promote the public policies to improve the quality of society—policies (A)–(E) listed above. Therefore, in order to make the new public policies viable, which become a kind of *second order policies*, another policy, kind of *first order policy*, should be promoted: replace the current power structure by a less concentrated power structure.

According to unified theory, the capitalist system operates with power relations. This is the essential factor in the long run. This makes capitalist society behave under particular traits. Capitalism is not a society of individual freedom—as the discourse preaches—but of oppression. It is not a society of wisdom but of egotism, opportunism, power relations, and blindness about the common good. It is not a society in which people's behavior reflect who they are, but who they have become. It is not a society that cares for the next generations, but mostly for today's individual interests; that is, it is not a society that cares for the environment, but for economic growth, which has become an addiction.

To be sure, economic growth is an entropic process, which implies an evolutionary process, with a finite period of collapse. Economic growth is leading the human species in an accelerated way to the brink of survival. The science-based public policies derived from the unified theory indicate that this form of capitalist system has come to an end and must go through a change, a re-foundation.

Neoclassical economics ignores the entropic nature of the economic process. The freedom discourse goes even further, as it negates some facts, like climate change, not to jeopardize pro-growth policies. Therefore, climate change is not internalize in public policies as it should, generating additional social costs.

Capitalism cannot but grow and hence will seek to grow until its own doomsday. Philosopher John Searle has recently argued that artificial intelligence poses a major problem for humanity. The machines so created have no consciousness about what they are doing; they just do. Another problem, a more risky one, is the conclusion reached here about the modern man and his intelligence, who influenced by society is becoming so egotistic that is being turned into that machine too.

To be sure, climate change implies a new stochastic distribution of weather events. However, if this fact is negated, people and governments will consider weather events, as changes in rainfall patterns, as part of the old distribution, not as events of the new distribution of climate change, and make no previsions for more extreme changes. As a result, innovations in prevention measures, individual and collective, are not promoted. The effect of this perverse incentive of the power elites worsens the effect of climate change upon human life and the quality of society.

POVERTY VS INEQUALITY

Further discussions about the positive and normative propositions in economics are in order. For example, which is more important for the quality of society, poverty reduction or inequality reduction?

Neoclassical theory's answer is none! The scope of neoclassical economics is the resource allocation problem, which calls for studying the ways human societies are organized to allocate scarce resources to alternative ends. The society's economic problem is the efficiency in the allocation of resources. The most accepted criterion of social welfare is the Pareto optimality. Income inequality has no role in Pareto optimality; poverty does not either. Transferring income from the wealthy to the starving poor does not imply social gain. It is a transgression against individual freedom and the individual gains and losses cannot be net out as social gain. Pareto optimality criterion is independent of the income inequality or poverty outcomes of the economic process. A society with a Gini coefficient of 0.70–0.80 in income inequality would still conform to a Pareto optimal situation!

However, the freedom discourse preaches that pro-growth policies are justified because they lead to poverty reduction. It does not matter if income inequality increases with growth. In this case, the normative principle is not exactly Paretian, but Rawlsian: Social welfare is superior when the utility of the most disadvantaged in society is higher, regardless of the situation of the rest. An increase in income inequality can then be justified if it leads to an increase in the real income of the poor. The increase in the *relative income* of the rich (implying higher income concentration) is justified if the *absolute income* of the poor rises. Thus, economic growth is good because real incomes of the poor increase with growth. The Rawlsian social welfare criterion does not contradict Pareto optimality criterion, for no one would suffer losses in the economic growth process.

These normative principles—called *welfarism* in the literature—follow from the neoclassical theory of capitalism. This theory assumes—although implicitly—that capitalism is an equal society and then Pareto optimality criterion is justified. Therefore, changes in the level of income inequality could not have consequences in the functioning of capitalism; any income inequality would be socially tolerated.

Even if capitalism happens to be very unequal, then the welfare criterion is also justified because the individual utility functions are not cardinal, thus not comparable; social gains cannot be net out from individual gains and losses. In addition, neoclassical theory assumes that individual utility functions are exogenously determined, in which the consumption levels of others do not count, only what the individual consumes, as in isolation. Thus, the individual makes choices with full autonomy.

Finally, neoclassical theory assumes that people care for their absolute real income only, not about their incomes relative to those of the others in society; hence, capitalism is a society in which any degree of inequality is socially tolerated, regardless of how concentrated income is. This is the Robinson Crusoe metaphor. These assumptions together predict that there is no social consequences of inequality. Income inequality is seen as something *natural* in society, no matter how high it is—similar to the idea of *natural* rate of unemployment, which can have any value, a tautological concept. This prediction is refuted by facts, for capitalism operates with social disorder. Welfarism follows from the wrong theory of capitalism; hence it has no much relevance for public policies.

Welfarism is nevertheless part of the current discourse that promotes economic growth. The so-called "problem of poverty" is thus the invention of the discourse. The engineering part of the discourse consists in setting a poverty line and then counting the people who are below it. If the proportion of the population below the poverty line falls, then it is said that poverty has declined. Data shows that indeed this particular measure of poverty shows declining trends in the process of economic growth. However, economic growth is accompanied by social maladies, such as social disorder, which refutes the hypothesis that poverty—not inequality—is the relevant variable for the quality of society.

The assumptions of unified theory of capitalism are different. First, the initial inequality is significant, which together with the fundamental institutions of capitalism—markets and electoral democracy—lead to a concentrated power structure. Second, individual motives and preference systems are not exogenous, but endogenous. Institutions are able to shape human drives; moreover, power elites are able to influence those drives in the directions of their own interests. As biology has showed, the individual is only partly himself, child of their biological parents (nature, genes), but partly is child of society (nurture). The preference system of individuals are endogenously determined by the capitalist society; hence, the behavior of individuals does not reflect who they *are*, but mostly who they have *become.*

Third, the unified theory assumes that people care about their relative position in society; hence, people tolerate inequality but limited to a certain threshold degree only. When inequality goes beyond their threshold of tolerance, individuals react and *seek* to restore inequality to the tolerable region by mechanisms outside the institutional rules—illegal activities. Therefore, not any degree of income inequality is socially tolerated, but only a strict subset of all possible distributions of income. Social disorder—a social malady—is the consequence.

Fourth, power elites have incentives to promote economic growth policies because they are the main beneficiaries, not only in maintaining relative income, but in maintaining the privileged position they have in society. Through the freedom discourse, they seek to legitimize the power structure and the economic growth policies by propagandizing poverty reduction.

Therefore, according to unified theory, an analytical distinction must be made between *absolute* poverty and *relative* poverty (inequality). The first category refers to consumption levels that do not satisfy threshold levels of the energy needed by the individual to work and survive as biological organism. This is a state that threatens life, a destitute situation, which cannot last forever and end up in the social statistics of death rates.

Relative poverty refers to consumption levels that do not satisfy threshold levels to attain social life enjoyment, social wants. Relative poverty is subjective; it is a non-tolerable income gap in comparison to others in society. People are no horses, seeking to satisfy only biological needs. According to theory of relative living standards (RLS), people have biological and social needs, the combination of which they order hierarchically; moreover, people seek to satisfy both at the same time as primary, secondary, etc. needs (Figueroa 2017, Chapter 4).

This assumption is contrary to Maslow's theory. This classical theory assumes that humans order their needs also hierarchically, but assumes that the biological needs (physiological needs) constitute primary needs, whereas social needs are secondary, and so on (Maslow 1970).

The assumption of limited tolerance for inequality is at play through the RLS theory. People's preferences are endogenously determined means that people seek to "keep up with the Joneses." Therefore, people seek to reach the consumption frontier of society, given by the consumption basket of the upper classes; that is, people seek to close the gap between their consumption basket and that of the consumption frontier. If the consumption frontier increases, the gap will rise, then people's relative poverty will increase (but absolute poverty remains unchanged), which will induce them to take actions directed to reduce the gap by different means, such as higher effort, but also by social protests, and eventually by illegal actions, which are conducive to social disorder. Illegal behavior of people would thus be endogenous.

The RLS theory is consistent with available facts. The imitation tendency—the so-called *demonstration effect*—in the behavior of people is indeed revealed in what empirical studies show. This theory explains the observed behavior of consumerism. Empirical data suggests that indeed people have no autonomy—or have little autonomy—in their economic choices.

The implication of the RLS theory is that the relevant concept of poverty is not absolute poverty but relative poverty (inequality), namely, the gap between the people's actual basket of consumption goods and that of the consumption frontier. Therefore, higher absolute income of the poorest groups of society may be accompanied by increasing relative poverty. This explains the fact that in the growth process, and spite of poverty reduction, social disorder does not fall or disappear.

Certainly, the proportion of people below a given poverty line can decline in the economic growth process, but this is just a statistical construct, with no scientific significance. The relevant question for the quality of society criterion is whether relative poverty—income inequality—declines with economic growth. Facts show that it does not.

The large majority of low income people belong to the category of low-relative income group rather than to low-absolute income group. The destitute situation threatens life and cannot last much, unless relieved; however, the relative poverty situation can, and constitute part of the general equilibrium outcome of the economic process. The observed stress consequences of poverty are usually related to the destitute situation only. However, these consequences also apply to those suffering relative poverty (outside destitution), for they are capable of struggling to overcome the situation, and thus generating social disorder. Hence, relative poverty (inequality) involves large segments of society—not just the destitute—and has consequences for social order. Inequality is the real social malady.

It is relatively easy to show that analytically there is no such thing as the "poverty problem." First, consider the case of a capitalist society in which economic and political assets were equally distributed, which would imply that incomes would tend to be equally distributed as well. Thus, there would not exist a problem of relative poverty. Would there be a problem of (absolute) poverty? Let the individual's subsistence income be defined as the level that can satisfy his or her biological needs of survival; hence, income below that of subsistence implies poverty. If the average income of society is higher than the subsistence income, then there will not be a problem of poverty, neither of inequality. If the average income is smaller, this only says that society is unviable; that is, this society in the long run will not exist.

Now consider a capitalist society that is very unequal (as current societies). If average income were smaller than subsistence income, as in the previous case, this only says that society is unviable; that is, this society in the long run would not exist. If average income is higher than subsistence income and, at the same time, income distribution is such that some people have incomes that are below the subsistence income (the destitute), then there would exist poverty from the individualistic viewpoint; however, from the collective or social viewpoint, there is no poverty, the problem is inequality, for some people are destitute, but some others are well-fed or even overweighed.

There are many examples in the public health area showing this principle. Children of poor households in the world are vulnerable to shocks and die from pneumonia, as they are undernourished and thus unable to generate good defense against germs. Tuberculosis continues to be the disease of the poor in the world, although the vaccination and the treatment exists. The cure and prevention of these diseases are relatively cheap; certainly, financing them would not force the country to go for foreign debt. The medical profession usually attributes these diseases to poverty. According to unified theory, these are the diseases of inequality. Social maladies are caused by inequality. The poor of the capitalism world are second class citizens.

It follows that, analytically, the problem of poverty does not exist. It is an invention of the power elites. It is a way to avoid their social responsibility of redistributing incomes, of attacking the income inequality problem; it is a way to place the responsibility instead in the individual—"you are poor, very sad."

Income Redistribution Effect vs Economic Growth Effect

After two hundred years of capitalist growth we have come to the situation in which inequality is high and persistent. It is not only that capitalisms operates with rich and poor people, but the gap is enormous, and the income concentration is then immense. Capitalism can be described as islands of prosperity in a sea of poverty. Not surprisingly, capitalism functions with social disorder—as the unified theory predicts.

Public policies derived from the unified theory promote no-growth policies, which would then have to include policies for redistributing income in the capitalist system so as to avoid congealing the current level in the degree of income concentration. No-growth policies may reduce income inequality endogenously, but it would be just around the current level, which is socially excessive.

The redistribution policy refers to redistributing income from the wealthy to the poor within Third World countries and from the First World to the Third World countries. Since the age of economic growth has come to an end, then the time of income redistribution has come by necessity.

The freedom discourse opposes income redistribution because it is an intrusion upon individual freedom—policy principle (D) of neoclassical economics. In addition, the discourse argues that redistribution of income just implies redistributing poverty, especially within the Third World; then the claim is that in order to raise the incomes of the poor economic growth should be promote—policy principle (A). Economic growth has not led capitalism to social progress, whereas at the same time natural resources have been degraded to the point of risking the human species survival. What a way to waste resources!

The argument that income redistribution would have low impact on raising the incomes of the poor is a fallacy. This can easily be shown. The redistribution effect would certainly depend upon the current degree of income inequality. The higher the degree of income inequality, the higher the redistributive effect upon the incomes of the poor would be.

Take the case of Peru and Brazil, the countries ranking among the most unequal in the Third World, with Gini coefficients around 0.60. The income share of the top 1% of households is about 30% and that of the bottom third is 5%. Then doubling the income of the poor group *now* would imply taxing the rich group by 16%. A tax rate that is not out of range nowadays. By comparison, doubling the income of the poor group through economic growth would have to wait for decades, depending on the growth rates for their incomes. At a growth rate of 2% per year, for example, it would take 36 years to see their income doubled. Therefore, it is untrue that income redistribution within the Third World implies redistribution of poverty.

The Gini coefficients of income inequality, measured from household surveys, shows a value for the *world society* that is currently around 0.60–0.65, depending on the assumptions made in their calculations (Milanovic 2016). The discussion in the literature is mostly about *changes*, whether this coefficient is increasing or decreasing by some points—marginal changes, that is. What is overlooked is that the *level* of this coefficient is very pronounced, making the discussion of changes by some marginal points of second order of significance.

Within the *capitalist system*, the current average Gini coefficient in the First World is around 0.30, whereas in the Third World is around 0.50, based on The World Bank-Milanovic data set. This source assumes that the household surveys are representative samples of income distribution in every capitalist society. However, it is known that the income of the wealthy are under-represented in household surveys. To be sure, it is not people that is missing in the household surveys; it is money. When including the income of the wealthy, these coefficients would certainly become much larger, especially in the Third World.

The WID data source is based on tax reports of countries. It is a much better source for calculating the income share of the top percentiles of the distribution, as these are the people who pay income tax; hence, Gini coefficients are not reported because they cannot be calculated. This data source shows that the income share of the top decile has increased since the 1980s, reaching currently to the figure of about 60% of the total world income (Alvaredo et al. 2017). This is a very high degree of inequality, for this figure was around 40–50% in the more unequal societies of the world in past decades (Brazil, Peru), when calculated from national accounts data.

For the sake of the argument, we may assume that the Gini coefficient of the world income inequality is similar to that of the capitalist system, even though the former calculation includes China and other communist countries that are relatively less unequal. Then we may assume that the Gini coefficient for the capitalist system is around 0.60–0.65, that is, similar to that of Peru or Brazil. Then the redistribution exercise shown above would also apply to the capitalist world as well. Therefore, the income redistribution effect upon raising *now* the income of the poor groups within the capitalist system would be significant as well; hence, the redistribution effect competes favorably with the growth effect even in this case.

These exercises show that, given the order of magnitude in the degree of income inequality in the capitalist system, the income redistribution effect upon raising the income of the poor is significant. It is a superior alternative to the growth effect, for it implies raising the incomes of the poor *now* and decreasing the degree of income inequality also *now*. In addition, the comparison with the growth effect ceases to be relevant in the Anthropocene age, where economic growth is not ecologically sustainable.

Therefore, given the high degree of income concentration, income redistribution is a powerful tool to improve the quality of life of society today. Thus a socially tolerable degree of inequality could be reached, and thus a society of higher social order and higher quality. The quality of society will improve without economic growth.

Public policies of no-growth together with income redistribution can thus attain higher degrees of quality of society, as they would be in favor of workers in the current and future generations. These policies, of course, are against the interests of the power elite; thus, they involve a problem of social conflict in the current capitalist system. The power elite would oppose them, as they prefer pro-growth policies together with pro-poverty policies, for in this may they are able to maintain their privileged position, not only in terms of income and wealth, but also as power elite.

It should be noted that, according to the Pareto optimality criterion, income redistribution brings no social improvement at all. This criterion assumes a highly equal society in the distribution of individual assets, economic and social. There would be no Pareto improvement with income redistribution in a rich and highly equal society, in which someone is taxed and thus has to reduce the vacations days in the Caribbean to transfer this amount to subsidize to another individual the purchasing of a luxury car.

The income redistribution policy in the capitalist system is of different nature. In this case, the income transfer through taxes from the rich to the poor would have the effect of reducing hunger and improving the social environment, with higher degree of social order and higher health status due to the lower pollution emissions. The redistribution effect implies improvement in the quality of society, the common good, which is the normative criterion consistent with the unified theory.

In sum, in the Anthropocene age, quality of society as policy objective has an ethical justification. This policy implies a combination of no-growth with income redistribution policies. These policies would be in favor of workers and against the elites of both the current and future generations, whereas maintaining the current pro-growth policies benefits mostly the power elites of this and future generations, even if it is suicidal, as it leads to the collapse of the economic growth process. This is the basic social conflict that is derived from the unified theory: The implementation of the new public policies would require reducing or eliminating the current power structure with which capitalism operates.

Conclusions

An economic theory is positive when it intends to explain the real social world. It does so, when its assumptions constitute a logical system, from which falsifiable predictions can be derived, and when facts do not contradict those predictions. Then the positive theory explains what the real world is. In order to derive science-based policies from such economic theory a normative principle is required about what the real world ought to be.

The essay has shown that indeed normative theory and positive theory are not independent. Therefore, normative propositions based on wrong theories are meaningless. This is the case of standard economics.

The unified theory of capitalism is able to explain the capitalist system. In particular, it is able to explain the fact that economic growth process leads to higher income levels, but accompanied by income inequality and environment degradation. To derive science-based public policies from the unified theory, a normative theory is needed to give them ethical justification. The essay proposes the principle that under situations of collective risk (the Anthropocene age), the common good *should* prevail over the individual interests. This principle is logically consistent with the assumptions of the unified theory. Therefore, science-based policies have logically been derived from the unified theory.

References

Alvaredo, F., et al. (2017, May). Global inequality dynamics: New findings from WID.world. *American Economic Review, 107*(5), 404–409.

Figueroa, A. (2017). *Economics of the Anthropocene age.* Cham, Switzerland: Palgrave Macmillan.

Maslow, A. (1970). *Motivation and personality* (2nd ed.). New York, NY: Harper & Row.

Milanovic, B. (2016). *Global inequality: A new approach for the age of globalization.* Cambridge, MA: Harvard University Press.

CHAPTER 9

Redistribution Through Labor Markets

According to unified theory, the science-based public policies in the Anthropocene age include no-growth, income redistribution, and technological innovations that are mineral resource saving. Among income redistribution, policies through labor markets was proposed (Figueroa 2017, Chapter 7).

This essay presents a more explicit elaboration of that policy proposal. The idea was to establish a guaranteed minimum income (gmi), which is different from legal minimum wages or poverty lines. It is not set as absolute income, but as *relative income*. It is not only national, but an *international policy* as well. At the same time, the policy must be consistent with the incentives needed for the well-functioning of labor markets.

In epsilon type societies (explaining the First World), where excess labor supply takes the form of unemployment, the gmi can be established as unemployment insurance. However, this insurance already exists in most First World countries. The insurance is set below the market wage rate so as to maintain the incentives for seeking

© The Author(s) 2019
A. Figueroa, *The Quality of Society*,
https://doi.org/10.1007/978-3-030-11656-9_9

wage-employment. To replace it or complement it with gmi does not present much theoretical problem, as has been discussed in the literature (van Parijs and Vanderborght 2017).

The more complex question is how to set the gmi in sigma type societies (the Third World), where excess labor supply takes the form of unemployment and underemployment, the latter being by large the more significant. The answer requires the scientific understanding of labor markets in sigma societies. This theory was developed and found consistent with facts in Figueroa (2015, Vol. 1 and Chapter 6). Now the task is how to use the theory to apply the said policy in the Third World. This is indeed the main objective of this essay. Thus, the gmi is discussed in the light of a short run model of the labor market in sigma theory.

A Short Run Sigma Model of the Labor Market

The model includes the following assumptions. The capitalist society produces only one good. The labor market refers to unskilled labor, where minimum wages are relevant. There are two groups of firms: large and small. In each category, the level of average productivity of low-skilled workers declines with the quantity of labor, for given technology, stocks of capital, and quantities of high-skilled workers. The average productivity level is higher in the large firms compared to the small firms, so are the corresponding marginal productivity levels.

The labor market is competitive; hence, the level of marginal productivity represents the labor demand curve. The labor market is non-Walrasian. The initial conditions are such that nominal wages are given and are sticky downwards due to social norms. There is overpopulation in the labor market, in the sense that the marginal productivity of the total labor is near zero.

Finally, the model assumes that the labor market operates with efficiency wages. Workers are not full partners of capitalists due to their alienation from the property of the firm; hence, firms must use devices to extract effort from them. In order to maximize profits, therefore, capitalist firms seek to pay workers market wage rates that are higher than their opportunity cost as a mechanism to extract effort from them.

Figure 9.1 depicts the labor market model. The quantity of labor supplied is equal to the segment OO'. The curve NN' represents the marginal productivity of labor in the

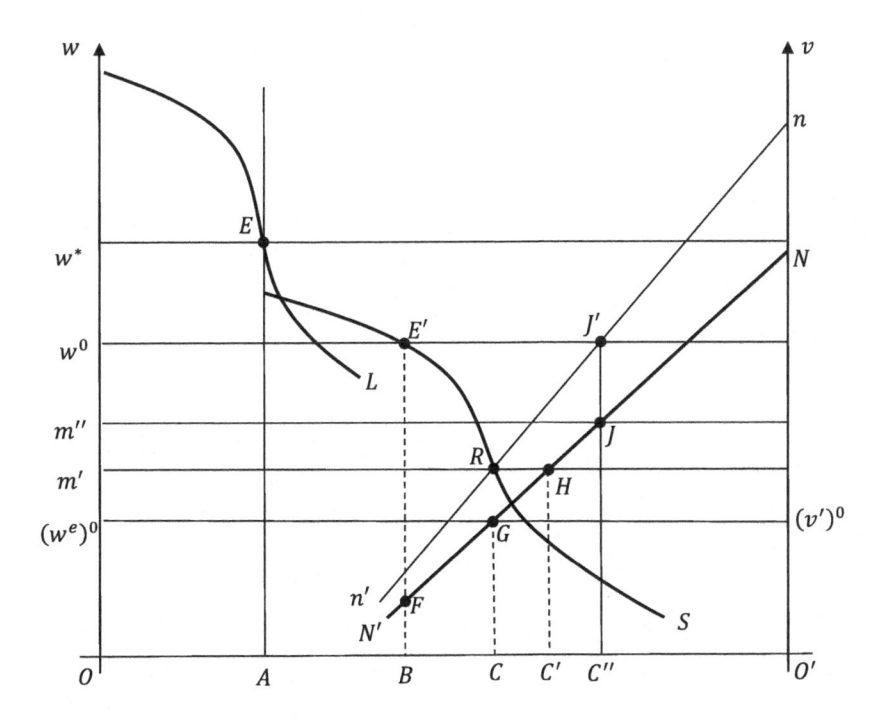

Equilibrium with three labor income layers: $w^* > w^0 > v^0 > (v')^0$

Fig. 9.1 The low-skilled labor market in the sigma society

subsistence sector or self-employment sector—measured from origin O'. This curve also represents the opportunity cost of wage-employment or the labor supply curve. On the labor demand side, the model assumes two sizes of capitalist firms: large and small firms. The average labor productivity curve of large firms has a higher level than the curve corresponding to small firms, which implies a difference in the corresponding marginal productivity curves, which in turn implies that the demand curve for labor is at higher level in large firms than in the small ones.

The rule of efficiency wages imply that firms, in order to maximize profits, would be willing to pay wage rates that are above that curve for each level of employment, which is represented by the curve nn', called the effort extraction curve. The gap between these two curves is a measure of the cost that the worker will suffer when dismissed from the job due to shirking behavior. This is the particular device firms utilize in overpopulated labor markets to maintain the needed labor discipline at the work place, which in turn will maintain high levels of labor productivity and profits in the firms.

Introducing Legal Minimum Wage

Let the state intervene in the labor market by setting a legal minimum wage rate. The logic of this policy of legal wage is to set a wage rate the value of which is above the market wage rate. It is a price policy. The nominal legal wage rate (P_h^*) is then set by the state, and given the price level (P_b), the legal real wage rate (w^*) is then determined, such that it is above the market real wage rate $(w^* > w^\circ)$. Consider the price level exogenously fixed in what follows, so nominal values will also measure real values.

Given the legal wage rate (w^*), and given the labor demand curve of large firms, labelled L, these firms will, in order to maximize profits, hire OA workers. At this wage rate, the excess labor supply is equal to AO' workers.

The labor demand for the workers in excess supply will come from small firms, along the curve S, the origin of which starts from point A. Therefore, there will exist a secondary labor market. Suppose the market real wage rate here is determined at $w° = P_h/P_b$, where the market nominal wage rate (P_h) is given in the short run $\left(P_h^* > P_h\right)$. This would be the equilibrium price of labor, whereas equilibrium wage employment would be AB. Certainly, small firms would increase profits if real wages were lower; profits would be the highest if equilibrium were at the point R, where the labor demand curve S crosses the effort extraction curve. However, this is socially unviable, for it would require the fall in the current nominal wage rate, which is against a social norm of the labor market.

The labor market therefore operates with two segmented markets: the primary and the secondary. These markets are however inter-related, as the equilibrium in both markets are determined simultaneously. The legal wage rate is determined by the market wage rate in the secondary market, the quantities of which are determined by the quantities of the primary market, which depends upon the legal wage rate. The exogenous variable is the real wage rate in the secondary market, determined by history. Hence, total wage employment in the capitalist sector is equal to OB and BO' is the excess labor supply.

If all surplus labor took the form of self-employment, then the marginal income in the subsistence sector would be given by the segment BF, which is below the both wage rates. This could be an equilibrium situation, for the market wage rate is an efficiency wage, so is the legal wage rate. However, this situation implies that workers would do nothing to seek employment in the capitalist sector, that is, they would wait passively to be hired, as they expect that the probability to find jobs (π), if actively searching for it, is nil (that is, $\pi = 0$). There is no incentive to be unemployed and equilibrium would imply zero unemployment rate.

However, the model assumes that workers expect a positive probability of finding a job, if actively searching for it ($0 < \pi < 1$), as workers in the capitalist sector rotate, retire, quit, die, or are dismissed, and thus job openings are created. There is competition for jobs in the labor market. The workers' expected wage (w^e), when searching for a job (staying unemployed), would be equal to the probability to find a job in the capitalist sector and get paid either salary.

Assume, just for simplicity, that workers take the secondary market wage rate as the relevant one, that is, the expected wage rate will be a fraction of the market wage rate there $\left(w^e = \pi w^\circ\right)$, and it will be uniform among workers. Therefore, there is an incentive to become unemployed and compete with the workers already employed in the capitalist sector. The consequence is that the expected wage rate will be higher than the marginal productivity of labor in the subsistence sector (segment BF) because now $\pi > 0$.

Workers excluded from the labor market now face a choice between unemployment and self-employment. Assuming that workers have no preference for either one, and that they are risk neutral, they would choose the higher income and stop moving from self-employment to unemployment when these two options provide them the same marginal income. Hence, the equilibrium takes place at point G along the curve NN', where the expected income when unemployed is equal to the sure marginal productivity of labor when self-employed, that is, when $(w^e)^\circ = (v')^\circ$. Therefore, in equilibrium, BC workers are unemployed and CO' are self-employed. The expected income is equal to the segment CG, which is consistent with the efficiency wage rule, for it is below the corresponding effort extraction value (on the nn' curve). Note that the equilibrium *average* labor productivity in the subsistence sector ($v°$) will lie above the *marginal* counterpart.

Therefore, the overall labor market equilibrium conditions are the following:

$$w^* \geq (1+p)w°, p > 0 \tag{9.1}$$

$$w° \geq (1+p')v'°, p' > 0 \tag{9.2}$$

$$v'° = \pi w° \tag{9.3}$$

Parameters p and p' indicate the premium required to attain labor discipline in the primary and secondary labor markets. These parameters are exogenously determined. The last condition says that the marginal productivity in the subsistence sector must be equal to the expected wage rate in the secondary labor market (of small firms).

Finally, the model assumes that governments are able to supervise the large firms only, which are relative few compared to the many small firms, the supervision of which would be very costly; in addition, the government has no incentives for doing more supervision either because if all firms were to comply with the law of minimum wages, then small firms would be unviable, and the excess labor supply would be even larger. The government would then face political costs. Therefore, it is in the interest of the government to maintain a secondary labor market, which may be called "informal wage-employment."

Hence, in this static model, the equilibrium values of prices and quantities in the low-skilled labor market will be reached as indicated above (points E, E', and G), and this equilibrium situation will be repeated period after period as long as the exogenous variables remain unchanged. Indeed, no social actor has the power or the will to change this situation. Capitalists would like to employ more workers and make more profits, but that would imply reducing the current nominal wages, which is against the institutional rules. Surplus workers have no choice, except to become unemployed or self-employed. Governments cannot reduce the current legal nominal wage for it is against the institutional rules, nor can increase it, for it would go against the interests of the economic elite; governments cannot enforce the law fully either, for it is costly and moreover would lead to an increase of the excess labor supply, which is against their interest to buy votes.

A significant trait of this labor market equilibrium is that unemployment originates from the free choice of the surplus workers—between unemployment and self-employment. Note however that this is a *second-best* choice, for the most preferable alternative would be to be hired in the capitalist sector, more preferable in large firms than in small ones. Hence, considering only second-best options, unemployment is voluntary, for workers could always find some income as self-employment (below the amount of CG, along curve NN'), but they prefer to seek actively wage employment instead.

Another trait of this model is that small changes in labor demand will not affect prices (wage rates), only quantities of equilibrium, and only changes in unemployment. This will be the case whenever the equilibrium quantity does not go beyond the quantity corresponding to point J', where the gap is just enough to maintain labor discipline and labor productivity level. If the upward shift in the demand curve is so significant that the equilibrium quantity goes beyond the quantity corresponding to point J', then both prices and quantities will rise. Firms will now have the incentive to raise nominal wage rates so as to maintain the needed gap that ensures labor discipline and the labor productivity level. If labor demand keeps rising, labor market equilibria will move along the effort extraction curve, segment $J'n$.

Empirical Consistency

The model predicts a labor market equilibrium with three labor income tiers. They are: $w^* > w° > v°$. These tiers correspond to three different labor productivity levels. The labor productivity level in large firms allows them to pay the legal wage rate. The labor productivity level of small firms is too low to pay it and thus they hire at lower wage rates than that established by law. Employment in small firms do not comply with the law and "informal wage-employment" is thus created, as opposed to the "formal wage-employment" in large firms.

Furthermore, this labor market model predicts not only inequality between capitalists and workers, but also inequality among workers of the *same* skills. Among workers, the poorest are those in the excess labor category (the unemployed and the self-employed), the richest are those employed in large firms, whereas those employed in small firms lie in between. Differences among these groups of workers also include labor standards. Workers employed in large firms have the highest labor standards, not only higher wage rates, but also other forms of legal social protection (health insurance, retirement funds, etc.). Those employed in small firms have lower labor standards, whereas the self-employed have the lowest.

These predictions are consistent with the facts of the Third World (Figueroa 2015, Vol. I and Chapter 6). Indeed, the excess labor supply takes the form of unemployment and self-employment, where the latter is the more significant. Inequality among workers of the same skills in income and labor standards are also observed. The self-employed work in precarious work places (marginal land in agriculture and marginal land spaces or at home in shanty urban areas), with very limited or nil social protection. Therefore, basic facts do not seem to refute the empirical predictions of the model; hence, on epistemological grounds, we can accept the model as a good approximation of the real world at this stage of our investigation.

Changes in the exogenous variables of the model will have effects upon the endogenous variables of the labor market—prices and quantities. To derive these causality relations would require a general equilibrium model. The low-skilled labor market interacts with other labor markets and also with markets for goods. However, the labor market model presented here is of the partial equilibrium type and will remain so. The main objective here is to explain the nature of labor market equilibrium in Third World countries.

The Legal Minimum Wage Effect

Under the assumptions of the labor market model of sigma theory, it is clear that state intervention leads to equilibrium with three labor income tiers. What would be the equilibrium situation if the state intervention to set legal wage rates were eliminated?

Figure 9.1 will also help us in answering this question. Let $w = w^°$ be the market real wage rate in absence of minimum legal wage policy. At this single wage rate, large firms will hire more workers, along curve L, and small firms will hire as before; hence, the total quantity demanded of labor at that price will increase (to a level higher than OB); consequently, the excess labor supply will decline. The expected wage will then remain and thus unemployment will fall and self-employment will remain unchanged. Equilibrium with two labor income tiers will now be the result: workers will be employed in the capitalist sector at wage rate $w^°$ and the self-employed will generate average income $(v^°)$ as before. (This new equilibrium situation follows directly from the graph, but it is not shown, just to avoid clouding the graph even more.)

There will be no primary and secondary labor markets, but just one single labor market, with one equilibrium price and one equilibrium quantity. Inequality among workers will be reduced, as the income of the richest workers have been reduced, some workers previously unemployment are now employed as wage earner, and the average income of the self-employed remains. However, the average income of *all* workers will not increase, as workers in large firms will have lower wage rates. Moreover, the elimination of the legal wage rate reduces unemployment but it does not imply the elimination of the excess labor supply. Finally, eliminating the legal wage rate would not improve the wellbeing of workers, for it leads to the elimination of the primary market, where wage rates and labor standards are higher; that is, all wage-employment in the capitalist sector will become of the kind of the current "informal wage-employment." Thus, changes in the average labor standards will fall.

Endogenous Three-Tier Labor Incomes

The labor market model has shown that the equilibrium with three tier labor incomes is the result of state interference in the labor market through legal minimum wages. This is a sufficient condition. Is it necessary?

Empirical studies on labor markets have shown a significant stylized fact: larger firms tend to pay higher wage rates than smaller firms even controlling for skills (Gibson and Stillman 2009). This fact can also be predicted from the labor market model presented above.

Given that the average productivity of labor is higher in larger firms than in smaller ones, and given that the marginal productivity of labor is a fraction of the average productivity, which must be equal to the wage rate in equilibrium, then higher wage rates can only be paid where average productivity is also higher. Therefore, the efficiency wage model may, in principle, lead to equilibrium with three tiers of labor incomes, as shown in the previous model, because of the difference in the capital endowments and thus in the levels in the average productivity of labor among the three sectors of the economy (large firms, small firms, and self-employment).

Now consider that the first tier in the model is not determined by state intervention, but it is endogenously determined by the large firms' behavior. Why would large firms be willing to pay a higher wage rate than the one prevailing in the market? Paying higher wage rates than the opportunity cost of the workers creates an incentive for labor discipline and loyalty because losing the job will be costly for the worker. The relevant opportunity cost is the worker's best alternative, which in this case is wage-employment in small firms.

Therefore, the new labor market model predicts that, in the absence of state intervention, the labor market equilibrium will also operate with three labor income tiers. This is a structural characteristic of the labor market in a sigma society. State intervention setting legal minimum wages is thus redundant. Figure 9.1 can therefore be read as a free competitive labor market structure, where w^* is endogenously determined by large firms. In this case, however, wage employment in small firms could not be called "informal."

Compared to the initial model with legal minimum wages, this would be the only difference.

It follows that the existence of excess labor supply is not generated by state intervention. The labor market in sigma society operates with excess labor supply; equilibrium with excess labor supply is its structural trait. It also follows that legal minimum wages has a political rationality, not an economic one.

Another prediction of the endogenous wage tiers is that this type of equilibrium applies also to high skilled-labor markets. Figure 9.1 thus represents the generalized labor market equilibrium in sigma societies, which are overpopulated. It shows how labor markets operate in such a social context, either for high or low skilled-labor, either with or without state intervention. Equations (9.1)–(9.3) show this generalized property.

By comparison, given the competitive labor market conditions, the neoclassical model would predict that the market equilibrium of price and quantity would take place at the Walrasian price of labor, which is, say, at point J—where the quantity supplied is equal to the quantity demanded, the horizontal aggregation of curves L and S. The unique market wage rate would be equal to the marginal income of the subsistence sector, but lower than the average income of this sector; hence, the wage rate would have to increase in order to attract workers into wage employment. This is full employment equilibrium, with zero unemployment and zero underemployment, which is refuted by facts. The existence of three income tiers in labor markets also refute this mode. Hence, the neoclassical model fails to explain the functioning of the labor market in sigma societies.

According to efficiency wage theory, full employment equilibrium is unattainable. What would be the incentive of workers to work hard if the labor market operates with full employment, meaning that they will always be able to find jobs? Workers need an incentive to work hard and full employment equilibrium is against this incentive. Therefore, labor market equilibrium wage rate will be set somewhere above the Walrasian price.

In the labor market models of sigma theory, unemployment still originates from the free choice of the surplus workers—between unemployment and self-employment. However, and as noted earlier, unemployment is the result of a *second-best* choice, for the most preferable alternative would be to be hired in the capitalist sector, more preferable in large firms than in small ones. Hence, considering only second-best options, unemployment is *voluntary*, for workers could always find some income as self-employment (below the amount of CG, along curve NN'), but they prefer to seek actively wage employment instead.

Neoclassical economics' standard argument is that unemployment is voluntary, as "the unemployed worker at any time can always find some occupation at once" (Lucas 1978, p. 354). Where? Certainly, not in another labor market. This proposition assumes the existence of a subsistence sector, in which the unemployed can always find some occupation at once, but as self-employed, generating an income that is lower than the market wage rate. The proposition then applies better to sigma societies, than to epsilon societies. However, to say that unemployment is voluntary—outcome of free choice in the labor market—does not change the quality that it is a social malady.

In sum, free competitive labor markets will also lead to equilibrium with three labor incomes tiers, that is, with inequality among workers. Actually, inequality among workers constitutes the general labor discipline device that capitalist firms use to maximize profits (Figueroa 2011).

Unemployment Insurance Policy

In the First World, the major labor market policies include unemployment insurance. This policy is not applied in the Third World. Why? The sigma model shows that it is unnecessary, for subsistence sector—where the surplus workers can generate their own income as self-employed—plays that role. If workers are dismissed from wage employment, then they would seek self-employment in marginal agricultural lands as peasants or in marginal urban lands as street vendors, as small shops, or in illegal activities, etc.

What if unemployment insurance were introduced? The principle of insurance as service is to protect a good or asset from the risk of losing it. If an individual suffers the loss of a property, which is insured, he or she will be compensated (totally or partially) for the loss. Similarly, if an individual losses his or her job, the worker will be compensated for the loss, and for a limited period. (Clearly, voluntary quits are not covered by the insurance.) Therefore, unemployment insurance operates for those that are already employed as wage earners and who run the risk of being dismissed from the job.

In sigma societies, the labor markets operate with significant excess labor supply, of which the largest segment is the self-employed; hence, the self-employed workers would be excluded from the insurance policy. Because the accumulation of human capital implies investments, the rate of excess labor supply is higher for lower levels of human capital. Therefore, the poor would be excluded in larger proportion from the insurance policy. Unemployment insurance could hardly improve the general wellbeing of workers in the Third World.

Introducing a Guaranteed Minimum Income (GMI)

Consider the labor market model in which free competition rules (no legal minimum wages exist). Let this be the case with competitive labor market equilibrium, given at points E, E', and G in Fig. 9.1, such that OA workers are employed in large capitalist firms, AB in small firms, BC are unemployed, and CO' are self-employed. The three tier labor incomes are $w^* > w^° > v^°$.

The effect of introducing a gmi as public policy instead of legal minimum wage can now be analyzed with the help of this model. The model suggests a simple way to do this. The gmi could be established as another kind of expected income, for it will play the same role in the labor market: It will be the opportunity cost of wage employment. Then gmi can be represented by a horizontal line in Fig. 9.1. At what level should it be set? Certainly, it could be set at level $(w^e)^°$. Workers can then choose the gmi if they are unable to find a wage employment or unable to make this income as self-employed; that is, the unemployed will receive the gmi. Hence, the equilibrium will remain at point G, and BC workers would receive the gmi.

Now consider setting the gmi at a higher level, but below $w^°$, say at level m'. Then the equilibrium will be at point H. The effects are the following:

> First, the market wage rates are not affected; then the size of the excess labor supply (BO') will remain, but its composition will change: the self-employed will diminish, whereas the unemployed will rise to BC' workers, who will receive the gmi.

Second, the average income of the workers in excess supply—both unemployed and self-employed—will increase. The gmi has an indirect positive effect upon self-employment income as well.

Third, inequality among workers will be reduced, and income gaps between capitalists and workers will also decline, as the fiscal cost of the gmi will come from taxing profits.

Fourth, general labor standards will also increase, as the unemployed are now covered with gmi, and self-employment will decline, where labor standards are the lowest.

It follows that levels of the gmi higher than at m' will increase further the average income of the surplus labor, maintaining the same market wage rates. Consider the level m'', which leads to equilibrium at point J. This situation still maintains the market real wage rates constant—the gap JJ' still makes the real wage $w°$ an efficiency wage rate. Thus, the excess labor supply will remain unchanged (BO'), but its composition will change: unemployment will rise to BC'' workers, who receive the gmi, and self-employment will fall further to $C''O'$.

Any gmi level set above m'' will however lead to an endogenous increase in the market wage rates. The overall labor market conditions stated above will breakdown. The opportunity cost of wage employment is now too high and to restore the gap that maintains the labor discipline will require a higher real wage rate in the small firms, which in turn will imply a gap that has become too narrow to attain labor discipline in large firms, which will also call for a higher real wage rate to maintain the same level of labor discipline. In short, firms will have the incentive to raise the market nominal wage rates in both sectors and thus raise both real wage rates—as price level is exogenously given.

At higher real wage rates, the quantity employed will fall (below point B in the graph) and thus the excess labor supply will rise, and self-employment will fall. Hence, unemployment will increase even further (larger than $E'J'$). In this case, the gmi has the effect of raising the market real wage rates, but at the cost of a higher fiscal expenditure on gmi due to the increase in unemployment. As can be seen in the graph, the rise in gmi has the effect of increasing the size of unemployment and thus the fiscal cost. Therefore, the limit to the gmi level depends upon the society's desire to redistribute income.

The higher wage rate in the low-skilled labor market implies a higher relative price. Firms will make adjustments to find the new set of optimal quantities of factors of production, including the mix of high-skilled and low-skilled labor, even in the short run. Just for the sake of simplicity, the substitution effects are ignored here—partial equilibrium analysis—and the labor demand curve is allowed to remain unchanged.

Note that the incentive system that the gmi introduces in the labor market is to encourage workers to seek wage employment, as market wage rates will always be higher than gmi. Therefore, the gmi policy is consistent with the efficiency wages rationality of firms. Capitalism needs to operate with excess labor supply and the gmi policy just seeks to protect workers against bearing the total cost of this social malady of capitalism.

The gmi policy seeks to give social protection not only to the unemployed, but also to the underemployed. The policy is intended to protect both, the first directly and the second indirectly. Actually, it is a mechanism to reach effectively the underemployed via the labor market. It is also a mechanism to break the link between production and distribution—a fundamental rule of capitalism—in a significant manner, which constitutes one of the new principles of the Anthropocene age economics.

Taxation is the standard mechanism that also leads to that break, but its empirical effect is known to be weak. Significant redistribution through fiscal policy (the distribution of the tax burden and of expenditure) is not an empirical regularity, according to the literature. The power elites have no incentives in following tax systems that are strongly progressive, which would go against their interests. Instead, they would proclaim anti-poverty policies, which need not derive from a strongly progressive tax system.

Figure 9.1 can also depict the effect of exogenous increases in the demand for labor. Take again labor market equilibrium at point J. An upward shift in the aggregate labor demand curve will lead to more employment at the given real wage rates, say, until point J' is reached. Further demand shifts would imply more employment but at increasing real wage rates. Then the effort extraction curve operates as the *effective* supply curve, which is represented by the segment $EJ'n'$. Therefore, the model predicts rising real wage rates in the long run, as labor demand expands. In the long run, in the economic growth process, labor demand expands not exogenously, but endogenously; hence, real wage rates will increase over time.

In a no-growth society, in which the labor demand is fixed, the model shows that real wages can be increased as well, by appropriate redistribution policies that lead to increases in gmi. Therefore, economic growth is not necessary for rising labor incomes, as long as gmi, and the redistribution it implies, are part of the new economic institutions in the Anthropocene age.

What would be the coverage of the gmi in the Third World? In principle, according to the static sigma model, the coverage would include those workers that are low-skilled and are part of the excess labor supply: the unemployed directly (who receive gmi) and the underemployed indirectly.

More significantly, the poorest in the Third World are different people, the *z-workers*, who will be reached by this income policy more than ever. Most z-workers—second class citizens, descendants of the populations under colonial domination—belong to this category of low-skilled labor, as they are discriminated against in the process of human capital accumulation. They are also self-employed in higher proportion to those non z-workers, as ethnicity also plays a role in the selection of wage employment. This selection does not operate through a random mechanism, so workers of the same skills are discriminated under some criteria, including ethnic social markers.

International data on these figures are unavailable. However, some order of magnitude can be established by looking at the situation of some particular countries. Take the case of Peru, as an example. Based on the official statistics, the estimates for the analytical categories of the labor market model presented here are as follows. For the *total* labor force, in 2003, the distribution was: 42% wage-employment in large and small firms (roughly in equal proportions), 51% self-employed or underemployed and 7% unemployed; hence, more than half of the total labor force constitutes excess labor supply. Defining low-skilled workers as those having less than secondary level of education (less than 10 years of schooling), this group represented 46% of total labor force, of which 78% were in the category of excess labor supply (Figueroa 2010, Tables 2 and 6).

Therefore, around 36% (that is, 46% of 78%) of the total labor force constitute the excess labor supply in the low-skilled labor market. This would be the group—mostly z-workers of Peru, indigenous and black populations—who would be affected with the gmi public policy, directly as unemployed (10%) and indirectly as self-employed (90%).

In the design of economic policies, detail is essential. The introduction of economic public policies can be seen as the engineering of the science of economics. Otherwise we could fall into the fallacy of *misplaced concreteness*, mistaking the map representing the reality for reality itself. The theoretical model has transformed the real world into an abstract, simpler world, just to be understood. Therefore, the introduction of gmi would require the elaboration of the engineering of the theoretical sigma model presented in this essay. Some examples follow.

Several schemes of income tax could easily be introduced with the gmi policy. The value of gmi is selective and could become the income level that marks the threshold of the tax-exempted income. Alternatively, gmi could be universal, going to everyone, and then income tax would be applied to everyone's total income—including here the universal gmi; therefore, in this case, gmi also operates as the level of tax-exempted income. However, the second scheme eliminates the stigma and the bureaucratic cost of claiming the benefits of gmi—as happens in the first case—because everyone gets the same amount, which is returned via taxes; thus, through taxation the beneficiaries will eventually be the targeted population; in addition, the benefit is not reduced if people earn more, creating incentives for seeking higher incomes.

The gmi policy does not intend to substitute the supply of public goods, such as education and health services; however, it can replace other forms of cash transfers that are common in Third World countries, the effect of which upon inequality are nil, even under economic growth, as the experience indicates.

Conclusions

A particular science-based public policy derived from the unified theory has been presented in this essay. Labor markets in the Third World are more complex than in the First World. The introduction of a gmi (guaranteed minimum income) in the Third World requires a valid labor market theory. A short-run labor market model of the sigma theory, the predictions of which are consistent with facts, has been presented here. The sigma model explains the fact that the excess labor supply is composed of unemployment and underemployment (the largest segment), and also the fact that inequality is pronounced among workers competing in the same labor market, such that the excess labor supply—the unemployed and the self-employed—constitutes the poorest group. In this essay, this model has been utilized to analyze the effect of the gmi policy.

The excess labor supply of low-skilled workers would be the target of the gmi policy. This policy would raise the income of the unemployed directly and also the income of the underemployed (self-employed in the subsistence sector) indirectly. The income of the poorest group of workers of society would thus be protected and raised, through income redistribution, and income inequality reduced. The z-workers, who are the descendants of the dominated populations under European colonialism, and are now second class citizens, would be targeted with this policy, as never before.

The income transfer through the gmi policy would be financed by taxing the profits of national and international firms, for gmi is part of the redistribution policies that no-growth in the capitalist system implies in the Anthropocene age economics. The gmi policy intends to reduce inequality between capitalists and workers and among workers as well. It is a relative income policy.

The short-run model assumes a no-growth society, in which the labor demand is fixed, and yet the model has shown that the gmi is an appropriate policy instrument to raise the average labor income of those excluded from the labor market, and even to raise real wages as well. Therefore, economic growth is not necessary for raising labor incomes in the overpopulated and very unequal countries of the Third World, as long as gmi, and the redistribution it implies, are part of their new economic institutions, according to the Anthropocene age economics.

REFERENCES

Figueroa, A. (2010, December). Is education income-equalizing? Evidence from Peru. *CEPAL Review, 102*, 113–133.

Figueroa, A. (2011). A generalized labor market theory: Inequality as labor discipline device. *Investigación Económica (Mexico), 70*(276), 163–185.

Figueroa, A. (2015). *Growth, employment, inequality, and the environment: Unity of knowledge in economics*. New York, NY: Palgrave Macmillan.

Figueroa, A. (2017). *Economics of the Antropocene age*. Cham, Switzerland: Palgrave Macmillan.

Gibson, J., & Stillman, S. (2009). Why do big firms pay higher wages? Evidence from an international database. *Review of Economics and Statistics, 91*(1), 213–218.

Lucas, R. (1978). Unemployment policy. *American Economic Review, 68*(2), 353–357.

CHAPTER 10

Epilogue: New and Old Economics

The essays presented in this book confirm in many ways that the unified theory of capitalism is a valid scientific economic theory. It has a valid epistemological justification. Their predictions are consistent with the basic facts of capitalism. Therefore, it explains the functioning of the capitalist system. The public policies derived from the theory are then science-based and, moreover, have ethical justification too.

The essays have clarified, extended, and elaborated further the initial findings of the unified theory. The main implications about the novelties of the unified theory of capitalism that can be derived from the essays are summarized now.

What Is the Nature of the Unified Theory of Capitalism?

As a scientific endeavor, it is an economic theory about the functioning of the capitalist system. As a unified theory, it is able to explain capitalism taken by parts—the First World and the Third World—through partial theories and then capitalism taken as a whole through a unified theory; it is a theoretical system. As any scientific theory, it has epistemological justification, given by the composite epistemology, which gives us the needed rationality to construct an abstract society intended to resemble the real world society, which by construction is testable, and the empirical predictions of which turn out to be consistent with facts—actually, with eight facts on capitalist production and distribution. The assumptions of the theory are proven to be appropriate. Hence, on epistemological grounds, the unified theory can be accepted as a good representation of the real world capitalist society.

Differences in the individual endowments of physical and social assets define capitalism. Capitalism is a society of class differences, capitalists and workers, because of the concentration of the physical capital endowments in the hands of capitalists. Differences in social entitlements makes capitalism also a society of citizenship differences—first and second class citizens. A capitalist society with class differences is analyzed through the epsilon theory, whereas a capitalist society with class and citizenship differences is done through the sigma theory.

The unified theory assumes that the First World is an epsilon society, the Third World is a sigma society, and thus the capitalist system taken as a whole is a sigma society too. The implication is that the functioning of the First World is qualitatively different from that of the Third World; moreover, the capitalism system taken as a whole operates basically as a Third World society, with social classes and also first and second class citizens. Capitalism is a hierarchical society. The unified theory intends to make economics a genuine social science.

The unified theory belongs to the new science of economics. The new foundations of economics indeed include the following: (1) scientific research needs epistemology, not methodology; (2) the economic process is entropic and evolutionary, not mechanical; and (3) an economic theory is a theoretical system, dealing with partial theories and a unified theory, which ensures unity of knowledge, not fragmented knowledge—one reality, one explanation. The new science of economics deals with the new social and environment context in which the economic process takes place—the Anthropocene age. Social reality is complex, but it has become even more complex. This new environmental context makes economics even a more sophisticated social science, in need of more sophisticated epistemology, Reaching scientific knowledge in economics is now harder, not easier.

What Is the Major Novelty of the Unified Theory of Capitalism?

It presents a new scenery of capitalism. Through the abstract society that the theory has constructed, then showing its essential traits, capitalism looks different from the standard economics view (neoclassical and Keynesian), which corresponds to the old economics.

According to unified theory, the capitalist system taken as a whole can be seen as a society of classes (of capitalists and workers) and as a society of citizens (first and second class). Hence, people participating in the economic process are endowed with two types of assets, economic and social. These endowments are unequally distributed, and constitute the initial inequality. This abstract society, representing the capitalist system, is a sigma society.

Two regions comprise the capitalist system, the First World and Third World countries, which differ by their initial conditions regarding factor endowments and initial inequality. The First World is underpopulated and socially homogeneous (social entitlements are equally distributed), whereas the Third World is overpopulated and socially heterogeneous (social entitlements are unequally distributed). Therefore, the First World is an underpopulated epsilon society, whereas the Third World is an overpopulated sigma society. To be sure, the capitalist system as a whole is a sigma society in that the workers of the Third World are second class citizens relative to the workers of the First World.

The fundamental institutions of capitalism include private property rights, market system, and electoral democracy. Given that the market system requires private property rights, the institutions are reduced to markets and electoral democracy as the fundamental ones.

With these basic assumptions, the unified theory is able to explain the capitalist system taken by parts (First World and Third World) through partial theories and then the capitalist system taken as a whole through a unified theory. Therefore, the unified theory constitutes a theoretical system—various partial theories, but a unified theory, which leads to unity of knowledge.

How Does the Capitalist System Operate?

The initial inequality in individual asset endowments lead to the existence of elites. These elites are then able to use the institutions of markets and electoral democracy to exercise power in markets and electoral democracy. Therefore, the initial inequality and the institutions together create a concentrated power structure, with economic and political elites. The power elites run the society seeking their own interests. In particular, the power elites promote economic growth public policies, which benefit them not only in concentrating income but in reproducing their privileged position in society.

According to unified theory, economic growth is an evolutionary process, not a mechanical one. Quantitative changes over time are accompanied by qualitative changes, and the process is subject to threshold values that set limits to the process; hence, economic growth cannot go on forever, and at some point will breakdown. The outcome of the economic growth process includes continuous increase in income levels together with rising income inequality and environment degradation, which implies economic growth with social maladies. The income level gap between the First World and the Third World tends to persist. On the other hand, growth of total output leads irrevocably to increasing pollution concentrations in the atmosphere and the consequent climate change.

In two centuries of capitalist development and output growth, not much social progress has occurred. The Third World countries continue to operate as sigma societies, that is, they have not become epsilon societies endogenously. Consequently, the capitalist system as a whole remains as a sigma society as well. Differences in the initial social assets, a legacy of European colonialism, remains unchanged.

Economic growth with social maladies is persistent under democratic capitalism. This is a paradox in a society that is supposed to be democratic and where individual freedom and equality is paramount. This fact just reflects the existence of a concentrated power structure. Regarding social maladies, the capitalist system is not self-regulating. The paradox is only apparent, as it has an explanation. The type of democracy is electoral, which is a distortion of the principle of democracy, for it implies the transfer of the political power of workers to the political elites who are then able to capture the state by buying votes.

The power elites use the mechanisms of capitalist institutions—markets and electoral democracy—to exercise their power. The power elites do not seek the common good, but their own interests. According to unified theory, power elites seek power as priority. They could even invent excuses to exercise their power, such as strong military states to maintain social order. The observed social disorder is then net of the state repression actions (more repression instead of more income redistribution), which the power elites take as excuse to exercise their power, and thus to intervene in the global capitalist society—the First World and the Third World. Even the communism threat was an excuse to seek higher degrees of power (through the arms industry). The fact that after the collapse of the Soviet Union, and the end of the so-called Cold War, the behavior of the power elites have not changed much in the global society is consistent with the prediction of unified theory.

Individual freedom under capitalism is limited. Firstly, it is subject to the constraints given by the initial inequality, which is not reduced, much less eliminated, in the growth process. Secondly, the power elite is able to control and change the behavior of workers, as they have the incentives, the power, and the instruments of behavioral engineering techniques. Individual freedom does not imply individual autonomy. Therefore, workers have been induced to become addict to economic growth, to the modernization and the consumerism that it implies; moreover, they have also been induced to strengthen their egotistic drive and weaken their altruistic drive. To be sure, workers' behavior reflect not much what they are, but what they have become.

The economic growth process has changed the planet behavior too. The Holocene age has been replaced by the Anthropocene age—the age of human activity influence. Now the economic growth process takes place under an ecological context of high stress. The dictum of the thermodynamic laws of physics (dealing with matter and energy relations) is that the higher the growth rates of total output, the sooner the collapse period will be reached.

The power elites however have the incentives to continue promoting economic growth, as they have become addicts to their benefits—profits and the privileged position in society. The elites only recognize poverty—not inequality—and unemployment as social maladies. This is opportunistic behavior because reduction in the rates of poverty and unemployment requires higher rates of economic growth (and so is promoted through the discourse), which benefits the elites themselves.

This is the scenery of the capitalist system of today. Even in the Anthropocene age, the power elites continue promoting economic growth policies ("business as usual"), even if they put the survival of human species into risk. Addiction to power is conducive to this economic suicidal. Economic growth is suicidal, but it is not the result of a collective decision.

Standard economics—neoclassical and Keynesian—actually gives theoretical support to pro-growth public policies. Economic growth should be maximized so as to reduce poverty and unemployment problems. This is because the theories of standard economics assume another type of abstract capitalist society. A society in which the initial inequality is not an essential factor, and the consequent concentrated power structure is not either. Income inequality can increase for it has no significant consequences on the functioning of society. Economic growth can also proceed forever, as it has no significant consequences on the environment.

In the case of neoclassical economics, economic growth could not be conducive to social maladies. Just the opposite, individual selfish behavior is conducive—as by an invisible hand—to the common good. Income inequality has no consequences on social order, no matter how high it is. Pareto optimality is independent of how concentrated income inequality is. Economic growth is a mechanical process. It is sustainable. However, the fact that economic growth is accompanied by social maladies refutes these predictions. The assumptions of these theories are thus proven to be inappropriate.

Keynesian economics recognizes the social malady of unemployment. All the same, the cure implies more output, induced by effective demand, which implies more environment degradation, which in turn generates other social maladies. In addition, Keynesian economics assumes ontological universalism, a uniform labor market theory everywhere, in which the only form of excess labor supply is unemployment. Indeed, international comparisons use only unemployment rates for the First World and the Third World. This ignores the different behavior of labor markets in the Third World, where excess labor supply takes the form of unemployment and underemployment, the latter being the more significant.

Marxian economics assumes that the economic growth process is evolutionary. The limit to the economic growth process is given by the workers' threshold of tolerance for pauperization and income inequality. The breakdown of the economic growth process will come from a revolution. Facts refute this prediction. Inequality keeps increasing and no workers' revolution has emerged to dethroned capitalism. The assumptions of the theory are proven to be inappropriate. The theory assumes the existence of a power elite, but ignores the power elite's capacity to use mechanisms—the behavioral engineering techniques that is continuously developed—to control and change the workers' drives, motivations, and thus their behavior.

Recently Marxian literature has incorporated works about the role of environment on the economic process. However, Marxian theoretical models of economic growth under environmental stress including their empirical testing—epistemologically justified knowledge—are not available yet.

What Are the Policy Implications of the Unified Theory?

It should be noted that unified theory has succeeded in explaining the functioning of the capitalist system by constructing models at a very high abstract level. Therefore, the derived science-based policies also correspond to propositions at the same high level of abstraction. The fallacy of misplaced concreteness will thus be avoided here.

Economic growth should not be promoted. Growth is ecologically unsustainable. Growth is also accompanied by social maladies. The economic and social cost of growth is the persistence of the social maladies and a sooner collapse period of the economic growth process. The expected positive growth effect upon poverty and employment is a mirage. There are two reasons for this. First, not poverty, but income inequality or relative poverty constitutes a social malady. It is the high degree of inequality that accompany economic growth what leads to the mal functioning of capitalism, with social disorder. Second, excess labor supply—a broader concept than just unemployment—has not been reduced with economic growth. Third, growth leads to environment degradation and the current situation of ecological stress, harming people's health.

The growth age of capitalism has come to an end. The only alternative left is to search for a high quality of society.

Firstly, income redistribution should be promoted. To stop economic growth and to congeal the current excessive income inequality would not help to have a better quality of society. This policy would involve redistribution within and between the First World and the Third World. Given the large current income gaps between the rich and the poor in the capitalist system, income redistribution would imply for the poor a significant gain, and *now*.

The excess labor supply problem is actually part of the income inequality problem. The overall income inequality arises from the significant income gaps not only between capitalists and workers, but also among workers. The latter effect is in turn due to differences in human capital endowments of workers and also due to income gaps among workers with similar human capital, which originates from the functioning of labor markets with excess labor supply. Income inequality is conducive to economic equilibrium with social disorder (illegal and corruption behavior), which means that economic equilibrium with excess labor supply is another significant factor that contributes to social disorder, to social malady.

Secondly, policies to break the link between production and distribution should be applied. The effective way to tackle the excess labor supply problem is then through income redistribution rather than employment policies. The current institutional rule by which the income of workers is connected to their access to wage employment would have to be replaced by another institutional rule. Income redistribution implies breaking the link between production and distribution, which requires another institutional rule.

According to unified theory, although labor market operate differently in the First World compared to the Third World, the generalized principle is that excess labor supply is required for the functioning of capitalism.

Unemployment is a social malady in the First World alone. Standard economics deals with this problem, assuming that capitalism functioning leads to full employment equilibrium everywhere. Hence unemployment is just either voluntary or incidental (neoclassical theory) or the result of bad government policies (Keynesian). The fact is that the First World always operates with unemployment, which refutes both theories. In contrast, this fact is explained by the unified theory as the social conflict nature of labor markets and the role of unemployment as the labor discipline device.

In the Third World, the excess labor supply takes the form of both unemployment and underemployment, where the latter is empirically more significant. The labor discipline device is the premium firms introduce in the labor market to generate a gap between wage rates and the income from self-employment (the opportunity cost). This is how labor markets operate in overpopulated societies. Reducing underemployment and unemployment would thus be the relevant policy objective. However, the size of the excess labor supply is too large to make any such policy objective attainable, for it would imply to nearly *double* the current wage employment level—since typically 50% of the labor force constitute today's excess labor supply.

Actually, the excess labor supply problem under capitalism has no solution because capitalism requires this excess to operate. Full employment equilibrium is not economically viable. Economic growth cannot lead to a full employment society, no matter how fast the growth rate is. Excess labor supply is the disease of capitalism. Indeed, the transition from communism to capitalism in the ex-Soviet Union implied the arrival of unemployment in the new social panorama.

Thirdly, policies directed to institutional changes should be applied. The ultimate factor that determines the outcome of economic growth with social maladies is the power structure. The trajectory of increasing per capita income over time, accompanied by social maladies, will go on—until it reaches its collapse—as long as the power structure remains unchanged. Therefore, in order to change the current economic growth process towards another process, which should reduce or eliminate the social maladies, and to postpone the collapse period, which in turn imply new public policies that promote no-growth and income redistribution, then the current power structure must be changed.

According to biology, human behavior is the result of two factors, nature (genes) and nurture (social influence). Human behavior can be controlled and changed. This theory implies that we humans are vulnerable to manipulation. This is very significant in the current capitalist system, where the power elites run the society. In the process of economic growth, the power elites have the incentives and the means to induce people to become increasingly individualistic and egotistic. The exacerbated selfish behavior we observe under capitalism is not what people are but what they have become. This leads to more stressful human life and implies a low quality of society. Reversing the relative strength of human drives—more altruism and less egotism in the Anthropocene age—would also require to weaken or eliminate the current power structure.

The current power elites have no incentives to promote these changes. The power structure is the combination of the initial inequality and the institutions of capitalism. Changing the initial inequality is socially unviable, as it would imply force, revolution. The concentration of capital into the hands of the capitalist class—given the class society—is the core of capitalism. The existence of first class and second class citizens is also part of the mechanisms that power elites utilize to exercise their power. Among institutions, the market system and the electoral democracy constitute the mechanisms through which the power elites exercise their power. Therefore, none of the components of the power structure seems to be amenable of change, much less by the power elites.

However, there seems to exist a possibility of change through the democratic institution. Democracy is the institution that is consistent with a free society. Democracy understood as the principle of *the government of the people, by the people, and for the people* implies that the political power lies in the masses, namely, the workers. Electoral democracy is an institution created to transfer the workers' political power to the political elite who can thus capture the state by buying votes. Hence, electoral democracy has become part of the power structure. It is a distortion of the democracy principle.

Dethroning the electoral democracy institution and replacing it by any form of democracy that is more direct, in which the political power is given back to the workers, would thus imply a change in the power structure. The capitalist class would still retain the economic power, but workers would now control the state and thus would hold the political power. Therefore, a workers' democracy would lead to a more balanced power structure under capitalism. Public policies could then follow common good objectives, rather than private interest as is the case now. The public policies of no-growth and income redistribution would become socially and politically viable.

Dethroning electoral democracy institution would certainly imply a re-foundation of the capitalist system. This in turn would come from the work of institutional innovators. It is usually recognized the role of technological innovators.

However, institutional innovators are also badly needed to solve the challenges of the new economic principles in the Anthropocene age.

What Is the Value of Epistemology?

Another novelty of the unified theory, a more indirect, refers to the use of epistemology in economics. How do humans acquire scientific knowledge? This is not different from the question of how people produce goods, to which we call *technology*. Of course, people at different time and places use different technologies; moreover, modern technology makes old technologies obsolete. Similarly, to the ways how people acquire knowledge we can call *methodology*. And, of course, people at different times and places use different methodologies; in addition, we could say that modern methodology makes old ones obsolete. Just call the modern and superior methodology by the term *epistemology*, which has solved the possible logical errors contained in the previous methodologies.

Science is thus epistemology. The unified theory is based on epistemology. It has utilized the composite epistemology—a combination of the epistemologies of Nicholas Georgescu-Roegen's abstract process and Karl Popper's falsificationism. The composite epistemology allows the researcher to study hyper complex societies, such as the social world together with interactions with the ecosystem. It has been made operational through the alpha–beta method, which provides the researcher with rules to construct economic theories, and then to accept or reject them.

The alpha–beta method has been applied to develop the unified theory. It allows the researcher to separate the real social world into partial worlds for analytical convenience (static, dynamic, evolutionary or First World and Third

World), and then to make them consistent in a unified theory, producing unity of knowledge—one single world, one single theory. It has also been utilized to compare the unified theory with other economic theories. The unified theory has been accepted on epistemological grounds.

The use of evolutionary models in comparison to mechanical models have also proved very productive. They all are useful, as they address different social contexts and different problems. However, analyzing the economic growth process as an evolutionary process, rather than as a mechanical-dynamic process, made it possible to discover and explain the outcome of economic growth with social maladies.

In particular, the evolutionary model allow us to understand the roots of the environment problem: The introduction of the thermodynamics laws of physics into the economic process made it an entropic process, which implies an evolutionary process. In the unified theory, these laws do not operate in a social void, but in a particular social context: capitalism. The unified theory is able to explain the transit from the Holocene to the Anthropocene, as an endogenous outcome of the capitalist economic process. The unified theory is an economic theory. It is not a multidisciplinary theory.

Researchers and practitioners of standard economics still use methodologies, not epistemology. They use mostly the methodology of deductivism, which takes as criterion of knowledge the theory itself. They assume (incorrectly) that the theory being a logical system cannot be empirically wrong. Therefore, the discussion is about the "realism" of assumptions.

Furthermore, if facts of the real world contradict the predictions of the theory, these researchers would argue that the real world must be wrong, and should operate as the theory says. Theories are thus protected from being destroyed via testing, which neglects the falsification principle: a scientific theory is created to be destroyed, if it is resistant to destruction, the theory must be very good. Or else the test is not statistical (based on random samples), but just based on a set of conveniently selected facts that protect the theory. Or else non-observable elements (such as expectations) are introduced into the theoretical models to make them immortal rather than mortal.

Another significant group of researchers do purely empirical research. This is theory-free research. The idea is to let data speak for themselves. This type of research is based on the methodology of inductivism, which takes as criterion of knowledge the existence of statistical relations. This is summarized in the commonly accepted fallacy that "the existence of correlation implies causality." There is no theorem that allow us to go from facts to theory and causality.

On epistemological grounds, the unified theory of capitalism appears to be superior to standard economics. The unified theory is able to explain facts that standard theories also do (economic growth: rising income levels), but the unified theory is able to explain facts that the other theories cannot (economic growth with social maladies).

The new science of economics is epistemology intensive to explain the social world, which is not only hyper complex, but increasingly so. The alpha–beta method help us to understand the hyper complex social reality, by the logical artifice of using theories and constructing abstract worlds, simpler to explain what causes what. Theories are testable by construction and can be accepted or rejected with this rule. Funeral after funeral of theories, economics can then make progress.

The use of epistemology reduces the risk of error. The appearance of superior epistemologies contribute to reduce that risk even further. Therefore, the acceptance of an economic theory is only provisional, until new dataset appears and superior economic theories or superior epistemologies are created. This is the limitation of economics, but it only says that scientific knowledge has no end.

The unified theory of capitalism intends to be the new economics, able to explain the new social and environmental world of the Anthropocene age. It attempts to challenge the old economics, dealing with the Holocene age, but on epistemological grounds.

Author Index

A
Alvaredo, F., 233

B
Bagchi, S., 184
Barrón, M., 11
Bernstein, A., 129
Billari, F., 127
Bonaiuti, M., 141
Brendon, P., 88, 179
Bulmer-Thomas, V., 11

C
Carroll, W., 184
Charles, A., 11
Chivian, E., 129, 163

D
Dalziel, N., 85
Dancourt, O., 11
Diamond, J., 102

E
Eichengreen, B., 196

F
Figueroa, A., 11, 13, 16, 17, 21, 26, 33, 44, 68, 70, 99, 115, 121, 125, 177, 184, 220, 227, 237, 238, 245, 250, 256

G
Georgescu-Roegen, N., 16, 44, 141, 145, 160, 274
Gibson, J., 248
Goodwin, G., 11

H
Hodgson, G., 104
Howe, S., 105

J
Jiménez, F., 11

K
Kholer, H.P., 127

L
Lucas, R., 250

M
Maseland, R., 112
Maslow, A., 227
Mayr, E., 68
McMullen, C.P., 162
Milanovic, B., 232
Myrskyla, M., 127

P
Piketty, T., 27, 127
Pinker, S., 102
Popper, K., 16, 44, 72, 274

R
Rentería, J.M., 184

S
Searle, J., 75, 100, 223
Sharma, K., 123
Silva Macher, J.C., 11
Smith, A., 106, 139, 173, 179, 198
Stillman, S., 248
Sweezy, P., 141, 145
Sweynar, J., 184

U
Upadhyay, U., 122

V
Vanderborght, Y., 238
van Parijs, P., 238

W
Wesseling, H.L., 85
Wilson, E.O., 79, 144, 161, 195

Countries Index

A
Africa, 14, 85, 101, 105, 112, 126, 133
Argentina, 85
Asia, 14, 85, 105, 133
Australia, 85, 90, 92, 105, 110

B
Belgium, 85
Brazil, 85, 231, 233

C
Canada, 85, 90, 92, 105, 110
Chile, 85
China, 127, 196, 233
Costa Rica, 85

F
France, 85

G
Germany, 85
Great Britain, 85

H
Holland, 85

I
Italy, 85

J
Japan, 111

L
Latin America, 14, 85, 105

N
New Zealand, 85, 90, 92, 105

P
Peru, 231, 233, 256, 257
Portugal, 85

S
Soviet Union (ex), 127, 271
Spain, 85

U
United States, 85, 90, 92, 105, 110
Uruguay, 85

W
Western Europe, 105

Subject Index

A

alpha-beta method, 2, 3, 8, 16, 17, 20, 44, 46, 47, 57, 67, 68, 70, 74, 76, 77, 79–81, 102, 103, 141, 209, 213, 274, 276
  derived from composite epistemology, 2, 44, 67, 68, 80
  as research rules for scientific research, 2, 17
Anthropocene age, 5, 6, 8, 9, 31, 37–39, 115, 135, 161, 164, 167, 169, 170, 174, 199, 201–204, 218–221, 233–235, 237, 255, 259, 263, 266, 267, 272, 274, 277

B

biodiversity, 128, 129, 132, 133, 142–144, 150–152, 154, 155, 160–163, 194
  and human health, 129, 132, 133, 154, 163
bio-economics, 8, 141, 144–147, 158, 163, 165–171, 194, 195
biology, 33, 68, 78, 79, 123, 169, 176, 191, 195, 226, 272
  and human behavior theory, 33, 272
  and two human drives: egotism and altruism, 33, 195, 272

C

capitalism
  citizenship differences, 65, 262
  class society, 90, 91, 272
  composed of *First World* and *Third World* countries, 1
  explained by partial theories and the unified theory, 1, 165, 261
Cold War, 127, 266
colonial institutions, 89, 90, 109–112
common good principle, 35, 220
competition under capitalism
  Darwinian competition, 111
  first order and second order, 183
  myth of, 205

composite epistemology, 2, 6, 16, 47, 68–70, 79, 180, 262, 274
corruption behavior, 95, 270

D

Darwinian competition of institutions, 104, 109, 183
depletion, 3, 4, 15, 19, 21, 29–31, 59, 128, 142, 147, 160, 161
discourse, 39, 97, 111, 177, 185–187, 189, 197, 200, 201, 222, 225, 231, 267. *See also* freedom discourse

E

ecological system, 1, 19, 128, 132, 142–144, 146, 152, 160, 161, 168, 195
economic assets, 93, 122
economic efficiency, 214
economic elites, 36, 37, 66, 95, 175
economic growth process, 1, 3–6, 12, 21–23, 25, 26, 30–34, 58–61, 63, 64, 92, 93, 95–97, 110, 115, 120–126, 129, 135, 146, 149, 156–161, 167, 169, 174, 176, 178, 179, 181, 188, 192–194, 197, 199, 200, 203, 204, 212, 214, 217, 218, 220, 224, 228, 235, 255, 265, 266, 268, 269, 272, 275
  as dynamic process, 61, 115, 169, 214, 275
  as evolutionary process, 22, 61, 218, 265, 275
economic growth with social maladies, 5, 7, 8, 15, 37, 38, 134, 173, 176, 181, 198, 204, 265, 272, 275, 276

outcome of the economic growth process, 5, 8, 15, 64, 176, 181, 204, 265, 272, 275
economic incentives, 192, 193, 196, 198, 199, 203
  vs social incentives, 192, 193, 198, 199, 203
economics
  a complex science, studying a hyper complex social world, 79
  in need of sophisticated epistemology, 79, 263
  a social science, 2, 12, 15, 44, 47, 79, 139, 145, 165, 168, 173, 204, 262, 263
  study of production and distribution, 2, 12, 19, 47, 147, 168, 171, 255
ecosystem, 28, 115, 131, 132, 135, 136, 139, 140, 142, 143, 147, 149, 152, 154–157, 159, 163, 164, 168–171, 194, 195, 274
electoral democracy institution, 4, 5, 17, 19, 22, 37, 63, 65, 95, 97, 127, 146, 149, 174, 175, 180, 181, 186, 197, 198, 201, 205, 226, 273
  vs democracy principle, 4, 5, 17, 19, 201, 273
endogenous preference system changes, 22, 56, 60, 226
endogenous technological change, 17, 22, 51, 55, 59–61, 66, 89, 109, 176, 212, 214
environment
  biodiversity, 128, 129, 132, 144, 152
  biophysical, 13–15, 21, 28–30, 32, 129, 139, 141, 142, 144, 145, 149, 152, 158, 159, 161, 163, 169, 197, 198

SUBJECT INDEX 285

ecological, 19, 32, 128, 142, 152, 269
ecosystem, 132, 136, 142, 149, 152, 159, 169
natural capital, 132, 149, 152
epistemology
  as formal science of logic, 43, 70
  vs methodology, 16, 68–72, 80, 102, 274, 275
  not part of philosophy, 70
  science of sciences, 43
  valid for any set of ethical values on science, 70
epistemology and ethical values of science, 70
epsilon society (abstract), 18, 21, 23, 24, 26, 37, 94, 115, 119–121, 126, 262, 264
epsilon theory, 18, 262
ethical values of science and epistemology, 70
European colonialism, 84, 87, 103, 109, 258, 265
excess labor supply, 20, 25, 27, 38, 71, 217, 237, 238, 241, 243–247, 249, 251–254, 256, 258, 268–271
  as unemployment and underemployment in Third World countries, 25, 238, 258, 268, 271
  as unemployment in First World countries, 20, 237

F

factor endowments, 22, 49, 54, 58, 62, 212, 214, 263
fallacy of misplaced concreteness, 257, 269
feudal institutions, 105
feudalism, 89, 91, 104, 110, 170
First World, 1, 13, 14, 18, 27, 85, 89–92, 94, 95, 97–104, 106, 108–111, 120, 121, 125–127, 133, 136, 165, 170, 183, 190, 191, 194, 231, 232, 237, 251, 258, 261–266, 268, 270, 271, 274
  explained by epsilon theory, 18
freedom discourse, 98, 111, 173, 177, 179, 181, 184–187, 198, 204, 223, 224, 227, 231. *See also* discourse
fundamental institutions of capitalism, 4, 17, 61, 65, 111, 181, 185, 197, 221, 226, 264

G

growth frontier curve, 23–25, 30, 32, 33, 54, 62, 103, 116–121, 124, 125, 156, 174, 175, 179
  level differences between First World and Third World, 125
  no convergence, 53, 126
  as temporary dynamic equilibrium of output per worker, 23, 24, 54, 62, 115, 116, 174
guaranteed minimum income (gmi), 237, 252, 258

H

healthy life expectancy, 5, 15, 31, 163, 220
  vs life expectancy, 5, 15, 31, 163
  measure of quality of society, 5, 31
Holocene age, 5, 31, 39, 161, 170, 171, 266, 277
human behavior evolution under capitalism, 33
human drives: egotism and altruism, 33, 272
  endogenous changes of relative strength, 179, 188, 192

I

illegal behavior, 14, 18, 178, 193, 194
income inequality
   in capitalist countries as a whole, 3
   in First World countries, 13, 18, 27, 98, 99, 265, 270
   vs poverty, 15, 102, 224, 228, 230, 267, 269
   in Third World, 13, 18, 27, 98, 99, 265, 270
   in the world society, 232
individualism, 174, 177, 186, 199–201, 203, 204
initial inequality, 4, 8, 18, 21, 22, 24, 25, 27, 34, 36, 49, 54, 58, 61, 63, 65, 87, 91, 93, 96, 98, 100, 110, 125, 146, 149, 174, 175, 186, 212, 226, 263, 264, 266, 267, 272
   includes economic and social assets, 8, 18, 65, 87, 146, 175
   unequal individual asset endowments, 93, 98, 174, 264
Institute for Health Metrics and Evaluation (IHME), 15, 163
invisible hand proposition
   and freedom discourse, 173
   and neoclassical theory, 173
   and unified theory, 198, 201

K

Keynesian theory, 139, 263, 267, 268, 271

L

labor markets, 17, 71, 237, 238, 240, 243, 246–251, 268, 270, 271
   in the First World, 258, 268, 271
   in the Third World, 238, 246, 251, 258, 268, 271
life expectancy
   vs healthy life expectancy, 5, 15, 31, 163
logic, 2, 43, 51, 70–73, 75, 78, 158, 209, 240
   and epistemology, 2, 43, 71, 158, 209, 211
   a formal science, 43

M

market institution
   as big computer, 36, 65, 158
   power structure included in equations, 4
   solving for prices and quantities, 36, 65
   and voluntary exchange, 4, 14, 36, 65, 108, 180
Marxian theory, 169, 269
mathematics, 157
   a formal science, 78
   includes assumptions (axioms), 78
methodology, 69, 71, 72, 263, 276
   vs epistemology, 16, 68–72, 80, 102, 274, 275
Mother Nature laws in economic process
   photosynthesis, 19, 143, 164, 165
   thermodynamics, 21, 28, 32, 59, 128, 143, 152, 156, 164, 165
myth of competition under capitalism, 205

N

natural capital, 131–133, 135, 142, 147, 149–155, 157, 160, 162, 194

neoclassical theory, 15, 17, 139, 140, 146, 181, 187, 198, 204, 205, 216, 217, 221, 224, 225, 263, 267, 271
nonrenewable natural resources, 151
normative economics
   vs positive economics, 207–209, 216, 223

O

overpopulation, 132, 135, 136, 238
   relative to capital stock, 120, 126, 133
   relative to natural capital, 133, 135

P

Pareto optimality, 35
path dependence
   or history matters, 96
   or social hysteresis, 89, 110
physics, 29, 68, 76, 78, 79, 162, 169
   and laws of thermodynamics, 267, 275
   and the law of photosynthesis, 19, 59, 143, 149, 164, 165
political elites, 4, 19, 34, 36, 66, 93, 95, 111, 175, 181, 184, 186, 188, 198, 199, 205, 264, 265
pollution, 3–5, 15, 19, 21, 28–31, 35, 59, 63, 128–130, 132, 140, 149–154, 156, 157, 160, 161, 163, 164, 169, 175, 176, 205, 217, 218, 220, 221, 234, 265
   irrevocable outcome of production, 19, 59, 149
   limited human health tolerance for, 19, 30, 31, 62, 63, 129, 153, 154, 217, 218
population density effect, 132, 133, 135

positive economics
   vs normative economics, 207–209, 216, 223
poverty
   vs income inequality, 15, 102, 224, 228, 230, 267, 269
power elites, 5, 6, 18, 19, 27, 32–36, 59, 60, 63–65, 86–88, 93–97, 109, 111, 112, 154–157, 165, 175–178, 180–187, 189, 192, 196–198, 200–202, 205, 221–223, 226, 230, 234, 235, 255, 264–268, 272, 273
   originated in initial inequality, 4, 18, 27, 36, 63, 93, 175, 226, 264, 272
power structure, 4, 6, 18, 30, 34, 35, 37, 63–66, 93, 96, 97, 104, 109, 135, 146, 149, 175, 189, 197, 200, 201, 204, 205, 212, 219, 222, 226, 227, 235, 264, 265, 267, 272, 273
   originated in initial inequality and institutions, 4, 18, 36, 63, 65, 93, 149, 175, 212, 264, 272
precolonial institutions, 109, 112
problem of the commons, 31, 32, 34, 154, 176, 188, 189, 199, 200, 203, 221
public goods, 3, 154, 176, 180, 182, 188, 189, 200, 215, 257

Q

quality of society (QoS), 64, 66, 129, 134, 135, 178, 202, 203, 217–220, 222, 223, 226, 228, 234, 269, 270, 272
   as common good, 35, 219
   declining (eventually) in the economic growth process, 3, 6, 30, 31, 135, 220, 235

measured by healthy life expectancy, 5, 220
quality of society and public policies, 6, 35, 235
quality of society in Anthropocene age, 115, 135, 219, 220, 234

R
redistribution effect, 234
  vs income growth effect, 231, 233
redistribution policies, 220, 231, 234
renewable natural resources, 22, 30, 131, 149, 219
Robinson Crusoe metaphor, 225

S
science-based policies, 6, 38, 210
self-employment as subsistence sector, 25, 240–242, 251, 254. *See also* underemployment
sigma society (abstract), 18, 21, 23–27, 37, 91, 93, 94, 98, 99, 106, 120, 121, 126, 174, 248, 249, 262–265
sigma theory, 238, 246, 250, 258, 262
social assets, 4, 18, 37, 65, 83, 89, 91, 96, 97, 200, 201, 262, 265
social hysteresis
  or history matters, 111
  or path dependence, 89, 110
social incentives
  vs economic incentives, 193, 198, 199, 203
social maladies, 3–5, 7, 8, 14, 31, 32, 34, 35, 38, 63, 64, 95, 102, 175, 176, 179, 181, 186, 193, 199–202, 205, 217, 218, 220, 226, 265, 267–269, 272

outcome of the economic process, 3, 5, 8, 31, 34, 37, 38, 134, 179, 181, 204, 265, 272
social markers, 18, 99–101
social order, 3, 23, 182, 200, 221, 229, 234, 266, 268
social sciences, 2, 12, 15, 73, 79, 145, 165, 168, 173, 198, 204, 262, 263
  as study of hyper complex social world, 79
society of shameless people, 203
standard economics, 12, 35, 38, 39, 44, 106, 139, 140, 170, 171, 183, 194, 201, 235, 263, 267, 275, 276
statistics, 81, 227, 256
  a formal science, 74
  includes assumptions (axioms), 74, 78
subsistence sector in the Third World, 27, 120, 251

T
theory of knowledge, 43, 69, 70, 75
Third World, 13, 14, 18, 21, 27, 35, 84, 85, 89–95, 97–104, 106, 108–112, 120, 121, 125–127, 133, 136, 165, 170, 190, 191, 194, 202, 231, 232, 238, 245, 256–259, 261–266, 268, 270, 274
  explained by sigma theory, 18, 238, 258
time
  chronological, 20
  historical (T), 14, 61, 167
  logical (runs), 20
  mechanical (t), 61, 96, 211

transition dynamics, 27, 52, 53, 62–64, 67, 119–121, 124, 125, 174, 175, 211–213
  observable and testable, 24, 54, 62, 120, 212
  spontaneous move toward the growth frontier curve, 24, 54, 62

U

underemployment, 13–15, 20, 192, 238, 258, 271
under-population, 126
unemployment, 13–15, 20, 25, 75, 117, 188, 192, 225, 237, 238, 242, 244, 245, 247, 249–251, 253, 254, 258, 267–269, 271

unified theory of capitalism: foundations, 17

W

wage employment, 241, 244, 248–254, 256, 270, 271
welfarism, 224, 225
Western supremacy as institution, 92, 93, 98, 102, 106, 111
women empowerment and fertility, 122
World Bank, 14, 15, 126, 127, 163, 232

Z

z-populations, 96, 102, 191
z-workers, 26, 27, 94, 256–258

Printed by Printforce, the Netherlands